THE UNCERTAIN SOUTH

THE
UN

CERTAIN SOUTH

SOUTH

ITS CHANGING PATTERNS OF POLITICS IN FOREIGN POLICY

BY CHARLES O. LERCHE, JR.

QUADRANGLE BOOKS • CHICAGO

CONTENTS:

Library of Congress Catalog Card Number: 64-10925

Designed by Joan Stoliar

Manufactured in the United States of America

First Printing

PREFACE

THIS VOLUME grows from the author's more than twenty years of residence in several parts of the South, his long personal history of interest in the problem with which the book deals, his conviction that the contemporary South deserves and requires greater study and understanding than it now receives, and his philosophic belief that objective analysis is a necessary prerequisite to value judgments on emotionally exciting problems of public policy. The research on which it is based was made possible by the support and sponsorship of the World Peace Foundation. Dr. Alfred O. Hero, Executive Secretary of the Foundation, has planned and is directing a broader inquiry into Southern attitudes toward world affairs of which this forms a part. The Foundation's interest in the South grew in turn out of an earlier series, *Studies in Citizen Participation in International Relations* (Boston: World Peace Foundation, 1959-1960), of which Dr. Hero was also director and editor.

Although the literature both on Southern politics and on Congressional behavior with respect to international issues is extensive, nothing existed when this project took shape that provided either a theoretical base or quantitative analyses of the relationship between Southern political action and the votes of Southern Congressmen on foreign policy questions. Of course, any student of Southern political life today is forever in the debt of two major studies, *The Mind of the South*, by W. J. Cash (New York, 1941), and *Southern Politics in State and Nation*, by V. O. Key, Jr. (New York, 1949). A pioneering evaluation of some of the points dealt with in the first part of this book was also undertaken by Paul Seabury, whose *The Waning of Southern Internationalism* (Princeton, 1956) alerted the author to several important analytical categories early in the project. These three works must be cited here, but the author must also pay tribute to the researches of the many highly qualified scholars whose writings enriched his understanding of a complex region and spared him the embarrassment that otherwise would have been the only prize to be found at the end of many blind alleys. Of the latter there proved even so to be an ample supply.

As Chapter I attempts to make clear, methodologically the study was designed to avoid preconceptions as much as possible and to construct theories only upon the basis of hard data. The volume incorporates only one admitted built-in bias: the author is convinced both of the necessity and the preferability of what the book identifies as the "multilateralist" approach to American foreign policy. Any other prejudices the reader may detect are inadvertent. Certainly the author would be disappointed if anyone considered the book as either "pro-Southern" or "anti-Southern" in its conclusions.

Acknowledgments for assistance given the author are always awkward in this kind of study, because so many people contribute in so many different ways to a final product. Many of the author's students and colleagues have patiently endured his tentative verbalizations of hypotheses for several years, some of which they unceremoniously exploded upon hearing. A number of public figures gave generously of their insights without the necessity of a formal "interview." Library staffs at Emory University, the United States Naval War College, and The American University were occasionally puzzled but never baffled by peculiar requests. At every turn the author has received both encouragement and assistance as he sought first to gather information and then to extract political meaning from the mountain of data.

Of those whose efforts have earned them the distinction (hopefully not dubious) of being singled out by name, the author owes first a debt of genuine gratitude to Dr. Hero, whose own vast knowledge of the South was always at the author's disposal and whose companion volume on Southern leadership attitudes toward world affairs incorporates his own recent researches.

Several of the author's graduate assistants—Messrs. James Cheek, Naryan Ghatate, Philip M. Burgess, and Gene E. Rainey—found themselves caught up in particular aspects of the project as it matured and made their unique contributions of energy and imagination. Mr. William J. Raiford, while preparing a Master of Arts thesis under the author's direction on "Southern Congressmen and Foreign Aid Legislation," upset a number of early hypotheses and suggested several fruitful lines of research.

The personnel of the Washington Office of the Americans for Democratic Action were especially courteous in making available their Congressional Rating Index for the period covered by the study.

Finally, the author's wife, Dr. Margaret Evans Lerche, has been a key participant in the study throughout. As the native Southerner in the family as well as an expert on Southern history, she contributed a perspective and a point of view all her own. As both a friendly critic and an active collaborator, she has made the author more conscious of his purpose and more convinced of the necessity of the very highest standards of accuracy.

The author also thanks the editors of the *Political Science Quarterly* for their permission to reprint material from his article, "Southern Congressmen and the 'New Isolationism,'" which appeared in that journal in September 1960.

Mrs. Elizabeth Forrest, with a sharp eye for grammatical and statistical consistency, prepared the final manuscript with exceptional accuracy.

It seems scarcely necessary to add, finally, that these acknowledgments in no way lessen the author's sole responsibility for the facts and the judgments that follow.

C. O. L., JR.

Washington, D.C.
January, 1964

THE UNCERTAIN SOUTH

FOREIGN POLICY
AND THE
CONTEMPORARY SOUTH

THIS is a book about American foreign policy, Congress and Congressmen, and the American South. More than anything else, however, it is a book about the South, that special part of the United States that comes equipped with its own history, its own folklore, its own social dynamics, and its own special brand of politics. The "nation within a nation" that was born during the early decades of the nineteenth century, enjoyed its brief noonday of glory during the Civil War, and has gone substantially its own withdrawn way ever since is again today the scene of great events. Massive social and economic changes are taking place below the Mason-Dixon line that carry immediate and far-reaching consequences for all Americans. One need only think of the worldwide distribution given to the famous photograph of Birmingham's police dogs lunging at Negro demonstrators to know that the South's problems are the problems of the entire nation.

The South has come a long way indeed since the 1930's when, as "the nation's number one economic problem," its sharecroppers, textile workers, downtrodden Negroes, and preposterous demagogues made the United States in general more conscious of the peculiarities of Southern life than it had been since Appomattox. The Roosevelt New Deal brought the TVA, the war brought industry, and the post-war boom brought progress. No longer a "problem" in the Rooseveltian sense, the South has instead become one of the nation's most hopeful frontiers. There is a buoyancy to the region's new cities, a climate of accomplishment and pride mixed with a faith in the future, that contrasts sharply with the aura of gentlemanly decadence so often portrayed in the literary romanticizations of the Southern dream.

The Southerner is a very different creature today than he was before World War II. He holds his head high now that he has finally shed the deadening consciousness of defeat that was the principal bequest of the Confederacy to later generations. He is apologetic no longer; he is bent on assuming the place in American life that he feels is com-mensurate with the importance and the strength of the new South that is being born. The day when Southern politics and Southern leadership could either be safely pat-ronized as of minor importance and dubious capability, or laughed at as beneath serious concern, has passed forever. The South has thrust itself onto the center of the stage of the national political drama and demands the same serious analysis and flexible responses that are granted any other politically relevant section of the country. Southerners can no longer be dismissed with a quip or classified as curiosities. Indeed, so significant has the contemporary South become that the United States cannot hope to put its own internal house in order or to face the world with clear purpose or full power until the nation grasps and copes with the South-ern metamorphosis in its full dimensions.

In no area of public policy—even including such highly-emotionalized questions as race relations and civil rights—has the new Southern self-assertiveness been more pronounced than in the field of American foreign policy. Although this study will make abundantly clear that Southerners show a wide range of attitudes toward world affairs and the place of the United States in the international system, in general terms it is self-evident that the decade of the 1950's was a period of major upheaval in the dominant tone of Southern opinion on world affairs. The South as a whole voices a very different foreign policy line than it did a generation or so ago.

Many Southern political figures, of course, have not changed. Especially among those veterans of the New Deal and wartime political battles who are still active today, no particular shifts in international attitudes can be found. Tradition still has its way in many parts of the South. Yet all Southern traditionalists—no matter what issue they may be addressing—are discovering to their dismay that today theirs is a minority position subject to continual erosion. The foreign policy ideas of the 1930's and 1940's have been outgrown in the South's frantic race to catch up with the rest of the country. New ideas are in the ascendancy and new men are taking on the burden of leading Southern opinion on international affairs as in so many other burning questions.

The new foreign policy attitudes of the contemporary South are intrinsically interesting and important for two different reasons. They represent in the first place a marked departure from the region's historic (if heavily stereotyped) position on international affairs and in that way furnish one index to the dimensions of the almost revolutionary changes through which the South is passing. Second, the general trend of Southern opinion on world affairs is running—and has run for more than a decade—in a direction substantially at variance with the prevailing tone of opinion throughout the United States. Whereas mass sentiment in the Northeast, in the West, and even in the Midwest is more and more accepting the larger implications of total American involvement in the course of world history, the hardening orthodoxy of Southerners now demands less American commitment than has been the case, fewer international adventures by the United States rather than more, and a simplification of the problems of foreign policy to the level of black-and-white choices implemented by techniques of direct action founded on overwhelming military power.

Thus the South remains a paradox to the end. At the very moment in history when the region is moving finally to merge its destinies with the rest of the United States in all important political, economic, and social terms, and with Southern society coming more and more to accept the same value structure and dynamics that characterize the nation as a whole, Southern mass opinion on desperately important matters involving national security, the preservation of peace, and world prosperity is diverging further and further from national norms. It would seem almost as if Southerners are determined that their distinctiveness must be preserved at all costs; the more they may look and act like other Americans, the more grimly they insist that they will never permit themselves to think like them.

This cleavage between the Southern view of world affairs and the prevailing opinion in the remainder of the country would be serious enough under any circumstances. Under conditions of cold war, nuclear stalemate, and constant tension, however, it becomes a matter of grave concern. The demands of leadership which an inexorable and inscrutable destiny has persisted in imposing on the United States ever since 1945 have made foreign policy formulation and execution an ever uncertain enterprise. The new and uncharted seas upon which the nation has been obliged to sail for more than two decades have given rise to a generous quota of uncertainties, regrets, nostalgic longings, and mercurial changes of mood in the body politic. The national consensus upon which effective governmental action in world affairs must depend has never been absolutely solid except in moments of tense crisis; the care and feeding of public opinion has therefore been a continuing task of all responsible foreign policy officials. If the South persists in moving outside the national circle of agreement on important issues of international affairs, the overall vigor of American action will obviously decline. If its example should prove attractive to significant portions of opinion in other parts of the country, the consequences—although unpredictable in detail—would certainly be massive and disruptive of whatever order and system there may be in American foreign policy.

So the foreign policy ideas of Southerners are more than merely interesting subjects for journalistic or academic inquiry; they are matters of immediate relevance to the practical task of devising an effective American response to the problems with which the world is so generous. The challenge the South presents to the political skill and courage of American political leaders and policy makers is immediate and clear. Some way of meeting it and containing its impact must be found if the worst consequences of its appearance and growth are to be avoided.

But any strategy, to be successful, must be based on as complete and accurate as possible an evaluation of the operational situation in politics as in war. Before the question of what to do about the South can be meaningfully discussed, some greater appreciation of the details of the problem is necessary. How does one measure the direction, the extent, and the magnitude of the new Southern outlook? Which of the many forces of change in the South today have brought about the new approach to international relations? How can the evidence of the shift be characterized, classified, and applied to deepen an obviously imperfect understanding of the South and its peculiar dynamics? What does the future hold; how far will changes go before coming to rest?

This book attempts to answer these—and a number of related—questions. Its emphasis throughout is upon prevailing trends of Southern political life, since the international attitudes of individuals are important only to the extent that they find political expression. Such relevance as this book may have to the problem of actually making American policy will probably flow from its diagnosis and tentative prognosis of the contemporary shape of the Southern phenomenon; it would require both greater sagacity and greater courage than the author claims to prescribe, even in the most general terms, any action formula for dealing with the theories of foreign policy that are finding expression in the South today.

CERTAIN NECESSARY DEFINITIONS

One of the difficulties intrinsic to the study of politics in the United States is the popular and journalistic proclivity (to which, it must be admitted, academicians and politicians are also addicted) to the loose use of descriptive terms. All political action involves choice and thus demands a value judgment among alternatives by he who chooses. It is natural that the names that people give to the choices and courses of action they face should reflect the preferences of the individuals involved. For short-term purposes of political disputation—elections, lobbying, and the like— no real harm is usually done if discussion takes the form of the embattled antagonists hurling imprecise but certainly emotionally stimulating epithets at each other. But this practice is fatal to serious analysis and rational understanding as well as to effective action in the real world. If elucidation rather than persuasion is to be the motive of any inquiry into political data, it is vital that descriptive terms be used that are as value-free as possible and that will mean at least roughly the same thing to anyone who might use them.

This difficulty is the hobgoblin of all social science research, but it is especially a stumbling block when popular opinions of American foreign policy are under examination. In this field longstanding shibboleths fly freely; here can be found easily available terms both laudatory and pejorative (although equally imprecise) to characterize almost any policy position. Here discussion, in which all parties insist that they have no purpose other than the advancement of the interests and the welfare of the American people and the government of the United States, tends quickly to bog down in words and to take on the form of the reiteration of fixed and emotionalized absolute positions.

As a result, in this book the analysis and description of foreign policy attitudes proceeds with virtually no reliance on the old and slippery terms "isolationism" and "internationalism," or their adjectival derivatives, "isolationist" and "internationalist." Neither "isolationism" nor "internationalism" has ever been as meaningful a way to classify or understand political thought and action as many of their manipulators think; neither concept, furthermore, is really relevant to the contemporary political pattern in the South (or elsewhere, for that matter). Both words, however, are so firmly imbedded in the working vocabulary of popular and political discussion in America, that their abandonment here with no explanation might be considered as leaving an analytical gap in the story.

If "isolationism" be taken in its common-sense meaning as referring to a belief that the United States should withdraw completely from international affairs, it has never—at least in this century—been an apt characterization of any sizeable body of opinion in the United States. Today all Americans are (and have been for years) "internationalists" in one real sense: everyone admits and recognizes the inevitability of the extensive participation of the United States in the ongoing course of world events. If almost no one who takes world affairs at all seriously is truly an "isolationist," and almost everybody is—even though often unhappily—an "internationalist," of what use are the terms?

The distinction they purport to draw is literally meaningless.

But the controversy about the nature of American foreign policy and the principles that should guide it, out of which the popular comprehension of the two terms originally grew, is real and fundamental. The basic issue that separates the two schools of thought, however, has never been a quantitative one. The longstanding issue in American life ever since independence has not been whether or not the United States should have any foreign policy at all; even the most rabid opponent of the League of Nations in 1919, for example, admitted that the United States would willy-nilly continue to have political dealings with the other sovereign states of the world regardless of whether or not it became a member of the world organization. The crux of the dispute between the so-called "isolationists" and "internationalists," then and now, has not been the quantitative level of the international involvements and relationships conducted by the United States, but rather a matter of the terms and conditions under which these contacts were to be initiated and carried on.

One strain in American thought, as old as the republic itself, emphasizes the special role of the United States. An articulate body of opinion has long denied that the nation has any permanent or vital stake in the international order as such, and argues that American is in right and in power free to pick and choose the extent and the occasions of its entry into world affairs. The isolation of the United States, therefore, is conceived of as being conceptual and intellectual rather than crudely physical. Americans are admitted to be unquestionably *in* the world but emphatically not *of* it. The United States, regardless of any arrangements of convenience it might be persuaded to make with other states, is thus in principle always dedicated to "going it alone."

The opposite point of view, to a very great extent a product of the twentieth century, sees the destiny of the

United States as inextricably tied up with that of the whole of mankind. American foreign policy does not really consist merely of the projection of an untrammeled national will upon an infinitely plastic environment as more simplistic formulations suggest, but rather the adjustment of the United States and its interests to the demands of an incessantly conditioning and often controlling international system. The important things Americans seek in world affairs—security, well being, and peace—they cannot by definition obtain by their own unaided efforts, since all of them are functions of the international order itself.

Thus the first position denies the centrality of the world political system to the choices facing the United States, while the second insists upon it; the first leaves no room for any community of American interest with the world outside, but the second makes such areas of common concern the very foundations of long-term American planning and action. The differences between the two are less those of detail or of recommended policy in a particular situation than they are functions of a deep-seated divergence in basic approaches. The two opposing philosophies of American foreign policy differ so sharply in their respective major premises that the diametrically opposing conclusions to be drawn from them should come as no surprise.

The real problem of definition, therefore, is to develop names for the two basic positions that both reflect their differences and suggest the fundamental point of view of each one. What is the distinguishing characteristic of each? The first, it will be recalled, contends that the United States should first and foremost retain and exploit the absolute maximum of national freedom of choice and action under any circumstances; its focus is therefore upon unilateral decision. The most communicative name is *unilateralism,* and this term is used consistently throughout the pages that follow. The second position, demanding as it does that American policy be built solidly upon a recognition of the

interdependence of all states for such security and prosperity as they may enjoy, is equally clearly a call for the
maximization of multilateral action. So the position is identified as *multilateralism.*

The unilateralist-multilateralist dichotomy is based on
principle rather than consistent practice. Politics being only
partially a principled exercise—expediency often demands
that a political figure "rise above principle"—it is perfectly
possible for a unilateralist adherent to advocate and support
a specific multilateralist enterprise. The opposite case is
also true: a convinced multilateralist may for any of a large
number of perfectly good reasons insist that the United
States in a particular case act entirely on its own. The support by large numbers of convinced unilateralists of the
major points in President Kennedy's multilateralist policies
during 1961, for example, is a clear case of the supremacy of
political expediency over doctrine, while one entire school
of Southern thought is solidly multilateralist on every issue
except the single politically explosive one of foreign aid. No
political classification can be foolproof, and there is no in-
tention here to argue that the unilateralist-multilateralist
duality covers all cases with mathematical precision. What it
does do, however, is to make possible the separation of
individual and group attitudes into analytically useful categories—which, after all, is the only real purpose to which
any abstract system of classification should be put.

As a result, in spite of the rhythmic appeal and conceptual simplicity of the seductive phrase "Southern isolationism," it will be used only rarely in the course of the
following discussion, and then never to refer to a specific
attitude or position. What has in fact been going on in the
South for some years is in no sense a return to any fantasy
of complete withdrawal from the world. The South sees
itself today as capable of projecting its values and its power
not upon the national scene alone, but in the larger world
as well; no Southerner feels any urge to huddle behind a

cotton curtain while occupying himself with the cultivation of his own soul. The South is as assertive in foreign policy matters as it is in many other areas, and for its spokesmen to argue for American withdrawal from the world would be effectively to deny the region's own dynamics.

The South is not "isolationist" in the literal sense of the term. The new attitudes becoming charcteristic of more and more Southerners today, however, constitute more than anything else a special Southern variant on the standardized unilateralist position. The traditional norm of Southern politicians, especially during the era of Nazi Germany, World War II, and the early cold war, was one that demanded and provided support for multilateralist moves proposed by the President, however many reservations in detail may have lingered in their minds. As a matter of fact, the much-praised "internationalism," long supposed to be rampant in the South prior to 1953, turns out on closer inspection to be rooted much more deeply in social and cultural biases and political expediency than in any particular commitment to multilateralist doctrine. Whatever the reasons for the stands they took, however, Southerners generally up to the opening of the Eisenhower era in 1953 were found on the side of whatever implementing moves were being made in behalf of the doctrine of multilateralism. That they are so no longer is the reason for this book.

The distinction between unilateralism and multilateralism as established here is maintained throughout the entire analysis. One special point of nomenclature, however, should be noted here, since much of the attempt at classification and characterization will make use of it. The extreme unilateralist point of view that shows no apparent willingness to accept even partially the implications of an interdependent world is additionally identified throughout as "ideological," for reasons that are probably self-evident but will be elaborated later on. Since no ideological characteristics can be clearly identified by even the extreme positions assumed by the adherents of multilateralism, the only "ideologists" met in the ensuing discussion are the hard-core and militant unilateralists.

SOUTHERN OPINION: THE CONGRESSIONAL SAMPLE

Probably the most visible and effective spokesmen for the Southern point of view on international affairs are the region's representatives in both houses of Congress. Only in Congress can a man whose personal roots and political loyalties are exclusively Southern have the opportunity and the duty to express meaningful opinions on American foreign policy. An executive official may himself be a Southerner, but holding federal office requires him (at least in theory) to serve a national rather than a regional constituency; a Southern politician operating outside the national government is literally irresponsible and free from the often embarrassing necessity of facing the operational consequences of his frequently carefree pronouncements. It is only through its Congressional delegation that the South can speak even quasi-officially on world affairs.

For the purposes of the discussion here, "the South" is defined as including fourteen states: the eleven that made up the Confederacy a century ago (Virginia, North Carolina, South Carolina, Georgia, Florida, Alabama, Mississippi, Tennessee, Louisiana, Arkansas, and Texas), West Virginia, Kentucky, and Oklahoma. From 1953 to 1962, the time span covered in this investigation, these fourteen states sent to Washington 28 United States Senators and 126 members of the House of Representatives. It is to these men and women that one must look for the hard evidence of the changing Southern attitude on world affairs.

Since the thesis of this book is that trends in the South as a whole are much more revealing than the performance records of individual politicians, furthermore, the somewhat scantier but more informative data drawn from the voting patterns of the membership of the several House delegations provide many more insights than does the rich tapestry of maneuvering on the floor of the Senate. The House figures tell much more about Southerners and the South for a variety of reasons.

In the first place there are simply more Congressmen from the South than there are Senators, and the sample is enough larger to be much more useful. Within the total of 126 Congressmen there is enough variation in points of view to permit the identification of several different attitudes along the unilateralist-multilateralist continuum. Members of the House, furthermore, are simply not permitted by their shorter terms and the controlling theory of representation in the lower house to be free agents, at least to anything like the extent Senators seem to enjoy. A Senator may go his own way for at least half and usually more of his six-year term, concerning himself seriously with constituent response only during the final two years before he must face the electorate again; the Representative, on the contrary, never dares for a moment to forget the folks back home. This fact of political life in the United States leads quickly to the valuable conclusion that voter revolts or even smaller shifts in mass opinion in the districts will quickly find registration in House roll calls, while their effect may be delayed or even avoided by more secure Senators.

The Senate of the United States is filled with strong personalities who take full advantage of liberal rules and procedures to express themselves in luxuriant detail. The House does not permit such freedom of individual self-expression; the working Congressman normally finds his choices sharply narrowed by the twin vises of party leadership in Washington and the demands of his followers at home. This difference between the two houses also serves as a supporting argument in favor of a concentration upon the Southern bloc in the House, as again the dichotomy

of a national multilateralist consensus confronting an evolving unilateralist movement at the grass roots faces dozens
of Southern Congressmen with the cruelest but most revealing of choices.

All in all, in almost every respect the 126 Southern
members of the House of Representatives furnish a reliable
weathervane by which to measure the winds of change in
their region between 1953 and 1962—the terminal dates of
the data used here. A focus upon the 28 Southern Senators
would be most informative about the Senate as a body and
the Senators as individuals, and would be a fascinating inquiry into political and interpersonal relations. But such
a project, in spite of the significance of its findings, would
be of only limited relevance to what has been and still is
going on in the South. The House members, with their roots
in their districts and their horizons necessarily circumscribed
by political realities, communicate (often without meaning
to do so) a very real sense of the contemporary Southern
dynamic and constitute the gateway into the main thrust
of this analysis.

GATHERING THE DATA

But the Congressmen themselves, however remarkable their
performances might seem, can do no more than suggest the
direction and the magnitude of the change in Southern
attitudes. It has already been made clear that the overriding
purpose of this investigation is to discover what sorts of
things Southerners generally are thinking about foreign
affairs and to try to connect these attitudes with certain
objective criteria of change. The records compiled by the
incumbents of each of the 126 House districts included in
the Southern sample, in other words, are only the starting
point; from the Congressman's office and the floor of the
House, the lines of inquiry run back to his district and into

the major trends of evolution and development that are operating there.

Inevitably, therefore, much more attention is devoted in later chapters to constituencies than to Congressmen. In many instances this has resulted in a substantial injustice as the role played by certain influential and powerful individuals has been necessarily minimized. But this is designed as a "macro-political" study aimed at an over-view of the entire South. Although several different theories of representation can be discovered at work among the 126 districts, by and large it is a safe enough assumption that the point of view expressed on foreign policy questions by any particular Congressman is determined more by the state of mind he senses among his constituents than by any other single factor.

This last point is fundamental to the entire argument, for almost all the conclusions drawn rest upon it. A second necessary postulate is that the way a district stands on foreign policy, particularly if its Congressman's position has undergone considerable modification, is in some direct or indirect way a function of the socio-economic changes that are at work among its people. Each of the 126 districts is therefore analyzed in terms of certain social, demographic, and economic criteria, using as raw data for comparative purposes the several publications of the United States Bureau of the Census. The first conclusions suggested by this initial comparison of the districts with each other are the base on which all the major lines of analysis eventually rest: several different kinds of changes are taking place in the South and the particular point of view expressed by any Congressman is in almost every case a calculated response to a complex of forces rather than a one-dimensional shift in reaction to a single overriding trend.

Once it had been established that there was probably a direct connection between what was going on in any Congressional district in the South and the position on world affairs taken by that district's Congressman, the remainder of the detailed analysis proceeded logically. The first set of data to be compiled and evaluated was obviously the record of how each Congressman had voted on foreign policy questions before the House, how this record compared with the overall Southern pattern, how the Southern performance had changed, and finally how the South stacked up alongside the rest of the House. Compiling these figures was not especially complex (although tedious), but their management and classification required that a time frame be established within which to work.

For a combination of reasons the ten years that began with the opening of the 83rd Congress in January 1953 and ended with the adjournment of the 87th Congress in 1962 was chosen as the period to be analyzed in detail. This was the decade in which the apportionment of seats followed the census of 1950; no changes in the size of any state's delegation and only one instance of redistricting within a state arose to complicate the strict comparability of the data. The ten-year period also comprehended the entire Eisenhower era and the first Kennedy Congress (the 87th), thus providing some bases for the evaluation of whatever differentials in performance might be discovered.

The most important justification for including the decade from 1953 through 1962, however, was the simplest and most logical: the great bulk of the shift in Southern opinion with which this book is concerned actually took place between these dates. The voting records themselves demonstrate that the movement away from the multilateralist orthodoxy of the South had not yet begun in 1953. It got under way only the next year, however, and reached its real peak between 1957 and 1960. The first two years of the Kennedy administration saw only a minimal reversal of trends of little significance.

Within the five Congresses (aggregating ten sessions)

that spanned the decade, roll call votes were recorded and tabulated on a number of issues that posed the unilateralist-multilateralist choice for all members of the House. These involved first and probably foremost the question of foreign aid, and the record of change in Southern attitudes on this one issue is a fascinating story in itself. But foreign aid, for all its centrality, does not tell the whole story. A second set of roll call records was compiled, this time covering a representative selection (actually more than half the total of roll call votes on foreign policy issues other than foreign aid) on other types of multilateralist proposals that came before the House during the decade. These latter issues were all one-time choices that lacked the characteristic repetitiveness implicit in the annual authorization measure for foreign aid. This group of votes threw the records of many Congressmen into a very different light, showing significant shifts in the position of many individuals and important patterns of development and change, whether viewed on a district-by-district, a state-by-state, or an overall Southern base.

The next step was to put all the roll call data together so as to see if any clear positions could be established. In the great bulk of the cases it proved relatively simple to classify each individual voting record in terms of its general pattern and to assign identifying characteristics and (hopefully) descriptive names to each cluster of districts and Congressmen. Six separate points of view were finally identified among Southerners, of which the four major ones comprehended almost 90 per cent of all the region's seats and the remaining two included only sixteen districts.

Among the four major groupings a curious but satisfying symmetry was remarkable. Two were clearly extreme, located as they were at opposite ends of the multilateralist-unilateralist range. The remaining two placed themselves immediately inside the extreme positions, one being almost multilateralist but with certain limitations, the other almost unilateralist but falling short in some key respects. The two smaller groupings were easily located in the central range between the extremes.

These clusters proved to be useful bases for both comparison and prediction. On the basis of the data employed, a generalized picture was constructed of the international outlook of each group. From this model its overall vote on any issue could be roughly predicted. As a check on the validity of the classifications, a number of roll calls not used in the original analysis were examined. It was discovered (happily for the theory being tested) that each group voted on these additional questions in almost exactly the way indicated by its general posture. So well did these data corroborate each other that the six points of view (and especially the four largest ones) became bench marks for all detailed evaluations in the investigation.

At this point in the inquiry, it became necessary to focus upon the Congressmen themselves. The primary concern here was the discovery of what personal and political characteristics of individual Congressmen could be correlated with each of the several points of view already established. A variety of political considerations—length of service, frequency and extent of interparty opposition, and so on—were evaluated for each group, and the results of certain interview data correlated in turn with these figures. Also a part of the general context of politics, a detailed examination was made of the record and the points of view expressed in the House by Southern Republicans during the decade.

Up to this point two sets of figures had been gathered: a group of roll call analyses and a variety of statistical data for each district. The next step was a crucial one: to combine the two so as to discover what sort of district was likely to be represented by a unilateralist, by a multilateralist, or by an adherent of any one of the intermediate positions. Various criteria were applied to each attitude grouping and proved to be of uneven relevance to the problem of measurement and prediction. One, however—per capita income per district—turned out to be astonishingly accurate as a reflection of or as a guide to the foreign policy position of that district's Congressman. From the combination of the several criteria it became possible to construct a model district for each of the important types, to identify the actual districts that most closely approximated the norms, and finally to locate, examine, and compare those districts that were obviously out of place and thus likely candidates for early change.

This analysis, in view of its criteria and its methodology, was in its essentials static. It was necessary at this point, therefore, to seize the dynamic factors and to seek to quantify the obviously central Southern phenomenon of change in political attitude, social and economic patterns, and international points of view. In order to gain some sense of how far contemporary trends were likely to go before some plateau of stability might be reached, both the extent and the pace of certain important dimensions of change in the South were analyzed. Among the most important and relevant aspects of the Southern metamorphosis considered were the parallel movements of people from the farms to the cities and from agriculture to industry. Also revealing and significant were the identifiable trends of Negro migration, both within the region itself and outward as well.

THE SEARCH FOR MEANING

Finally, with the data gathered, the problem of meaning had to be faced. Do all the data add up to anything; is there a thread that links the great changes in the South to the shift in the international outlook of Southern Congressmen? What translates social pressure into political attitudes?

Certain preliminary negative conclusions were easy to draw. The answer to why the Southern outlook on world affairs has become so uncertain cannot be found in any

study, however detailed, of the international issues them-
selves. Neither does the voting record of any particular
Congressman furnish many explanations or good reasons.
The key to the riddle lies neither in the problems nor in the
Congressmen, but rather in the South itself and in the dis-
tricts racked by crisis and torn by change.

The most significant single political fact about the contemporary South is the reappearance of protest as a political
force and of a new generation of Southern demagogues as
the spokesmen and manipulators of that mass unease. The
Southern readjustment is painful. As a reaction to the
strains and dilemmas history has forced upon it, an entire
stratum of Southern society has become politically activist
as the best way of expressing its discomfort. The new unilateralism of so many Southerners is less a judgment on the
nature and the course of world affairs than it is a reflection
of their own dismay at what is happening to them at home.

Looked at in this way, the appearance, rise, and apparent predominance of unilateralism in Southern thinking
about world affairs is not an aberration that can be dealt
with by clever techniques of political leadership or ignored
as fundamentally irrelevant. It is a completely understand-
able and often (in a special way) justifiable response to a
highly complex situation, and in a larger historic context
may possibly be sympathetically accepted as a part of the
price Americans must pay for the advantage of having the
South at last an integral part of the nation. Unilateralist
ideology among Southerners cannot be argued with, cannot
be crushed, cannot be ignored, and cannot be laughed out
of existence. Its effects on its adherents are one of the stark
political facts of our time. In the foreseeable future its impact may be expected to grow rather than to decline; its
militant advance guard will be strident in advocacy and
bitter in defeat. But although it must be endured, it cannot
be permitted to triumph.

This view of the Southern phenomenon, the major conclusion of the entire book, is perhaps less sensational and yet less optimistic than many other judgments of recent years. But in defense of the conclusion advanced above (which may be read in greater detail in the final chapter), it must be emphasized that the facts of Southern political life today do not really permit any other interpretation.

It is a curiously sobering thought that the South has been "rediscovered" by successive generations of non-Southern intellectuals for more than a century, and yet this perplexing region remains virtually as mysterious as ever. No outsider can really grasp the peculiar flavor of the Southern way of life; no Southerner, on the other hand, can fully communicate to a Northerner the full range of the political emotions that seethe in his subconscious. This book, written in a mixture of affection and bemusement by a native of the North who has lived most of his adult life in the South, does not seriously pretend to get inside the skin of the very Southerners with which it is concerned. Its purpose is description and analysis, not condemnation or exhortation. Its methodology is as rigorously quantitative as its subject matter permits; its point of view as objective as its author can maintain during a critical period of American national life; its conclusions as firmly based on the data as the figures themselves allow. The final verdict upon methodology, point of view, and conclusions alike will be rendered by future generations of Southerners themselves.

SOUTHERN
INTERNATIONALISM—
MYTH AND REALITY

A PART of the working image of the American political process that has long been widely shared by most concerned, articulate, and mass media-sensitized Americans is that the South has long been the home of something they persist in calling "internationalism." The impression that south of the Mason-Dixon Line lives a people more aware of the responsibilities of the United States to the world community, more willing actively to support a policy designed to fulfill those responsibilities, and more inclined to participate personally in the implementation of those decisions with their money, their time, and their sons has had a firm grip on the imagination of much of the American body politic. Because this idea has won such wide acceptance and because the contemporary attitudes of Southerners in and out of Congress are so at variance with the image, the myth and the reality of the "traditional" Southern position must be examined before the deviations from this norm can be treated.

For many years, and especially since the era of 1939-

1941 preceding the entry of the United States into World War II, casual political discourse has assumed the existence of deep splits within the American consensus on certain issues of foreign policy, largely in terms of the isolationism-internationalism antinomy referred to in Chapter I. As a starting point, it has been axiomatic that the seat of "isolationism" in the United States has long been in the Midwest, and that the excesses of the 1920's and the 1930's—the rejection of the League of Nations, the failure to enter the World Court, the Neutrality Acts, the equivocation during the Spanish Civil War, and so on—were more than anything else the results of the pernicious doctrines of isolationism as preached across the prairies and the plains. Offsetting this baleful influence to some extent, however, was the consistent (if often ineffective) counterforce of the South, whose spokesmen—according to the myth—consistently fought the good fight for a reasoned, pragmatic, yet ultimately idealistic American commitment to a working international order.

This version of history, which tends subtly to relegate the other sections of the United States to a relatively minor role as spectators of the battle between the major ideological opponents, received much of whatever empiric validation it may boast during two brief periods of recent American history: the League debate in 1919, and the immediately pre-war controversy that began in 1939 and climaxed at Pearl Harbor. In these two situations that mark the beginning and the end of the "interwar" era, there is little doubt that the Midwest (largely if not completely) and the South (also largely if not completely) took opposite sides and attempted to lead their respective camps. During 1940 and 1941, for example, the America First Committee (the holding company for all shades of isolationism, withdrawal, and non-participation in the war) became almost entirely a Midwestern organization, while it had virtually no supporters in the South. Southerners in Congress, on the other hand, were well ahead of any other regional delegation in their advocacy of measures of national defense, of proposals to aid the allies, and of early American entry into the war. All of these points are part of the record and cannot be gainsaid.

But myth-making requires oversimplification, and the actual position of Southern Congressmen and the attitudes among Southerners which provoked this regional posture were much more complex than they might seem to have been on the basis of the highly selective evidence usually advanced to support the general thesis of Southern multilateralism. The South's approach to foreign policy, like its approach to so many other issues of public affairs, has long been special. The unique ingredients in its own brand of "internationalism" clearly distinguish the traditional Southern view (or, more accurately, the view articulated by traditional Southern politicians) from the concepts of foreign affairs shared by the bulk of the leadership of the more complex societies in the Northeast, the Midwest, and the West.

ELEMENTS OF THE SOUTHERN POSITION

What are the data that lend credence to the myth of Southern internationalism? What was the traditional Southern outlook on world affairs that was held generally throughout the interwar years, was brought to a peak during World War II, and remained controlling in the postwar era up to the beginning of the first Eisenhower administration? Just what has the South done to deserve its reputation as an enlightened region on international affairs, always alert to advocate and support multilateralist foreign policy ventures?

Probably the most solid ingredient in the Southern approach to foreign affairs has been a consistent commitment to free trade as a general economic principle and low tariffs as a political goal. So strong has the Southern position long been on this point and so influential were Southerners in the councils of the Democratic party that for generations tariff policy was one of the very few legitimate differences that could be discovered between the two major political parties. The South's delegation in Congress after the Civil War (to say nothing of the violent Southern objections to Whig tariff policy in the first half of the nineteenth century) was always in the van of the continuing Democratic attempt to roll back the level of protectionism. The one-party system in the South, rooted though it might have been in the bitter memories of war, defeat, and occupation, nevertheless had this practical issue on which to feed for many years. The Republicans were the high-tariff party, and immediate Southern interest dictated the continuation of the region's historic identification with the low-tariff Democrats.

The Smoot-Hawley Tariff of 1930 was anathema to Southerners, but the Reciprocal Trade Program of 1934 almost immediately became a shining symbol to them. It was after all the work of Cordell Hull, himself a Democrat and a Southerner, and—whatever the limited results the program actually may have had—it was unquestionably a step in what the South conceived to be the right direction. Even today, when the magic of Roosevelt and the New Deal has tarnished in a very different South, the two monuments of that era that yet evoke fond memories are TVA and the Trade Agreements Program.

A second characteristic of the Southern approach to foreign policy for many years has been a consistently sympathetic attitude toward the symbolism of "a strong national defense" in general and toward virtually any and all specific proposals aimed at increasing or strengthening the armed forces. Always alert to the emotional impact of military power as an expression of national personality and will, Southerners in Congress have consistently been defenders of the armed forces and advocates of a greater place for them in American society.

Although the South, as cruelly injured by the depression of 1929 as any region of the country, went along with the early New Deal in its attempt to reduce the size and cost of the military establishment, it greeted President Roosevelt's rediscovery of military power with great enthusiasm and no little relief. With Southerners sitting in key positions on Congressional committees and with almost the entire Southern delegation united in support, the military measures looking toward the American entry into World War II were enthusiastically accepted. On seven important bills of this type between 1939 and 1941, Southern support outstripped that from any other region of the country: the fortification of Guam (1939), the revision of the Neutrality Acts (1939), the Lend-Lease Act (1941), the British Aid Bill (1941), the Draft Extension Act (1941), the Ship Seizure Bill (1941), and the repeal of the Neutrality Acts (1941). The strong Southern position on preparedness during this era, particularly in view of the intensity of the crisis of conscience which gripped so many Americans at the time, went far to shape the dominant Southern image of internationalism in the minds of an entire generation of Americans.

In the immediate postwar era, the South's orientation and commitment to affairs military did not diminish. Throughout the entire cold war period, to the limited extent to which there has been any serious Congressional conflict over the overall size of the nation's military establishment, Southerners by and large have been on the side of opposing any reduction and of demanding steady increases. The Armed Services Committees in both houses have for several Congresses been chaired by Southerners, and the same has been consistently true of the other committees and subcommittees strategic to the Pentagon. The South's deep dedication to national defense, it must be admitted, has both ideological and highly practical roots, and seems beyond either question or imminent change. To the extent that promotion of a large and powerful military establish-

ment and the willingness to use it freely in support of
national objectives is a component of an "internationalist"
point of view, the South has been and may today claim to be
highly qualified on this count.

A third ingredient in the traditional Southern position
has been a relatively benign attitude toward northern and
western Europe in general, and in particular toward Great
Britain. Again, this leaning showed up most specifically
during the two high points of Southern involvement in world
affairs in the interwar years, at the end of World War I
and on the eve of World War II. During the debate on the
League of Nations, many Southerners voiced a clear Anglophilia and argued that the United States was and would
remain in good hands so long as it remained closely allied
with Britain. In the confusion of the war debt and depression
eras the preoccupation lapsed, not to reappear in any major
way until the fall of France and the Battle of Britain
in 1940 forced the entire nation to re-examine its identification with Europe. Southerners, especially those most closely
identified with the regional tradition, did not hesitate; from
mid-1940 onward they were consistently in the vanguard
of those arguing for extensive aid to the United Kingdom,
not excluding American entry into the war.

The Southern preoccupation with Europe as the appropriate battleground for America continued throughout
the war and projected itself almost unmodified into the cold
war era. Southern support of the Truman Doctrine, the
Marshall Plan, the North Atlantic Treaty Organization, and
the United States military commitment in Europe during
the late 1940's was almost complete and unquestioned. The
student may search in vain for any Southern counterpart
(at least prior to 1953) of the raucous Anglophobia and fear
of Europe that dominated, for example, the pages of the
Chicago Tribune and the public utterances of most Midwestern Republican Congressmen during this period.

It was not until the major focus of American policy

began to swing away from Europe toward the non-western world that the marked Southern shift began. Although it is somewhat ahead of the story, it is nevertheless interesting to point out that even during the period of the great swing in Southern attitudes during the 1950's, only a very few Southern Congressmen voiced any qualms about the "mutual security"—that is, military assistance—aspects of foreign aid. Their objections tended to center on the increasing non-European orientation of the program and the dominant place in policy calculations gradually assumed by considerations of economic aid and development. A significant rebirth of Southern interest in aid programs took place when in 1962 and 1963 United States relations with Europe again became complicated by the issues of nuclear deterrence and the Common Market. This was a return to the familiar for many Congressmen from the South, and on these questions they had a ready-made tradition to guide their deliberations.

An economic commitment to a multilateral system of international trade, a preoccupation with military affairs, and a half-hidden sense of allegiance to Great Britain: these then were the traditional components of the Southern posture on world affairs. Do they add up to an acceptance of any abstract doctrine of "internationalism"? The proposition, even put in the most favorable terms, seems a doubtful one.

What is clearly lacking in the traditional Southern exegesis of foreign policy is what was identified in Chapter I as a sense of "multilateralism." There is nowhere in the Southern ethos any appreciation of the interdependence of states and peoples and the necessity facing the United States of adapting itself and its desires to the demands of a normally intractable environment. The point of constant reference of Southern spokesmen between 1919 and 1953 was in almost every case ostensibly "what is good for the United States," cast normally in terms xenophobic and unilateralist even when the rhetoric was the most flamboyant in calling for support of America's allies. The standardized image of "going it alone" even within the bounds of an international organization like the League of Nations or the United Nations was always implicit—and frequently explicit—in Southern discourse. There is in the traditional Southern outlook, in other words, no commitment to any generalized ideal of a world order; there is only the belief that complete fulfillment of American aspirations is possible in a world that can eventually be arranged to suit the purposes of the United States.

One is struck today by the naiveté and provincialism of even the most "internationalist" of the Southern spokesmen of the interwar period. Although they professed selfless dedication to the welfare of the United States and all its people, their working frame of analysis was forever and unquenchably Southern. Each of the issues that arose was evaluated in a peculiarly regional way and each found its resolution in Southern terms. Foreign affairs, in other words, passed through a distinctly Southern filter and was finally reduced to the foreign policy of the South. The fact that in certain crucial periods the South and the remainder of the nation agreed on particular action programs should not mislead the observer into thinking that the South reached its conclusions in the same way or for the same reasons as did other parts of America.

The explanation for this divergence in foreign policy atitude is part and parcel of the special role that the South has played in American history. A different social order, a stubborn and anachronistic adherence to a rural-oriented economy, a constant and insoluble racial problem, a distinct political system based on one-party dominance, and a festering pessimism born of separation, defeat, and exclusion all contributed to the conditioning any Southern leader brought to his contemplation of world affairs. It would have required supermen to transcend their regional roots in order to adopt an enlightened and broad approach to international issues; the South, like the nation at large, does not breed an especially large supply of supermen, and of these only a few eventually find their way into Congress.

SOURCES OF THE SOUTHERN POSITION

Thus the elements in the traditional Southern position can be identified with certain long-standing strains in Southern political life. Several contributing factors led Southern leaders to take the positions they did, forces indigenous to Southern life and deeply imbedded in the region's political code. Each of these—of which none is entirely dead today and of which several are still of major significance—played its own part in shaping the dominant attitude.

The economic internationalism intrinsic to the Southern position was legitimate and practical. Committed, alone among the major regions of the United States in the late nineteenth and twentieth centuries, to primary reliance upon cash-crop agriculture, the South had an immediate and continuing need for access to overseas markets. Exporting cotton and tobacco to Europe and importing European manufactures freed Southerners to some extent from the dominance of Northern industry and gave them a sense of being participants in a broader economic system. The Confederacy ultimately based its hopes for victory on the sovereign role of King Cotton in bringing about British intervention, and the South never wavered in its confidence that its capacity to produce certain agricultural products of guaranteed international demand was its own and the only available route to prosperity. Southern cotton and tobacco farmers, particularly the former, were throughout the bulk of the interwar period entirely without real price protection by the federal government and were, therefore, at the mercy of the world market. Up to the very eve of World War II, therefore, the South and its spokesmen were almost unanimous in eschewing protectionism and in insisting on the progressive liberalization of the terms and conditions of international trade.

But, even in dealing with such immediately practical and hard-headed matters as finding export markets for their cotton in an increasingly competitive system, the South remained incurably romantic and myth-ridden. The low-tariff position was a principle of faith and doctrine as much as it was the result of realistic calculation. Low tariffs were defended heatedly by many who had little or no appreciation of their real economic implications; it was sufficient for the quixotic Southerner to know that Northern manufacturers and Midwestern wheat farmers were on the other side. From this he could quickly deduce that they were, therefore, at bottom aiming at the further suppression and impoverishment of the South. A titillating air of unreality still clings to the official record of several of the tariff debates of the early years of this century. Many Southerners in Congress consciously evoked recollections of Shiloh and Chancellorsville as they encouraged each other to do battle with the forces of Northern bourgeois capitalism.

A second element, difficult to quantify but immediately obvious to anyone who becomes aware of the climate of Southern political discourse, is the impact of Woodrow Wilson as man and memory on Southern foreign policy attitudes. It is impossible accurately to verbalize the sense of pariahdom shared by politically sensitive Southerners during the long years from the Civil War to the election of Wilson. The region felt—with considerable justice—that after the war it had never been really readmitted to the inner circles of the national government where its sons had earlier bulked so large. The Republicans (at least after 1876) would have nothing to do with the South, and the national leadership of the Democrats, secure in the region's "solidity," saw no reason to make special concessions to a bloc of states already hopelessly committed to the party. The South's political frustration seemed complete.

Woodrow Wilson, although elected from New Jersey, was a Southerner by birth and rearing, and the South adopted him immediately as one of its own. When as President he showed a tendency to rely on Southern advisors and to listen sympathetically to Southern leaders, his victory over the South became complete. As the region's "first President since Jefferson Davis," Southerners gave him their hearts.

As a result, Southern support of Wilson was generous, undemanding, and in retrospect almost touching. Wilson, whose historic image in the North is that of a cold if liberal intellectual, emerges from Southern folklore as a romantic conservative, a true *beau ideal* of the Old South. And it is undeniable that his "New Freedom" domestic program made few embarrassing demands on Southern society while simultaneously serving to some extent to redress certain rankling injustices under which Southerners felt themselves burdened. In foreign policy, influenced as he was by such sons of the South as Colonel Edward House and Ambassador to Great Britain Walter Hines Page, Wilson approached his major crises completely in harmony with Southern predispositions. When the showdown finally came in the aftermath of the war, the South was prepared to go all the way with Wilson.

The fight for the League, and the eventual victory of the Senate Republicans both at the moment and in later years, quickly found their places as further installments in the history of the Lost Cause. The opposition to Wilson's grand design and to the Treaty of Versailles was in Southern eyes part of the continuing campaign against the South, and to argue in favor of the League was also to continue the struggle for the vindication of the peculiar values of Southern society. Very few of the dedicated battlers for the Covenant seem to have grasped the fact that Wilson's own image of the League as a body that would tie the hands of all sovereign states, including the United States, clashed directly with the regionalist and nationalist symbolism of the South. It was enough that a Southern President was demanding an international organization; no committed Southerner was interested in asking too many questions.

Since Wilson's fight became the South's fight as well, his ultimate repudiation was also accepted as a Southern defeat. The mythmakers thereupon went to work, and Wilson and the League became part of the interwar weaponry of Southern political leaders. Roosevelt, although welcomed as a Democrat, faced certain handicaps in winning Southern support: he was identified with the urban Northeast, he relied heavily for support upon organized labor, and he launched programs of reform that carried very disturbing implications for Southern society. Except for reciprocal trade, therefore, Southern acceptance of the Roosevelt foreign policy before 1938 was limited, cautious, and tentative.

The failure of the 1938 purge of conservative Southern Congressmen, the virtual abandonment of the reform phase of the New Deal after that date, and the approach of the war all changed the South's attitude toward Roosevelt and the President's own response. As the New Deal became engrossed in international crisis, the assumptions and the language of Wilsonianism again became common currency in the American body politic. To the South this was like coming home again, and its citizens responded almost unanimously.

The problems of World War II, whether of preparedness, prosecution, or settlement, were to the South a "second time around" on the issues of the age of Wilson. Finally, it seemed, the arguments of 1919 and 1920 were going to be repeated; this time, however, the side of reason, right, and justice was going to win. From the debate with the America First Committee on through the ratification of the Charter of the United Nations, Woodrow Wilson played a major role as silent advisor and constant inspiration to most Southern leaders. Wilsonianism, and with it the South itself, was finally to be vindicated.

Closely connected in the long-term outlook of the South with the imagery of Wilson is the particular mythology of national party politics that has long been dominant in the South. During the long drought that began with the election of Lincoln and really endured until Franklin Roosevelt forged the new Democratic coalition in 1932, there were only two Democratic presidents. Under both Cleveland and Wilson, therefore, the South (playing such a major role in Democratic politics as it did) saw itself in the unusual position of being central to national affairs. The special significance attached to Wilson (and Roosevelt, at least immediately prior to and during the war) was in large if indefinite measure a function of his role as a Democratic president.

This would suggest that the Southern approach to foreign affairs owes a great deal to the pervasive effect of party regularity. It is a quirk of history that the first three Democratic presidents of this century—Wilson, Roosevelt, and Truman—all had their respective administrations capped by a major international war. Whatever thoughts this coincidence—never made overt, but today part of the folklore of American politics—might induce in other Americans, it has no way proved to be a difficulty for the Southern traditionalist. As successive Democratic presidents have been drawn into major wars, Southerners have followed unquestioningly.

There is a curious symmetry in the patterns formed by the administrations of Wilson and Franklin D. Roosevelt. Both presidents took office committed to domestic reform; both felt, on assuming office, that foreign affairs was of secondary importance. Both faced a series of international crises that gradually forced them to abandon the bulk of their domestic program in favor of deeper involvement in international affairs. Both achieved climax by military victory; the programs of both suffered postwar repudiation. The parallels are striking indeed.

Almost as interesting is the way in which the South's Congressional delegations throughout both periods reacted to the President. In neither case, for example, was the South's "internationalism" especially obvious (even to the Southerners themselves) until after the chief executive had made his own turnabout; in neither instance, furthermore, did the South ever go beyond the President in charting a positive course. The conclusion is easy to draw that just how far the Southern group was willing to go toward multilateralism in either case was determined more by what the President wanted in any situation than by independently-exercised Southern judgments on the merits of the case.

It was quite another matter, however, when Southern Democratic Congressmen were in positions of responsibility and leadership during periods when the White House was occupied by a Republican. Here the more revealing dimensions of the Southern thinking on foreign affairs can be found, freed as the Southerners were from the necessity of supporting a fellow Democrat. Here instances of partisan opposition—not a peculiarly Southern phenomenon by any means—are frequent; here also, however, can be found cases in which leading Southerners placed themselves behind Republican presidents who were following a course deemed satisfactory to the South. Perhaps the most striking recent example of this was the courageous and unremitting identification of Senator Walter George of Georgia with the Eisenhower foreign policy during the mid-1950's.

One anticipatory word might be said here about the decreasing effectiveness of party regularity in keeping Southerners in line behind a Democratic administration. The Democratic party, ever since the election of 1936, has not been dominated as it was for so long by Southern leadership and Southern ideas; on the contrary, the tendency has been quite in the other direction. Southerners, particularly since 1945, have found themselves increasingly at odds with a party leadership depending for so many of its votes on minority groups, organized labor, and urban party machines. A conservative coalition of Southern Democrats and Midwestern Republicans has largely dominated the House of Representatives ever since 1938 and has sporadically extended its influence to the Senate. Coincidentally, the rise of the Republican party in the South, although not spectacular, has been steady in the increasingly urbanized region.

All these factors have largely undermined the appeal of party solidarity to Southern Congressmen on any kind of issue, and on foreign policy in particular. The Kennedy administration, thoroughly and admittedly party-oriented and partisan in outlook, had in its three short years only limited success in winning Southern support for its foreign policy moves, and the 88th Congress elected in 1962 showed unmistakable signs of being even less amenable to this appeal than its immediate predecessor. No more graphic demonstration of the changes in Southern society that form the base of the argument in this study could be advanced than the tarnished symbolism of the Democratic party in the once-but-not-any-more solid South.

Another element in the Southern tradition that contributed to the region's composite foreign policy attitude is its philosophical view of violence. Also an exceptionally difficult concept about which to be specific, there is no doubt that Southern culture has long had a different attitude toward interpersonal violence than has had the remainder of the nation. Whether one analyzes the upper-class code of chivalry that still lingers on in many parts of the South or the cruder principles of man-to-man relations that govern poor-white (and poor-Negro) behavior, the phenomenon of violence bulks large.

Without attempting to speculate on the personality

structure of Southerners—a fascinating but obviously inconclusive venture, at least in the present context—it is
evident from the historical record that Southerners are
willing to accept violence as a tolerable way to conduct
international affairs much more readily than are most non-
Southerners. Military establishments do not exist, the South
insists, merely to provide satisfying careers for men with
a stronge sense of *noblesse oblige* (and, it may be cynically
pointed out, relatively poor economic prospects in any other
career); they should be used freely in the national interest.
The United States maintains an army, a navy, and an air
force in order to win victories over the nation's enemies and
to accomplish the nation's objectives. For a president to
neglect his duty to use military power with determination
and courage is for him to fall short of what the American
people should expect of their public servants.

Thus the military fixation of Southerners has a profound cultural root, and Southern conduct in a moment of
crisis is highly predictable. During the prolonged crisis of
the cold war Southerners have led not only in the steady
escalation of the size, complexity, and expense of the armed
forces of the United States, but also in the flaming rhetoric
of the final "showdown" with communism, filled with gloomy
but exciting forecasts of inevitable war.

A fairly abstruse point in this connection might help
to throw the Southern approach to international violence
into deeper perspective. Force is the only technique of true
finality available to states in the international order. When
a state goes to war, the correctness of its position and the
persuasiveness of its public relations are substantially irrelevant; the only consideration that really matters is
whether or not its will and its armed strength will be
adequate to bring about victory on the battlefield and the
submission of the enemy. In other words, in strict conceptual terms, violence in international politics may be
viewed as the highest form of unilateralism, as the state

seeks to have its way in the face of adamant and active opposition. The theory of warfare long accepted by sovereign states and the political order from which this elaborate doctrine depends both presuppose that in any military conflict there is always a winner and a loser, and furthermore, that the stakes of war themselves are of a sort that permit "victory" and "defeat" to be meaningful terms.

These abstractions lead to a concrete point. The extent to which Southerners are distinctive in their early and heavy reliance upon the calculus of violence in international affairs is a measure of the extent to which they are instinctively predisposed toward unilateral formulations of American policy choices. In war the unilateralist can see himself (and his nation as well) "taking arms against a sea of troubles" and reducing all the ambiguous and complex choices of politics to a simple we-or-they dichotomy. This is the unilateralist's view toward foreign policy matters of all sorts in any case—the United States against the world— and it is of special relevance in military crises only to the extent to which it is made explicit. No single proposition cuts so deeply into the image of Southern "internationalism" as the region's clear preference for military implementation of unilaterally-determined policies.

A word should also be said here about the regional Anglophilia to which some attention has already been paid. This visceral orientation seems to come from two sources, both today of markedly less influence than heretofore. The first is the South's remarkable immunity from the waves of immigration that rolled over American shores between 1860 and 1920. It must be admitted that during this era the South was much less attractive as a new homeland than were the rural Midwest or the urban East, nor was there much inclination in the South itself to welcome such immigrants as found their way there. In any case, at least until the onset of World War II, the South was ethnically the most homogeneous region of the United States, with a population (except, of course, for the Negroes) heavily Anglo-Saxon in origin, broken only occasionally by pockets of Latin (French or Spanish) influence. Although for most Southerners the British Isles were far away and long ago, the ethnic unity of the South contrasted so sharply with the diversity characteristic of most of the rest of the nation that it became a point of Southern pride to retain the memory of their British roots long after the notion had any social validity.

A second cause, less specific but of great value in developing the ideal of a "Southern way of life" as a combined palliative and stimulant to political action, was the fancied identity between the British and the Southern aristocratically-dominated social systems. Born in the days of the plantation aristocracy, the ideal of a propertied leisure class governing in the name of all for the common good had a profound and long-lasting effect on Southern attitudes generally. British upper-class sympathy with the Confederacy during the Civil War and British leadership in both world wars played their parts in contributing to the identification of Southern leadership with British traditions. Sympathy for and active support of British policy could thus easily be made into a matter of simple obligation rather than of complex and calculating policy.

A consequence of the South's racial homogeneity, however, was the region's leadership in the almost totally successful attempt to restrict immigration. Cultural isolation and political unsophistication led easily into a narrow xenophobia, and the national government's program to keep foreigners out received and still receives general approbation among Southerners. Strange disparities appear in the reasoning used, however; some Southerners broaden their preoccupation with racial "purity" from the Negro to include Orientals, Slavs, Jews, and Latin Europeans in the general category of undesirables, while other Southerners are opposed to further immigration on the simple and pragmatic

ground that immigrants are low-wage workers who take
jobs away from natives. In either case, however, the result
is the same: the picture of the United States as the haven for
the oppressed is sharply conditioned by restrictions and
limitations.

THE DEMAGOGIC ABERRATION

Running alongside the traditional Southern approach to
foreign policy as outlined above, sometimes coinciding but
more often clashing with it, has been the second strain of
Southern thought about international affairs. This has been
more than anything else the voice of social and economic
protest rooted in the discontent of the poor-white stratum of
Southern society. Although as authentically Southern as the
more orthodox attitude analyzed above, and although sharing a number of specific points of view with it, demagogic
foreign policy pronouncements over the years have had a
very different impact upon the political thinking of the
South and ultimately the nation.

The phenomenon of protest, so central to the contemporary behavior of the South, is analyzed in some greater
detail in Chapters VIII and IX. In this introductory discussion it is necessary only to clarify one or two of its
salient features so that its aberrant foreign policy posture
can be thrown into the sharpest possible contrast with the
traditional points of view.

Probably the most important characteristic of demagogic protest in the South prior to World War II, at least in
terms of international attitudes, was that it was a function of an activist climate of politics. The traditional foreign
policy outlook of the Southern leadership elite was normally,
as one writer put it, "laid athwart apathy" in the body politic
and was viable only to the extent to which the masses of
Southern citizenry did not feel themselves directly involved in the policies their own Congressmen were pro-

mulgating and supporting. As soon as individual awareness and identification replaced mass non-involvement among large numbers of voters, the easy upper-class formula of interventionism, militarism, and free trade became complicated and difficult to apply. The Southern demagogue of the interwar years, speaking for a social group ordinarily outside the scope of the Southern foreign policy consensus, had little patience with traditional formulas.

Protest was necessary to the demagogue because only in a crusade to rectify injustice as they saw it could the bulk of the Southern white population muster enough energy to go on the political warpath. Demagoguery was thus a result rather than a cause; no demagogue could hope to bulk large in the affairs of his community or his state without an aroused body of citizens mobilized behind him. Once he had his mass movement in operation and in hand, the peculiar dynamics of Southern politics made his importance inevitable and his victory probable.

The demagogue, in the course of feeding the appetites while continually sharpening the hostilities of his poor white, rural, unsophisticated, racist, and low-income constituency, tended to level his heavy guns at all "outsiders." The catalogue of his targets might be conceived as a set of concentric circles drawn around the rural South, with the Southern aristocrats receiving the first volleys and, as the range lengthened, other deviants such as the Northeastern United States, all large cities everywhere, all religions outside the narrow range of fundamentalist Protestantism, and all foreigners brought under fire. Thus the demagogue, in spite of his own exceptionally limited and parochial horizons, was almost inexorably drawn into the arena of foreign policy discussion.

Southern demagogues from the Populist Tom Watson of Georgia to the buffoon from Buncombe County, North Carolina, Robert Rice Reynolds, all preached a militant and obscurantist doctrine of total withdrawal and non-involvement in international affairs. Like their co-ideologists in the Midwest, they combined reformism with isolationism (in a literal sense, these are the only true *isolationists* in recent American history) and fused a demand for economic justice at home with a disavowal of the outside world, all in the grand tradition of American radicalism. The Southern demagogue differed from his Northern colleague primarily in his involvement in the issue of white supremacy, a key to the Southerner's political methodology but of virtually no relevance to the Northern rabble-rouser, except during the brief and ugly episode of the Northern Ku Klux Klan in the late 1920's.

The demagogues of the interwar South were in a real sense prosecuting a class war, and they spared no aspects of upper-class Southern life in their effort to set the poor whites against both the Bourbons and the Negroes simultaneously. This brought them into collision with the foreign policy symbols of Southern aristocracy, and the demagogue was openly Anglophobic, anti-Wilson, on occasion pacifist, and anti-League of Nations. No one can be certain today to what extent the foreign policies advocated by the demagogues of that era were sincere and the result of personal conviction, or were instead only convenient springboards from which to mount assaults against their local opponents. But the effect of this tactic is clear: audiences did not bother to question the demagogues' sincerity but tended instead to accept as revealed gospel their formulations of the nature of the world and the task of the United States.

In truth it is inaccurate to classify the demagogic aberration as a "foreign policy" position at all. Its overall effect was to deny the necessity of the United States conducting anything like a real foreign policy in the world. Consistently contradicting either the necessity or the desirability of American entry into world affairs, and projecting an image of a nation kept pure and strong by turning its back on the temptations of diplomacy, the demagogue argued that the world could be kept forever from America's doorstep if only the people remained alert and dedicated enough to see and avoid the peril. The interventionist proclivities of the traditionalists and the Bourbons were devastatingly easy to portray as sinister plots to deliver the United States (especially the rural South) to the mercy of London politicians and Anglophile New York (and Atlanta) bankers. Foreign affairs was not a continuing responsibility of the national government, but was instead a temporary process of exercising a finite set of devils, after which therapeutic effort the nation could relax secure in its strength and prosperity.

In the face of overwhelming Southern support for World War II, some of the prewar demagogues—notably Senator Reynolds—maintained their true and radical isolationist position on into the era of active combat. This was perhaps the truest test of demagogic consistency: if a leader of protest was willing to fly in the face of his constituency's traditional support of militarism and war, he was beyond doubt outside the pale of the Southern norm even in its most generous dimensions. But by and large the demagogic thrust in the interwar South had been largely stilled before the crisis of 1939-1941, and the voice of protest, although not stilled, did not ring quite so loudly after the New Deal had begun to chip away at the discontent that was its source.

The South in the last years before World War II, in other words, had returned almost completely to the stewardship of its traditional ruling class; only a few of the old demagogues like Reynolds and Martin Dies were functioning at the time of the fall of France. The region's response to the threat of war was more in keeping with the long-term predilections of its leaders than had been its overall outlook only some half-dozen years earlier. The demagogic approach to foreign policy largely lapsed after the mid-1930's, to reappear only in the aftermath of the school desegregation decisions two decades later.

The firm grip of the traditionalist approach to world affairs that permitted Southern Congressmen to vote for multi-lateralist measures continued unshaken throughout the war and the early stages of the cold war. There was nothing surprising in the Southern response to the demands of World War II itself, comporting so neatly as this great enterprise did with both the South's ego-image and the requirements of simple electoral politics. The traditionalists likewise greeted the United Nations warmly as a final if delayed vindication of Wilsonianism, but found little difficulty in combining the idealism of the United Nations with their simultaneous advocacy of a higher level of national defense expenditure than either President Truman or the majority of Congress accepted.

The onset of the cold war as well caused few problems for Southern leadership. Newly proud of their "conservatism" and with the exotic, baleful, and frightening specter of the Communist conspiracy to spur them on, the traditionalists found it simple to follow administration leadership into the programmatic implementation of the anti-Soviet campaign. Europe's centrality to at least the early phase, already noted, contributed to the ease with which the Wilsonian image of international co-operation in the United Nations was transmuted into a naked power struggle reminiscent of the titanic crusade against Hitler.

Disillusion began to set in even among the staunchest supporters of American cold-war policy when the struggle gave signs of being inconclusive and inordinately expensive. The Marshall Plan, originally accepted by the South as a one-time expedient to fill a temporary need, gave way to an apparently permanent Mutual Security Program; the Korean War, coming so close on the heels of the victory over the Nazis as to disconcert many normally military minded Southerners, reached its frustrating climax and dragged on in the slow agony of Panmunjom. The focus of American efforts shifted from Europe to strange battlefields in Asia, the Middle East, Latin America, and ultimately Africa. Gradually, the disinclination of successive administrations to seek final and complete victory as prohibitive in cost and unbearable in risk began to corrode many Southern attitudes, even as it was to do in other parts of the nation.

The regional disposition to support multilateralist efforts, never especially strong since it demanded a measure of perceptive "world-mindedness" that very few individual Southerners could muster, began to crumble in the face of time and bemusement. But even the frustrations of the Korean War, whatever their effect on the popular consensus, brought about no real Southern secession from the Congressional majority supporting the general line of American foreign policy. The time sequence argues that the true cause of the contemporary Southern shift is not to be found in the host of contradictions besetting the conduct of American foreign policy, however annoying the international environment might be. The breakaway of the South is the result of forces within Southern society itself rather than an outcome of any developments in international affairs.

Subsequent chapters recount an effort to determine what these forces were and are and to point out the direction in which they have and are yet moving the Southern mind. Fewer and fewer Southern Congressmen have been supporting the genuinely multilateralist aspects of current American policy, while more and more have been accepting the premises and some of the conclusions of the more militant, demagogic brand of unilateralism. This is the major element in the contemporary Southern shift.

THE REVOLT
AGAINST FOREIGN AID

THE CHANGE in the international outlook of
the South is nowhere more clearly documented than in the
record its Congressmen have made on the question of that
hardy perennial of recent American foreign policy, foreign
aid. When the United States launched the Truman Doctrine
and the Marshall Plan in 1947 and 1948 and thus committed
itself to furnishing extensive assistance to friendly foreign
countries, it was quite apparent that the South produced a
disproportionately large share of the House votes necessary
to enact these bold new policies into law. The fourteen
Southern states held then (and hold now) slightly less than
30 per cent of the 435 seats in the House of Representatives,
the exact percentage varying slightly with each decennial
reapportionment. In 1948, the South was almost twice as
favorable toward the Foreign Assistance Act (the Marshall
Plan) as the House as a whole; less than 16 per cent of the
74 negative votes cast on final passage of the bill came
from Southern seats.

Thus identifying itself at the beginning so conspicuously

with the principle of foreign aid, the South remained true to its pledge throughout the second Truman administration and the Korean War. Even though some doubts were apparent and although it was clear that the pro-foreign aid position did not necessarily carry over in every case into other multilateralist policy endeavors, the South's Congressional delegation during these years was generally assumed to be safely in the multilateralist camp and was counted on largely to offset any potential danger of a renaissance of Midwestern "isolationism."

With the opening of the Eisenhower era, however, and probably connected in some way with the reappearance of a Republican administration in Washington after twenty years of exile, the Southern consensus on foreign aid began to dissolve. Beginning in 1954, the number of Southerners in the opposition column began to increase each year as the annual request for a renewal of the program reached the floor of the House. Once set in motion, the trend gained momentum rapidly. By 1962 the South had earned—and was apparently quite proud of—the distinction of being the most anti-foreign aid region of the United States; its representatives surpassed those of any other part of the country not only in the vehemence of their objections during debate and in the submission of restrictive amendments but—even more significantly—in the percentage of their number that made their positions unmistakable by voting "nay" in the showdown of a roll call vote. The mercurial quality of Southern politics and the volcanic rate of change in the region's mass attitudes are both dramatically illustrated by the South's remarkable feat of changing itself from a source of overwhelming support for foreign aid to the program's most extreme opponent in the short space of eight years—or, as the figures make clear, actually bringing about this metamorphosis within the span of a single presidential term.

FOREIGN AID AND THE SOUTH

In thus turning their backs on their own past position, Southern Congressmen were also going counter to the trend in the nation at large. This can be most simply demonstrated by an examination of the series of votes that furnish the clearest and least equivocal cross section of attitudes from one year to the next: the annual roll call on the "authorization" bill for foreign aid in the House. The authorization measure is a more accurate indicator of basic attitudes than any of the other votes taken during the annual aid cycle, in part because by its nature it tends to stress principles and policies rather than financial details. This is the central consideration, as shown by the consistency with which the authorization draws a larger total of votes than the appropriation bill or the adoption of a conference committee report.

Five Congresses, the 83rd through the 87th, span the decade from 1953 through 1962. During these ten years, overall support in the House for the foreign aid program (and opposition to it as well) remained remarkably consistent in the face of a rapidly changing international environment. Table 1 suggests how little the figures changed over the years.

Over the ten years covered here, the figures show a total margin in favor of foreign aid of almost exactly two to one. Furthermore, the vote in 1953 was the most lopsided in favor of the bill, with over 72 per cent of the total being affirmative; in 1962, on the other hand, the percentage of "yeas" dropped to its lowest during the decade, only marginally better than 60. During the intervening eight years, however, it is remarkable how little the affirmative percentage varied from its median figure of approximately 66.

TABLE 1 *

ROLL CALL VOTES ON FOREIGN AID AUTHORIZATIONS,
HOUSE OF REPRESENTATIVES, 1953-1962

YEAR	YEA	% OF HOUSE	NAY	% OF HOUSE	% YEA
1953	280	64	108	25	72.1
1954	260	60	126	29	67.3
1955	273	63	128	29	68.1
1956	275	63	122	28	69.2
1957	254	58	154	35	65.4
1958	238	54	134	31	63.9
1959	271	62	142	33	65.6
1960	243	55	131	30	64.9
1961	287	66	140	32	67.2
1962	250	57	164	38	60.3

* A word or two about the rationale of this table and those that follow is appropriate here. In order to have the data strictly comparable, the only positions considered in the analysis in this chapter are those that found their way into a formal roll call "yea" or "nay." Pairing, by means of which a Congressman may absent himself from a roll call but still make his position a matter of record, and other indices by means of which a member's stand on a measure might be ascertained, are all ignored in these calculations. The votes used here, in other words, are drawn from the official record only.

The corresponding data for the 126 Southern Congressmen, however, show the outline of a completely contrary evolution (Table 2).

Here the story of the Southern revolt against foreign aid is spelled out. The first year covered by the table, 1953, was the last in which the Marshall Plan consensus remained operative, and the South showed its earlier colors by turning in a moderately higher percentage of support than did the House as a whole. In 1954, however, the first great secession took place as roughly twenty regular supporters of the program dropped away into opposition, but overall the

Southern contingent remained perceptibly if no longer over-whelmingly in favor of the idea for the next two years. The second—and really determining—shift in voting patterns took place in 1957 as another twenty-odd Southerners moved into the negative column. There was a slight swing backward from the high point of opposition after 1957; not until 1963 did the Southern affirmative percentage drop as low again.

TABLE 2

ROLL CALL VOTES ON FOREIGN AID AUTHORIZATIONS,
126 SOUTHERN CONGRESSMEN, 1953-1962

YEAR	YEA	% OF SOUTH	NAY	% OF SOUTH	% YEA
1953	84	67	29	23	74.1
1954	62	49	48	38	56.4
1955	66	52	50	39	56.9
1956	65	52	54	43	54.6
1957	41	33	76	60	35.0
1958	48	38	60	48	44.4
1959	46	37	69	55	40.0
1960	43	34	62	49	40.9
1961	61	48	61	48	50.0
1962	49	39	68	54	41.0

The only year after 1957 in which the South did not show its opposition to foreign aid in unequivocal terms was 1961. In that first year of the New Frontier, President Kennedy was in the first flush of his honeymoon with Congress and the people and was determined to establish the primacy of his leadership beyond question. He and his associates therefore committed themselves to an all-out effort to rally Congressional support that would lead to a reassuring and vindicating heavy affirmative margin for foreign aid. A well-organized campaign of pressure and persuasion was mounted against the principal centers of opposition to the aid program, particularly in the South and in the Midwest. The drive to pile up a massive vote was far more intense and administration agents far more active than at any time under President Eisenhower.

But Southern stubbornness proved to be a match for the New Frontier's mixture of blandishments and coercion. President Kennedy was able to increase the total affirmative vote in the House by 44 votes over 1960 and to raise it to the largest figure for the decade, but—far from reducing opposition—he drew a total of 140 "nays." This figure was well above the ten-year average of 135 and larger by 9 than had been cast against President Eisenhower's request the year before. The affirmative percentage of the House vote was only 2.3 percentage points higher than in 1960.

Mr. Kennedy's less-than-convincing victory was made so in large part by the performance of the South. Under administration urging, Southerners increased their total of "yea" votes from their near-low of 43 in 1960 to 61 in 1961— the largest number of "yeas" since 1956. But he had almost no effect on the negative side, as the figure dropped from 62 in 1960 only to 61 the next year. In the meantime, Republicans were resisting the leadership of a new and self-confident Democratic administration by a significant abandonment of the program themselves. The upshot was a one-time triumph for the President; his effect on the South—such as it was—was almost entirely dissipated the next year. In 1962 Southern figures, both affirmative and negative, slipped back to their post-1957 norm.

Thus the conclusion suggests itself that the relatively consistent pattern of House voting on foreign aid during the ten years under consideration here was the result of two contrary trends which canceled each other. If the South, in other words, was increasingly in opposition while the House as a whole remained consistent, it would follow that somewhere in the membership increases in support were taking place to offset Southern declines. During the years in which the South was revolting against foreign aid, were there in fact countervailing forces at work elsewhere in the House?

For this purpose the House may be divided into two groups, the South and the "non-South," the latter consisting of the 309 seats outside the fourteen Southern states.

TABLE 3

CUMULATIVE VOTES, FOREIGN AID AUTHORIZATIONS, HOUSE OF REPRESENTATIVES, 1953-1962

YEARS	WHOLE HOUSE	SOUTH	NON-SOUTH
1953-62	2631-1349	565-577	2085-767
(10 years)	(66.1%)	(49.5%)	(72.6%)
1953-56	1088- 484	277-181	811-303
(4 years)	(69.2%)	(60.5%)	(70.9%)
1957-62	1543- 865	288-396	1255-469
(6 years)	(64.0%)	(42.1%)	(75.8%)

This brief table contains a good deal of information and suggests some interesting relationships. The figures in the first place confirm the hypothesis stated above: during the latter part of the decade there was indeed a marked increase in the affirmative percentage for foreign aid from the non-South that almost offset the growing animosity toward the program that Southerners were demonstrating. From a percentage base of less than 71 in favor during the first Eisenhower administration, the non-South increased its overall support by almost exactly 5 percentage points during the latter six years of the decade, thus holding the overall decline in House support to the minimum figures advanced in Table 1.

A second proposition that the table makes explicit is the date at which the South seceded from the consensus.

During the 1953-56 period, the Southern bloc remained generally in support of foreign aid by roughly a three to two margin, while the non-South was running somewhat stronger at almost three to one. After President Eisenhower's second inauguration, however, the Southern affirmative group lost almost half its 1956 membership and the region fell back into a three-to-two opposition majority. In that same period the non-South went over the three-to-one mark overall in the face of a significant recession in 1961 and 1962.

It is also significant that the non-South as defined in this discussion includes the 129 seats from the Midwest, long regarded as the true seat of unilateralism and myopia in foreign policy. Some greater attention will be given to the Midwesterners in a moment, but the dimensions of the Southern revolt against foreign aid are impressive in themselves. From 1953 through 1956 the average number of "nays" from the South was only 45, while from 1957 onward the average leaped to 65; on the other side of the equation, the Southern bloc cast almost as many affirmative votes on the program during the first four-year period as were forthcoming during the entire second Eisenhower administration *and* the first two years of the New Frontier.

Overall the opposition to foreign aid averaged 134.9 votes per session; to this figure the South contributed an average of 57.7 votes. The actual figures, of course, have moved up or down from one year to another, as has also the South's portion of the overall opposition. It is instructive to note the increasing share of the burden of hostility the South has borne, at least until the advent of the Kennedy administration in 1961 (Table 4).

From this table one conclusion may be quickly drawn: ever since 1957—the crucial year—the South has been the source of nearly half the total opposition to foreign aid authorizations in spite of the fact that only slightly more than a quarter of the seats in the House are held by

TABLE 4
"NAY" VOTES ON FOREIGN AID AUTHORIZATIONS,
HOUSE OF REPRESENTATIVES, 1953-1962

YEAR	HOUSE	SOUTH	NON-SOUTH	SOUTH'S % OF TOTAL
1953	108	29	79	27
1954	126	48	78	38
1955	128	50	78	39
1956	122	54	68	44
1957	154	76	78	49
1958	134	60	74	45
1959	142	69	73	49
1960	131	62	69	47
1961	140	61	79	44
1962	164	68	96	41

Southerners. In 1957, 1959, and 1960 the South came closest to breaking through the 50-per-cent-of-the-total opposition barrier, but never quite reached the critical point. Under President Kennedy the regional share of opposition declined perceptibly, but this was due to an increase in the negative votes from the non-South rather than to any change in Southern thinking.

Now that the place of the South in the anti-foreign aid bloc in the House has been quantitatively defined, it becomes necessary to develop some comparisons in detail. The "non-South" as a residual category is not sufficiently discriminating to serve as a valid base for comparison; there is far too much heterogeneity in American political life and patterns to trust a residual category such as this for any meaningful conclusions. The greatest concern in this connection, of course, is the place of the Midwest, both in terms of its level of support of foreign aid as compared with the

South and of its share of the overall non-South record. How in fact does the South measure up to the performance of the American midlands on the issue of foreign aid?

Here the contrast can be most graphically demonstrated by breaking the House down into three voting groups. The first is of course the Southern sample of 126 seats from fourteen states. The second is the Midwest, comprising twelve states (the two Bureau of the Census categories of "East North Central" and "West North Central") with 129 seats during the period under discussion. Finally, the third category is still residual, called here the "two coasts," consisting of the Northeast, the Mountain West, the Pacific Coast, and (after 1958 and 1959 respectively) Hawaii and Alaska. This third group held 180 seats in 1958, 181 in 1959, and 182 from 1960 through 1962. Table 5 shows the results of comparing the way the three sub-groups voted on foreign aid authorizations over the decade.

These figures, covering the crucial years of the 1950's and the early 1960's, pretty effectively lay to rest the ghost of Midwestern isolationism—at least in foreign aid and at least in comparison with the South. Although the Midwestern states continued throughout the decade to provide some significant portion of the overall opposition, never after 1954 was a hostile majority registered from the region—although it must be admitted that the affirmative margin almost disappeared in 1962! Even so, the different directions of evolution taken by the Midwest and the South during the period show in clear and unambiguous contrast.

The table also confirms the suspicion that the House majorities for foreign aid across the years owed their impressive size primarily to the almost solid support of the delegations from Northeastern and Western states; in only six of the ten years covered by the table did the Midwest and the South combined show an overall affirmative majority, and then only twice after the South made its great shift in 1957. On the other hand, only a relative handful of

TABLE 5
ROLL CALL VOTES AND PERCENTAGES, FOREIGN AID AUTHORIZATIONS
BY GROUPS OF STATES, HOUSE OF REPRESENTATIVES, 1953-1962

YEAR	WHOLE HOUSE			SOUTH			MIDDLE WEST			TWO COASTS		
	Y	N	%Y	Y	N	%Y	Y	N	%Y	Y	N	%Y
1953	280	108	72.1	83	29	74.1	54	59	48.1	142	20	87.7
1954	260	126	67.3	62	48	56.4	54	58	48.2	144	20	87.8
1955	273	128	68.1	66	50	56.9	62	57	52.1	145	21	87.3
1956	275	122	69.2	65	54	54.6	64	48	57.1	146	20	87.9
1957	254	154	65.4	41	76	35.0	65	58	52.8	148	20	88.1
1958	238	134	63.9	48	60	44.4	68	54	55.7	122	20	85.9
1959	271	142	65.6	46	69	40.0	69	54	56.1	156	19	89.1
1960	243	131	64.9	43	62	40.9	66	51	56.4	134	18	88.1
1961	287	140	67.2	61	61	50.0	70	55	56.0	156	24	86.6
1962	250	164	60.3	49	68	41.9	64	63	50.4	137	33	80.5

Congressmen from the "two coasts" groups voted "nay" in any roll call; further analysis also reveals that these approximately twenty votes came each year from the same districts.

It has already been pointed out that the aid program began in 1961 and 1962 to draw increasing negative totals, but the figures advanced here show no significant increase in either the Midwest or Southern totals. The bulk of the new "nay" votes came from the two coasts, as the total jumped moderately (from an average of less than 20, to 24) in 1961 and then significantly to 33 in 1962. In part this possibly portentous swing was due to Republican resentments against the Kennedy leadership, in part to the growing unpopularity of the aid program in general, and in somewhat larger part to the increasing activity of the "radical right" fraction in American political life that found foreign aid a convenient and vulnerable target. In any case, the solidity of Southern opposition, the ominous decline in Midwestern support, and the growing minority of "nay" voters along the two coasts made the future of the aid program dark indeed. In 1963, as a matter of fact, the first really successful House revolt against any administration aid proposal occurred. This development, although beyond the time frame of the present study, will be examined below.

The extent and direction of the Southern divergence from the Midwest and the two coasts is shown best by cumulative percentages (Table 6).

Although the overall ten-year record of the South is not markedly different from that of the Midwest—the latter is more than half affirmative, the former less than half, but there is only a matter of less than 4 percentage points separating them—the differences between the two periods into which the decade is divided here are relevant. In 1955 the Midwest crossed into support of the program while the South maintained its traditional stand in favor of foreign aid; as a result in 1955 and 1956 the House total showed

TABLE 6

CUMULATIVE AFFIRMATIVE PERCENTAGES BY GROUPS
OF STATES, FOREIGN AID AUTHORIZATIONS,
HOUSE OF REPRESENTATIVES, 1953-1962

YEARS	WHOLE HOUSE	MIDWEST	SOUTH	TWO COASTS
1953-62	66.1	53.3	49.5	86.9
(10 years)				
1953-56	69.2	51.3	60.5	87.8
(4 years)				
1957-62	64.0	54.5	42.1	86.4
(6 years)				

larger affirmative percentages than were ever to be achieved
again. In the final six years, on the other hand, the falling
away of the South was the single variable operating against
the program, yet this single region's defection was sufficient
to work perceptible change in the overall record of the
House.

Unless the 1962 change in the vote of the Midwest
portends a fundamental readjustment of regional attitudes
toward foreign aid rather than merely an election-year
demonstration of Congressional independence of an assertive Democratic administration, the South will continue to
enjoy indefinitely the lonely eminence it has occupied since
1957 as the only major region of the United States whose
Representatives in Congress regularly cast a majority of their
votes in opposition to the principle of foreign aid. Ever since
the first philanthropic flush of the Marshall Plan wore off,
foreign aid has been generally agreed to be politically
"unpopular." But although many Congressmen from all parts
of the country have long been articulate—often eloquent—
on the political difficulties inherent in a consistent advocacy

of foreign aid, nowhere except in the South and in the Midwest (and especially in the former) has public resistance to the program been translated into actual roll call votes on any large scale.

THE STATES AND FOREIGN AID

Up to this point in the discussion, the unit of analysis has been "the South," a political entity with 126 votes of which to dispose in a roll call vote. But even the most casual acquaintance with Southerners will suffice to make the observer acutely aware that the South, in spite of its significant cultural homogeneity and its peculiar history that combine to make it distinctive and distinguishable from the rest of the nation, is itself a richly varied region. Its political, economic, and social composition is far too complex to permit any but the roughest kind of comparisons with other parts of the United States. Any conclusions that begin with the words, "The South is . . ." can never be any more than tentative and non-specific.

The more complete analysis and evaluation of the Southern revolt against foreign aid, therefore, requires that the lump of 126 votes be broken down into more digestible portions. Here the Southern norm of political identification and the base of practical political calculation coincide to furnish a most convenient avenue into more precise and discriminating figures. The Southern tradition and the rules of politics in the United States make the state a valid unit of investigation. The figures for each of the individual state delegations as they faced the recurrent necessity of voting on foreign aid throw the Southern performance into new and in many ways unsuspected perspective.

Table 7 summarizes the way each of the fourteen states voted on the foreign aid authorization bill in each of the ten years. In each individual vote, of course, the affirmative vote is placed first. Once the data are presented in this way, it becomes apparent that the summary figures used earlier served at least as much to obscure meaning as to elucidate it. There is some measure of consistency within certain groups of states that can be discovered from the table, but the general impression is one of remarkable diversity. State-by-state and year-by-year analyses make it possible for one to pinpoint tides of change—which, be it noted, do not all run in the same direction. With the table as a guide, what patterns of state behavior are the most immediately identifiable?

During the ten-year period, Kentucky was beyond doubt or comparison the most pro-aid state in the South; in company with Alabama it made up the two-state group

TABLE 7

ROLL CALL VOTES ON FOREIGN AID AUTHORIZATION BILLS, HOUSE OF REPRESENTATIVES, 1953-1962

STATE	1953	1954	1955	1956	1957
Alabama (9)	8-1	5-3	6-1	7-2	6-2
Arkansas (6)	5-1	4-2	3-3	4-1	3-3
Florida (8)	6-0	3-5	4-4	4-4	3-4
Georgia (10)	8-2	7-1	8-2	7-3	2-6
Kentucky (8)	6-1	8-0	6-1	7-1	7-1
Louisiana (8)	2-5	2-4	2-5	3-4	1-6
Mississippi (6)	1-5	1-4	1-5	1-5	1-5
North Carolina (12)	10-2	1-10	1-8	4-8	1-10
Oklahoma (6)	5-1	4-1	5-1	4-1	0-6
South Carolina (6)	4-1	2-3	3-2	2-4	0-6
Tennessee (9)	6-1	6-1	7-1	7-2	6-3
Texas (22)	11-7	11-7	11-10	6-12	4-16
Virginia (10)	9-1	5-5	4-6	4-6	4-6
West Virginia (6)	3-1	4-2	5-1	5-1	3-2
TOTALS	84Y	62Y	66Y	65Y	41Y
	29N	48N	50N	54N	76N

whose delegations have never "joined the opposition" by casting a majority of their votes against foreign aid in any year. Kentucky, Alabama, Tennessee, West Virginia, Oklahoma, Arkansas, and Florida (in descending order) all had a cumulative affirmative percentage of more than 50. This fairly creditable showing of seven pro-aid states out of the fourteen must be downgraded, however, by several considerations. In the first place, Arkansas and Florida qualified by only narrow margins; second, of the other five in the group, three had shown wide fluctuations in sentiment; third, the list included none of the South's largest states—Texas, North Carolina, Georgia, or Virginia. Actually, on the basis of the record itself at the close of the

1958	1959	1960	1961	1962	YEA	NAY	% YEA
7-2	6-2	5-1	7-2	5-2	62	18	75.5
5-0	2-4	2-4	3-3	2-3	33	24	58.0
5-3	4-3	5-3	5-3	4-4	43	33	55.2
1-9	1-8	1-8	1-9	1-8	37	56	39.8
6-1	6-2	7-1	7-1	7-1	67	10	87.0
1-3	1-4	1-4	3-5	3-3	19	43	30.6
1-5	1-5	1-5	1-5	1-5	10	49	16.9
3-4	1-9	1-7	6-6	1-11	28	75	27.2
3-2	3-2	3-3	5-1	2-4	34	22	60.7
0-5	0-5	0-6	0-6	0-5	11	43	20.4
4-5	5-4	3-4	5-3	4-3	53	27	66.3
8-10	8-13	7-7	12-11	10-12	86	105	45.0
3-6	4-5	4-6	4-5	4-6	45	53	45.9
1-5	4-2	3-3	4-1	5-1	37	19	66.0
48Y	46Y	43Y	61Y	49Y	565Y		49.5
60N	69N	62N	61N	68N	577N		

87th Congress, only Alabama and Kentucky could be safely classified as having a solidly favorable record on foreign aid (and both were to reverse themselves in 1963).

On the negative side, the picture is simultaneously clearer and yet more complex. Mississippi was for all ten years the Abou Ben Adhem of the anti-foreign aid camp; its record of well over 80 per cent opposition is far beyond all others both in magnitude and in year-by-year consistency. Its closest rivals (although both trail by considerable margins) are South Carolina and North Carolina. Grouped some 10 percentage points still lower, but equally deserving of membership in the hard-core opposition to foreign aid on the basis of their performance during the latter years of the decade, are the remaining states of Georgia, Virginia, and Louisiana, all well below 50 per cent affirmative and none showing particular flexibility in its pattern.

There remains only Texas. Thanks to the pervasive effect of a Texan as Vice-President in the Kennedy administration, the Lone Star State's performance during 1961 and 1962 provided a sharp contrast to its generally hostile position on aid during the bulk of the Eisenhower years. Yet even its one-vote affirmative majority in 1961 and its near-even split in 1962 are not especially impressive, and Texas (with an overall affirmative percentage a fraction of a point below even Virginia's) must be figured as an opposition state—but perhaps not as a key element in the dedicated opposition.

A tantalizing story unfolds as the chronological vote of each state is read across the table from left to right. Almost all have undergone some change in their positions: some swing back and forth, some tend to go steadily in the same direction, others go one way and then reverse themselves. Each state's experience is unique; all are interesting in themselves and provocative of extensive speculation.

Alabama is one of the simplest cases to analyze, at

least during the ten years covered in the table (its record after 1962 showed some interesting aberrations as a result of its racial crises and its failure to solve its redistricting problem after the census of 1960). Its original commitment to foreign aid did not vary after it recovered from its momentary and slight slip in 1954. From 1955 through 1962 its delegation consistently cast six or seven affirmative votes each year as opposed to only one or two negatives.

Arkansas also boasts an affirmative percentage overall, but this represents an arithmetical summary rather than a settled position. Not once during the ten years did all six of its Congressmen cast all their votes on either side of the foreign aid vote at one time, but every other possible basis of division for a six-seat delegation shows up at least once in its record. During the latter years of the decade, however, its votes tended to be more negative than otherwise.

Florida slipped from its unanimous affirmative stand in 1953 to a near-even split for the remainder of the period. After 1953, as a matter of fact, its cumulative totals show only four more "yeas" than "nays"—an affirmative margin of less than half a vote a year. Nevertheless, the state avoided casting a negative majority after 1957.

Georgia offers an almost classic example of a state delegation making a deliberate, all-at-once, and apparently permanent shift in position. The state was heavily in favor of aid up through 1956. The next year the Georgians moved, virtually in a body, into the negative and remained there (in spite of considerable change in the actual incumbents) through the end of the decade. The almost 40 per cent cumulative affirmative vote of the state was a product of its earlier years. From 1957 onward Georgia has been and is today one of the centers of deep and unyielding hostility to the aid program.

Kentucky offers the least difficulty of all the fourteen states, remaining almost unanimously in favor of the program throughout the decade. Of the total of ten "nays" from the state during the five Congresses, nine came from one single district.

Louisiana was one of the two states that were already in opposition in 1953. Its ten-year record demonstrates few signs of any real change. It should be noted, however, that its actual voting record is not as trustworthy a guide to the attitudes of the delegation as in the case of several other states, due to the unusually high incidence of non-voting among its eight Congressmen. Three of the group, for example, avoided going on the record for as many as three consecutive years, and only in 1961 (when the Kennedy administration was making its all-out effort to corral all possible votes) did all eight vote at the same time.

Mississippi's case is the exact reciprocal of Kentucky's. Probably the most consistent of all fourteen and with an enviable percentage of participation in the roll calls (only one of the six did not accumulate a perfect voting record on the question), its annual 1-5 split was a standard feature of every vote during the decade. Equally impressive was the tenacity of the single Congressman who withstood what must have been powerful pressure from his state and his own constituents and persisted in voting in favor of the program every year. It is an eloquent commentary on Mississippi politics that when the state lost a seat after the 1960 census, it was this particular Congressman who was returned to private life by way of an electoral defeat.

North Carolina is by all odds one of the most interesting and perplexing states of the entire fourteen. With the second largest House delegation during the decade, and with an old and well-deserved reputation for liberalism to its credit, the state might have appropriately been expected to be found in company with Kentucky and Tennessee as a leader in support of foreign aid in particular and the general principles of multilateralism as well. Instead, its delegation proved to be among the bellwethers of the anti-foreign aid trend. North Carolina was the first Southern state to go all the way into opposition, reversing itself completely between the votes of 1953 and 1954. After a partial recovery in 1956, it fell back again the next year and never again contributed to any extent to the passage of any foreign aid authorization until it showed itself especially susceptible to the Kennedy blitz of 1961. Its 6-6 split that year, however, was converted in 1962 to the familiar 1-11 division, and the state's outlook on foreign aid was apparently well fixed as the decade drew to a close.

Oklahoma, like Arkansas, was a waverer. Its six-man delegation split 4-1 or 5-1 in favor of aid until 1957; that year, as the wave of secession swept the South, Oklahoma voted like South Carolina and lined up unanimously against the measure. Recovery, however, was swift; from 1958 onward the state—again except for a temporary response to New Frontier pressure in 1961—remained evenly divided.

South Carolina's record is the virtual twin of its neighbor to the north, although its initial shift in 1954 was not as complete as was the case among the North Carolinians. Not until 1957 did the Palmetto State become solid in its opposition, but after that year it seemed to be seeking to make up for lost time. Not one South Carolina Congressman voted affirmatively on foreign aid in any year after 1956 until the end of the period.

Tennessee, except for its aberrant votes in 1958 and 1960, remained consistently on the affirmative side. In the second half of the ten-year period, however, two of its delegation in the House changed positions from approval to opposition, thus increasing Tennessee's "normal" output of "nays" from its original low of one in the early years to at least three. The behavior of the Tennessee vote during the final years of the decade provided strong grounds for a suspicion that the cycle of change had not run its complete course by 1962.

Texas is, with North Carolina, the great mystery in the South. A sizeable body of opposition existed within the

Texas delegation already in 1953. This minority became a majority in 1956 and after that year only in 1961 did Texas turn in an affirmative vote for foreign aid. But the yeasty nature of Texas politics is underscored by the wide swings in the respective totals of "yeas" and "nays"; obviously more than a handful of the Congressmen from Texas are of divided opinions on the question and therefore subject to constitutent pressure from year to year. It was already noted, furthermore, that Texas has proved to be amenable to New Frontier pressure as indicated by its drastically different patterns in 1961 and 1962.

Virginia, in keeping with its tradition of decorum in politics, quietly abandoned its early support of foreign aid in 1954 and after 1955 remained admirably consistent in maintaining an almost unvarying 4-6 division in opposition.

West Virginia, with a percentage of overall support surpassed only by Kentucky, Alabama, and Tennessee, nevertheless shows two quirks in its otherwise steady level of affirmative commitment: a 1-5 negative vote in 1958 and a 3-3 split in 1960. The loyalty of West Virginia Democrats to the Kennedy administration is widely known, and showed up in the area of foreign aid by solid voting support in 1961 and 1962.

The table is equally as interesting when the data are read from top to bottom as from left to right. Looking at the figures one year at a time, it is possible to develop a sense of the shape of change within the Southern group as a whole from year to year. Here the interrelations among pairs and groups of states begin to become clear.

1953: The Eisenhower years began with significant opposition to foreign aid coming from only the three contiguous Gulf Coast states of Mississippi, Louisiana, and Texas. The remaining eleven were all pro-aid by a wide margin. This situation was a replica of the attitudes of the latter years of the Truman administration and provided a literal point of departure for the changing Southern position during the ensuing nine years.

1954: In this year the first inner shift took place. North Carolina executed its complete about-face and Florida, South Carolina, and Virginia either divided equally or showed negative majorities. To the original three more or less hostile states of Texas, Louisiana and Mississippi were thus added four new ones. In terms of the number of states on either side, the South was already halfway to opposition.

1955: The total change from 1954 was only minimal, but three new and portentous developments occurred. Arkansas began the gyrations that were to continue for the remainder of the decade, Virginia took its definitive position in a 4-6 split, and the Texas figure changed appreciably (a foretaste of what was to come the next year).

1956: Only one major shift can be found in this election year as the overall affirmative and negative totals changed only slightly from 1955. The single transfer of allegiance, however, was a most important one: Texas, almost without warning, turned in a two-to-one negative vote. In addition to the Texas vote, other significant developments were North Carolina's partial recovery and the continued evidence of instability in the position of Arkansas.

1957: The first year of the second Eisenhower administration saw the Southern storm break in full fury. Georgia's secession from the affirmative majority was the largest single element in the new situation, but the trend of rejection affected four other states as well. North Carolina rebuilt its solid negative front, Oklahoma unexpectedly cast all six of its votes in opposition, South Carolina completed the transformation that it had begun the year before, and Texas dropped to its ten-year low point of support. All told some twenty-five Congressmen from the South changed their 1956 votes of "yea" to "nay" in 1957—a blow from which neither the House of Representatives nor the Southerners themselves have recovered to this day.

1958: This was the year in which the losses of 1957 were partially recouped. Arkansas unpredictably voted 5-0 in the affirmative (the year after Little Rock); Florida clambered painfully back to the "yea" side; North Carolina's vote, thanks to wholesale absenteeism, was much closer to an even division than had been the case earlier; Oklahoma went back to supporting the program; and the Texas figure also approximated an equal split. Offsetting these positive gains in large measure, however, were two new defections that, although temporary, nevertheless unhinged both Tennessee and West Virginia from their hitherto solid base of affirmative commitment. Overall the South's vote in 1958 swung back sharply from its 1957 extreme, the affirmative total increasing only by six over the previous year but the negative figure decreasing by sixteen.

1959: The tide turned again, however, in 1959. Arkansas slipped once more, the North Carolinians who had missed the 1958 vote turned up this time to vote "nay," and even Texas turned up a few more negative votes. Even the repentance of Tennessee and West Virginia for their peccadilloes of the previous year could not prevent the Southern total from almost equalling its configuration of 1957.

1960: This year of presidential campaigning found the House considerably more reluctant than usual to put itself on record on the issue of foreign aid; sixty-three members, including twenty-one Southerners, failed to answer the roll call. With so much absenteeism, the 1960 vote is relatively uninformative except for minor modifications in position by Tennessee and Oklahoma and the return of Texas to an even division. In the cases of Tennessee and Texas, however, absenteeism was clearly a major contributing factor to the position of both states; actually the 7-7 division in Texas accounted for only two-thirds of the state's total of Congressmen.

1961: The first year of the New Frontier, it will be recalled, was one in which the administration made an all-out effort to make major changes in the votes of those Southern states thought to be amenable to persuasion. In Arkansas, Florida, Oklahoma, and Texas the Kennedy influence was clearly marked, but nowhere was it more obvious than in

North Carolina. Mr. Kennedy's success in changing that state's vote on foreign aid from its adamant and solid opposition of the preceding seven years to a 6-6 standoff stands on the record as one of his most impressive—if short-lived—feats of legislative leadership. But North Carolina was the only hard-core state in which the New Frontier made any real headway in winning new support for foreign aid; the other states in which the administration scored heavily were all divided to begin with and had histories of considerable change. As indicated earlier, the administration's work resulted in a major increase in the number of affirmative votes from the South but virtually no decrease in the number of "nays," for the only even split the region can show after 1956.

1962: The decade ended with unmistakable evidence of the transitory nature of Mr. Kennedy's work in 1961 clear for all to see. In essence, the voting pattern of 1962 was astonishingly similar to that of 1959. Louisiana, with two absentees, managed an even division at 3-3—its strongest affirmative showing of the entire ten years. On the other hand, Arkansas, Oklahoma, and Texas all slipped back from their 1961 positions (Texas, however, only minimally), and North Carolina furnished an almost classic example of backsliding. That state, except for one hardy holdout in the delegation, turned its back on the President and retreated into uncompromising opposition.

Another way of throwing the geographic bases of opposition to the aid program into high relief is to combine the fourteen Southern states into three sub-regions. The first of these groupings, the South Atlantic states, consists of (from north to south) Virginia, North Carolina, South Carolina, Georgia, and Florida. The second is made up of the Gulf state group: Alabama, Mississippi, Louisiana, and Texas. The final sub-region is called here the "border states," including West Virginia, Kentucky, Tennessee, Arkansas, and Oklahoma.

The first two of these sub-regions are fairly well accepted in social-science inquiry into American life; the third, however, lacks such familiarity. Everyone seems to agree that there is something called a "border" between the North and South, and that the border area is not quite as "southern" as its neighbors to the south. Here, however, the rationale of the border-state group is neither geographic, socioeconomic, nor cultural, but rather political. Each of the states included is part of the political South with a difficult racial problem and a tradition of one-party rule. Yet the outlook of each of them is at least partially non-Southern on international questions and differs in important ways from the states of the "inner South" that lie below them on the map. Perhaps the most dubious member of the border-state group is Arkansas; it could possibly with as much justice be included in the group of Gulf states—although it obviously is *not* a Gulf state. Its border-state identification is preserved, however, for several reasons: its behavior on foreign aid during the decade was more characteristic of the border states than of the other two groups, it shared with the other border states the common characteristic of at least one non-Southern boundary, and—methodologically speaking—its total, added to the other border states, made up a sample sufficiently large to be usefully compared with the remaining two.

When the vote figures for the states in each of the three groups are totalled on an annual basis, the following table results.

The meaning of these three columns of figures can best be grasped by imagining three broken lines plotted on a graph. The curve representing the affirmative percentage of the Gulf states would begin only slightly above the middle and drop swiftly to just under 50 per cent. There it would remain—except for the one sharp jog downward in 1957—until the end of the decade. The line for the South Atlantic states would begin with the highest percentage figure to be shown on the entire graph, drop

TABLE 8

ROLL CALL VOTES ON FOREIGN AID AUTHORIZATIONS,
HOUSE OF REPRESENTATIVES, BY GROUPS OF STATES, 1953-1962

YEAR:	GULF STATES			SOUTH ATLANTIC STATES			BORDER STATES		
	Y	N	%Y	Y	N	%Y	Y	N	%Y
1953	22	18	55.0	37	6	86.0	25	5	83.3
1954	19	18	51.3	17	24	41.5	26	6	81.3
1955	20	21	48.8	20	22	47.6	26	7	78.8
1956	17	23	42.5	21	25	45.7	27	6	81.8
1957	12	29	30.0	10	32	23.8	19	15	55.9
1958	17	20	45.9	12	27	30.8	19	13	59.4
1959	16	24	40.0	10	31	24.4	20	14	58.8
1960	14	17	46.6	11	30	26.8	18	15	54.5
1961	21	23	47.7	15	30	33.3	25	8	75.8
1962	19	22	46.3	10	34	22.7	20	12	62.5
TOTAL	177	215	45.2	163	261	38.4	225	101	69.0

to a level only half as high for a three-year period, and then drop again to a level at or more often below 30 per cent. The border states, finally, would show a line that also begins quite high but remains so for a much longer period. When this curve finally falls it does not drop as far as did the other two, stabilizing between 55 and 60 per cent.

Put this way the crucial significance of the two years of 1954 and 1957 shows up even more clearly. The 1954 decline took place only within the first two groups, the border states remaining substantially unchanged; in point of fact, furthermore, the 1954 drop was almost entirely within the South Atlantic cluster as the Gulf state percentage decreased only 3.7 points. In 1957, in contrast, the decline was much more general: the Gulf states fell off 12.5 points (all of which, incidentally, was recovered the next year), the South Atlantic states 22.9, and the border states 25.9 (the largest decrease of all three, since this group had the longest distance to fall).

The Kennedy administration's effort in 1961 was similarly geographically concentrated. It had some little impact on the South Atlantic group (actually only in North Carolina; it will be recalled that in 1961 that state voted 6-6 instead of its usual 1-10 or 1-11 split) but struck home most directly in the border states. The affirmative percentage of the latter group increased 21.3 points in 1961 over the previous year. On the other hand, the Gulf states responded to the administration's pressure in 1961 by a much larger total vote, but—to the administration's undoubted disappointment— the percentage overall remained substantially unchanged. The affirmative total increased by seven, the negative total by six, and the net effect of the New Frontier's campaign was virtually self-cancelling.

The Gulf states were the source of whatever opposition existed to foreign aid before 1953; since 1956 this group (even in the face of the broad swings in the Texas vote) has been the most consistent in its performance. The South Atlantic states, on the contrary, have been the most elastic, with a net spread in the affirmative percentage of the group of nearly 50 points in ten years. Yet a second look at the metaphorical curve of the South Atlantic group suggests that, once its two-step decline had been completed in 1957, its more or less definitive plateau of support had been reached. Even so, however, in 1962 the South Atlantic group set two records for the period: its percentage of "yeas" was the lowest ever achieved and its gross number of "nays" the largest.

The border states, of course, show their less "Southern" orientation by the relatively late date at which they yielded to anti-foreign aid pressure, the much more limited extent of their shift, and their great responsiveness to the Kennedy counter-effort in 1961. In the latter year, the New Frontier succeeded in changing percentages of support in the Gulf and South Atlantic groups only by inducing would-be non-voters to stand up and be counted on the affirmative side; the negative totals for these two, however, remained almost unchanged. In the border states, on the other hand, the great shift of 1961 was due largely to the much more difficult feat of changing erstwhile "nay" voters into supporters. The increase of seven affirmative votes in the border group was matched by an equivalent decrease of seven on the negative side.

Put in these terms, the center of opposition to foreign aid in the South is beyond question the South Atlantic states. The border states as a group—in spite of individual cases of adamant hostility—constitute no real threat to the consensus, and the Gulf states would appear to have long ago struck their final balance. In the arc of seaboard states that runs from Virginia to Florida, there were in 1962 few signs of hope for the better on the issue of support for foreign aid, especially in view of the fact that opposition in this group reached its absolute and percentage peak in the final year of the period. This solid base of anti-aid sentiment in the South Atlantic region, when added to the more than half of the Gulf states' votes and the roughly 30 per cent of the border group, constitutes the core of the problem.

FOREIGN AID AND THE DISTRICTS

Any comparisons and conclusions that rely on "the South" or its fourteen component states as analytical units must rely upon summary figures of some sort. The South never votes *en bloc* nor do state delegations on foreign aid; each Congressman votes as an individual, and the only truly meaningful voting records are those compiled by individual members of the House as they put themselves on the record. From these figures come the several levels of summary generalization used in the discussion up to this point. Appendix II in the rear of the book gives a district-by-district record of the votes for each of the ten years. The figures there take no account of changes in incumbency, since they are for districts rather than for Congressmen. Even so the individual district histories revealed in the votes are impressive in their variety and in the extremely suggestive patterns many of them form. It is remarkable how few of the districts have maintained an unbroken front on foreign aid (on either side of the question). And it is interesting to note the number and the location of those whose record shows a marked change after the inauguration of President Kennedy in 1961.

Of the 126 districts, twenty-seven boast of a record featured by no negative votes on foreign aid. Entirely unsurprisingly in view of the overall performance of the two states, Kentucky with six and Alabama with five are the leaders in this category; Texas also has five districts of unbroken support, but the size of its delegation makes this a not noteworthy record. No other state except Virginia has more than two.

On the other side of the coin, twenty-two districts did not, during the decade, cast any affirmative votes on aid. In view of the already demonstrated fact that the great Southern shift on foreign aid occurred *during* the ten-year period between 1953 and 1962, it is not remarkable that only twenty-two districts were solidly opposed throughout the decade. In 1953, for example, there were twenty-nine negative votes from the entire South; included among them were certainly the twenty-two in question. Of this group of confirmed anti-aid Congressmen, Texas provides six and Louisiana and Mississippi each five. Georgia contains two, and Alabama, Kentucky, North Carolina, and South Carolina one each.

Thirty-one additional districts show on the record

solid evidence of a clear and definite change of heart from support of to opposition to aid, up to and including resistance to New Frontier arguments in 1961. Seven of these districts were in Georgia, six in Virginia, and five in South Carolina—three South Atlantic states that with North Carolina (which had three definite shifters) made up the firmest body of opposition to foreign aid to be found in the entire South. Most of these made their move fairly early in the decade and should be counted as being as deeply involved in the opposition as the twenty-two districts who never did support the program during the period.

In contrast, only four cases can be found of districts whose representatives moved firmly from a position hostile to aid to one solidly in favor. At least two of these shifts can be identified with changes in incumbency, the other two resulting apparently from a fresh reading of the winds of national and local opinion.

The detailed tabulation of votes by district will be referred to extensively and the conclusions drawn from it explained in detail below. It is from these data and those in the following chapter that criteria are selected by which to type and classify the districts in Chapter V. The figures are also utilized to a major degree in characterizing different categories of Congressmen in Chapter VI.

APPROPRIATIONS AND CONFERENCE REPORTS

There remains only one important point of which to dispose in this review of the Southern revolt against foreign aid. The story so far has been told in one dimension; the votes analyzed and the general conclusions drawn have been based on the way the Southern members of the House responded to the annual *authorization* bill. Is this a valid guide? Is it not possible that other conclusions might be drawn from an analysis of the analogous roll calls on the appropriation bill that annually accompanied the basic authorization, and on the House votes approving the report of the conference committee that reconciles the differences between the Senate and the House versions of either bill?

These are fair questions; answers to them are necessary before the data advanced here can be accepted as reliable and truly indicative of Southern Congressional attitudes. Fortunately for the investigator who thus finds his task made simpler, however, the similarity in the configuration of Southern votes on authorizations, appropriations, and conference reports is remarkable.

Table 9 demonstrates how close together the authorization and appropriation bills for each year remained:

TABLE 9

AFFIRMATIVE PERCENTAGE OF VOTES CAST,
FOREIGN AID AUTHORIZATIONS AND APPROPRIATIONS,
HOUSE OF REPRESENTATIVES, 1953-1962

YEAR	HOUSE:		SOUTH:	
	Auth.	*Appr.*	*Auth.*	*Appr.*
1953	72.1	71.5	74.3	70.4
1954	67.3	67.5	56.3	61.9
1955	68.0	67.1	56.8	54.3
1956	69.2	70.2	54.6	52.2
1957	62.2	65.6	35.0	41.3
1958	63.9	66.4	44.4	41.1
1959	65.6	67.2	40.0	42.0
1960	64.9	67.5	40.9	38.3
1961	67.2	68.7	50.0	47.0
1962	60.3	61.6	41.8	42.3
1953-56 (4 years)	69.2	69.2	60.5	59.7
1957-62 (6 years)	64.1	66.5	42.1	46.2
1953-62 (10 years)	66.1	68.0	49.5	49.4

It would appear from these figures, and especially the cumulative totals at the bottom of the table, that the widespread popular and journalistic impression that many Southerners (and Congressmen from other areas as well) voted in favor of the authorization bill but then showed their true colors by voting against the appropriation necessary to make the program effective is almost entirely without foundation. The data themselves suggest that the South's shift during the decade was quantitatively smaller with regard to appropriations than it was on the principle of foreign aid, but the actual differentials are so small for any year and especially with regard to the cumulative figures that they can hardly serve as a basis for any judgments. The simplest and most probable explanation of whatever variation may be found is mere absenteeism; very few actual instances could be found during the entire ten years of Congressmen who voted "yea" on an authorization but "nay" on the corresponding appropriation.

The same close correlation exists between the authorization roll calls and the several votes on conference committee reports. In general, since there is little opportunity to debate a measure of the latter sort and none to offer amendments, since conference committee reports are put to the House on a take-it-or-leave-it-basis, both interest and participation in such a vote were usually considerably below those surrounding the initial passage of a bill. Both the opponents and the supporters of foreign aid, and especially Southerners of both types, seemed to avoid these roll calls in about their appropriate proportions, and the statistical evidence indicates that the results in percentage terms are much the same as on the other measures.

Nor do the simple roll call data on authorizations convey either the flavor of the debate on aid in which Southern spokesmen have usually bulked large—increasingly so on the negative side in recent years—or the many amendments aimed at cutting out vital parts of the program, at placing limits on executive authority in its administration, or—always—at reducing the funds to be made available. In no area is the much-discussed but often difficult to discover coalition between Southerners and Midwestern Republicans more apparent than in the floor fight over foreign aid each year. Congressmen with little otherwise in common find it relatively simple to join forces in a usually futile but always pyrotechnic combat against foreign aid.

But however interesting these details may be—and many of them will be considered in a somewhat different context in subsequent chapters—they serve here only to underscore a point that has already been amply demonstrated. Regardless of how the figures and the speeches and the amendments and the votes may be added up, they all point the same moral, one already deduced from the simple roll calls on the authorization bills. Southern Congressmen generate the loudest and the most articulate anti-foreign aid voice and turn in the largest identifiable bloc of negative votes in the entire House of Representatives.

These, then, have been the ingredients of the South's revolt against foreign aid in Congress. The magnitude of the Southern shift of attitude is indeed impressive, but no more so than the degree of deep commitment many Southern Congressmen (or, as will be demonstrated later and which may be even more important, their *districts*) have developed to the crusade against the very principle of aid to foreign countries. No matter how the data are analyzed, one major point comes through: the opposition to foreign aid is not a tactic, not a temporary shift, and not merely a reaction born of short-lived passion and frustration. A major modification in the international outlook of Southerners has taken place that, although epitomized in the issue of aid, nevertheless spills over into many other areas. Some of these broader implications of the new Southern point of view will be examined in the next chapter.

A NOTE ON THE 1963 VOTE

The foreign aid authorization roll call votes of 1963 taken on August 23 provided a dramatic confirmation of the trends discovered and the conclusions reached in this chapter that were based on earlier data. The 1963 votes, however, merit special attention here because of their peculiar significance in two ways: first, in 1963 the South slipped to its lowest point of overall support of foreign aid since 1957, with certain unprecedented breaks in the ranks being especially noteworthy; second, for the first time Southerners constituted part of a victorious anti-aid coalition on a record vote.

As the foreign aid authorization bill of 1963 neared a final vote in the House late in August, it was obvious that the measure was facing serious difficulty. Administration ineptitude and broad popular disillusionment with the program combined to put the President's proposals in real danger. After beating back several initiatives by anti-aid forces on August 22, the next day the bill's sponsors and the Kennedy administration took a severe defeat.

On a Republican motion to reduce the authorized aid figure by nearly six hundred million dollars, a roll call vote produced the surprise: by a vote of 222-188 the amendment was accepted. The hostile coalition was made up of an almost solid Republican phalanx joined by sixty-six Democrats—all but six of whom were Southerners (and four of these six were from Missouri). That done, the House then immediately passed the reduced authorization measure, 224-186. Fifty-two Republicans this time joined 172 Democrats to provide the margin, the narrowest the program had ever enjoyed.

Thus in 1963 there were two roll calls on foreign aid on the same day. These two votes provide the base for some interesting comparisons. The House, for example, voted 54.1 per cent in favor of the cut and then reversed itself by casting a 54.6 per cent affirmative vote in favor of the bill on final passage—a swing of 10 percentage points almost entirely accounted for by the thirty-seven non-Southern Republicans who switched sides. The South, on the other hand, remained impressively consistent on the two votes.

On the motion to reduce the authorized funds, the Southerners (reduced in number of seats from 126 to 124 by reapportionment after 1962) voted 74-40 in favor, or an affirmative percentage *on the administration's position* of only 35.1. On the authorization bill itself, the South's position remained amost unchanged: 41-73, an affirmative percentage of 35.9. Only in 1957 had Southern support of foreign aid dropped so low; never except for that one year, as a matter of fact, had the percentage gone below 40. The vote also showed the second highest number of roll call "nays" ever recorded and equalled the lowest number of "yeas."

On a state-by-state basis, the vote also showed some provocative changes. In the table that follows, it should be kept in mind that in the first column a "yea" vote is a vote against the principle of aid.

Undoubtedly the most important single entry in this table is Kentucky's 7-0 vote in favor of the reduction in funds and the state's unimpressive vote on final passage. The Alabama delegation also broke away from its pattern of the previous decade if by a narrower margin. Also note-worthy was the Florida vote, particularly on final passage; the addition of four seats to the Florida delegation would appear to have strengthened the anti-aid forces rather than weakened them. The second largest House delegation from the South in 1963 joined the opposition to aid with un-mistakable emphasis. Other interesting defections included the loss of one of Virginia's steady four affirmative votes

TABLE 10

ROLL CALL VOTES, FOREIGN AID AUTHORIZATIONS,
HOUSE OF REPRESENTATIVES, 1963

STATE		AMENDMENT TO REDUCE FUNDS	FINAL PASSAGE
Alabama	(8)	3-2	3-2
Arkansas	(4)	3-1	2-2
Florida	(12)	5-6	3-8
Georgia	(10)	8-1	2-7
Kentucky	(7)	7-0	4-3
Louisiana	(8)	2-4	3-3
Mississippi	(5)	5-0	0-5
North Carolina	(11)	9-2	1-10
Oklahoma	(6)	2-4	3-3
South Carolina	(6)	5-1	0-6
Tennessee	(9)	4-3	3-4
Texas	(23)	12-10	10-12
Virginia	(10)	8-2	3-7
West Virginia	(5)	1-4	4-1
TOTALS		74-40	41-73

(the 10th district) and the apparently significant shift in the position of Tennessee.

On the positive side there is less to note. The administration's strong effect on the Texas delegation remained apparent, as the group split along the familiar lines it had followed after 1960. Also noticeable was Louisiana's maintenance of an even division in the face of a general Southern falling away, matched in large measure by Oklahoma and West Virginia that also remained true to their stance in the latter years of the previous decade. It should be noted, too, that the affirmative side also garnered the vote of the new

Congressman from Georgia's fifth district that includes Atlanta.

Except for Kentucky's aberrant performance, the record suggests that in 1963 the Southern vote was little more than a continuation of trends already apparent several years earlier. The South increased its expressed animosity toward foreign aid, but the negative side won its victory on the amendment and made its strong showing on final passage only by means of votes from the Republican contingent outside the South (none of the fifteen Southern Republicans, be it noted, voted in favor of aid on either roll call). Thus the projection advanced earlier in this chapter is more credible than ever; the South cannot defeat foreign aid by itself, but any major accession in anti-aid strength outside the region will make the Southern fraction exceptionally strategic.

IV
THE SOUTH AND
INTERNATIONAL
CO-OPERATION

ALL NEGATIVE VOTES look very much alike when enshrined in the dusty immortality of a roll call. It is impossible to draw meaningful conclusions about the international outlook of a single Congressman or even about an entire state's delegation from the record of a "yea" or a "nay" in any particular instance. Even when a single issue is followed over a period of years—and even when the issue is as important and as emotion-filled as foreign aid—the resulting conclusions must be so narrow as to be almost one-dimensional. The preceding chapter threw the South's position on foreign aid into perspective and indicated some high spots and some shadowed recesses in the region's outlook on world affairs. But the story must be filled in in more detail before the crucial question to which this book is addressed—"Why?"—can be answered with any confidence.

Foreign aid, although the most persistent and often the most exciting of the international issues with which the House of Representatives was confronted during the decade 1953-1962, was of course by no means the whole story. The massive program of international assistance of many types in which the United States has been engaged ever since 1947 has been no more than one extremely important part of a much broader enterprise. In general this larger area of American foreign policy may be fairly termed that of "international co-operation."

In view of the nature of the contemporary world and the ambiguous nature of many of the challenges with which the United States has been faced, the nation and its government have felt for many years a clear interest in and a powerful compulsion toward institutionalizing an elaborate network of co-operative international arrangements. This judgment had little of the philanthropic and nothing of the charitable about it; it was instead the result of the most hard-headed and crass calculations of which the American government was capable. Only by formalizing and structuring multilateralism, American strategists reasoned, could the long-term interests and aspirations of the United States stand any real chance of achievement. The upshot of this preoccupation has been a proliferation of military, political, economic, social, cultural, and humanitarian enterprises in which the United States has joined since the late 1940's and to which it has given continuous—if sometimes uneven —commitment. Although none of these programs has involved such relatively large sums of money or such long-term and extensive commitments as has foreign aid, all flow from the same general perception of the international environment and all involve the same kinds of decision and action.

Many of these moves required Congressional action of some sort during the decade being examined here. Each such question as it arose in the House offered the Southern bloc an opportunity to put itself on the record as either favoring or opposing the specific measure—as well as the broader philosophy of foreign policy upon which all of them rested. In these votes the 126 Southerners in the House, in other words, covered much the same policy area as they did in voting on foreign aid, but usually with some broader scope, a much less concentrated involvement in details, and usually with much less political excitement.

In this chapter, therefore, a parallel analysis of Southern roll call voting on a series of such multilateral issues is undertaken to serve as a basis of comparison with the foreign aid patterns noted in Chapter III. In general the votes, covering as they do such a broad gamut of issues, may be fairly considered to constitute the judgment of individual Congressmen on the principle of international co-operation as a fundamental part of American foreign policy in the latter part of the twentieth century. This is by no means to suggest that each vote by each Representative is to be considered as a referendum on a theory; rather the aggregate of his votes may be considered as incorporating such a judgment. The votes included in the list for analysis are of several sorts; when a high measure of consistency or a unifying pattern is discoverable in the votes of individual Congressmen or particular state delegations, one may fairly conclude that the motivation behind the votes was based more on abstract principle than on the details of individual measures.

Thus the conclusions in this chapter, although in a basic sense complementing those of Chapter III, may nonetheless be considered as moderately more fundamental than those suggested in the discussion of foreign aid. As will become apparent in the general and specific breakdown of the votes, there is considerable coincidence between the opponents of foreign aid and those Congressmen who reject the co-operative (hereafter consistently called "multilateralist") aspect of contemporary American policy. These obdurate Congressmen who are filtered out by the double grid of foreign aid and miscellaneous multilateralist measures represent one pole of Southern opinion; at the other, of course, is the bloc that supports both foreign aid and other multilateralist enterprises with equal fervor. In between, however, is a limbo of divided voting records and presumably less solidified views; in many ways these are the most interesting of all.

Foreign aid is therefore conceived as the most polarizing international issue Southerners faced during the decade, the one to which they tended to respond the most forcefully in either direction. The votes analyzed in this chapter, however, call more directly into question matters of basic points of view and attitudes, and in that way provide a cross-check on the results derived from the figures on foreign aid. From the two is developed later a scheme by means of which to arrange and order the several positions on international affairs held by each Southern Congressman.

THE FOURTEEN VOTES

From approximately three times that number of roll calls during the decade that involved a clear choice for or against the principle of multilateralism in action, fourteen have been selected for the detailed analysis made here. These particular votes were, it seems scarcely necessary to point out, not selected because of the particular conclusions they permitted; instead several other criteria of selection were applied, the combined effect of which was hoped to be the presentation of a genuine panorama of Southern opinion and the formulation of some testable generalizations.

The first point that should be noted is that the fourteen votes selected span the entire decade but concentrate at certain crucial points in time. Three, for example, are drawn from the single year of 1953, when the South had not yet abandoned its support of foreign aid and the Eisenhower era was just beginning. Two are from 1957, the high point of anti-foreign aid voting among Southerners. Four are from the late Eisenhower years, two each from 1959 and 1960. Finally, five are drawn from the first two years of the

Kennedy administration and include the major foreign policy undertakings of the New Frontier's first Congress.

Second, the votes were selected so as to cover a broad variety of issues. Several call for the commitment of funds, others for the implementation of relatively non-political humanitarian principles, and still others for the acceptance of an obligation to co-operative government action.

Third, all but two of the fourteen consist of the roll call vote on final passage of the measure in question. The two exceptions are in the first place a motion to recommit a bill to committee—a frequently used device by means of which a bill is in effect killed but without the necessity of the House formally voting "nay," and second, an amendment offered to reduce the funds contained in an appropriation bill. The reason for preferring final passage votes was identical to that applied in the case of foreign aid: it was assumed that a vote on the final pasage of a bill would more likely represent a choice of the principle incorporated in the measure rather than details of finance, implementation, or administration. The two exceptions noted above were chosen as particularly significant on other grounds.

Finally, partly for simplicity in tabulation but—to be frank—also in response to a quasi-esthetic urge for symmetry, generally votes were selected in which a "nay" was a vote against the principle of multilateralism. In only two cases—the same two mentioned above as not involving the final passage of a bill—were roll calls utilized in which the anti-multilateralist position was taking the initiative and in which therefore a "yea" was analogous to a negative vote on the co-operative principle of the bill.

The fourteen measures subjected to detailed analysis in this chapter and which make up the raw material of the unilateralist-multilateralist dichotomy on the principle of co-operation in American foreign policy, are identified in the following list. They are in chronological order; the number each bears is also the identifying figure used to refer to it in the tables below. The issues on which the House and the South expressed themselves during the decade are as follows:

1. Wheat for Pakistan (1953), a proposal to make available government-surplus wheat to Pakistan on very favorable terms.

2. The Refugee Act of 1953, permitting the immigration of a limited number of *bona fide* refugees.

3. A motion to recommit the Emergency Famine Relief Act (1953) with instructions to kill; this bill would authorize Congress to make surplus agricultural products available to meet famine in friendly countries.

4. An amendment to a supplementary appropriation act, to reduce by 7 million dollars the United States contribution to international organizations (1957).

5. A proposal to revise the immigration laws in order to relieve certain "hardship cases" (1957).

6. A measure to increase the United States subscription to the International Monetary Fund and the International Bank of Reconstruction and Development (1959).

7. A bill to permit United States participation in the Inter-American Development Bank (1959).

8. The International Health and Medical Research Act (1960), permitting United States participation in a broad but not especially extensive international effort in medical research.

9. A bill to permit United States participation in the International Development Association (1960).

10. The Alliance for Progress (1961), President Kennedy's ambitious venture in development in Latin America.

11. The Mutual Education and Cultural Exchange Act (1961), putting United States action in this field on a statutory footing.

12. The Peace Corps Act (1961), creating this well-known and interesting venture in people-to-people foreign assistance.

13. Creation of the United States Arms Control Agency

(1961), the first time arms control and disarmament had even been placed on a fully statutory basis.

14. The authorization measure permitting the United States to purchase United Nations bonds (1962).

In the list above, numbers 3 and 4 are the two exceptions to the principle that a "yea" vote is in effect an approval of the multilateralist premise in American foreign policy. Although when these two votes are analyzed in detail, the true "yea" and "nay" totals are retained, in all summaries a "yea" on votes 3 or 4 is counted as a "nay" in the total, and *vice versa*.

THE SOUTH AND MULTILATERALISM

The overall Southern record on the fourteen bills is shown in Table 11 below, compared in each instance with the House as a whole and with the non-South as a bloc. Even as generalized a set of figures as is contained in the table provides the basis for some provocative generalizations.

Probably the first conclusion to be drawn from the data is somewhat paradoxical. It would appear from the relative times and dates involved that the assumption that foreign aid was the catalyst that led to a wholesale revision of Southern attitudes is actually without foundation. Instead, the figures suggest the contrary: the Southern resistance to foreign aid actually seems to be a derivation from a more basic (and earlier developing) philosophical rejection of multilateralism in almost any form. The real Southern revolt against aid does not begin until 1954, but the three votes from 1953 found in the table (numbers 1-3) reveal that the South was showing hostility on these issues well before the regional rejection of foreign aid. As a matter of fact, never again during the decade were the Southerners to show such near-unanimity on a foreign policy bill as they did in their overwhelming vote against the International Refugee Act in 1953 (number 2).

Another point worth pondering is this: never once in

the fourteen cases cited did the South support the principle of multilateralism as strongly as did the non-South. It would seem logical to assume that somewhere in the list there should be one measure or one proposal of a multilateralist nature that appealed to Southerners more than it did to the other groups represented in the House, but from the first to the last the South lags behind. In a few cases, including, for example, the vote on the International Health and Medical Research Act of 1960 (number 8) or the roll call on the creation of the Arms Control Agency in 1961 (number 13), the South's figures come closer. But Southerners set great store by consistency, and in this particular case the region's spokesmen remained true to their beliefs. With the South always less enthusiastic about multilateralist measures than the non-South, it is no surprise that the percentage figure in each case for the House as a whole falls between the respective affirmative percentages of the two groups.

In four cases (numbers 2, 3, 4, and 9) the South broke with the majority of the House; in these votes a majority of the Southerners found themselves in the overall minority (as was the case usually on foreign aid). In five of the first six votes, the South provided more than half the total vote of the anti-multilateralist group. After that point, however, only once—in the case of the Mutual Education and Cultural Exchange Act of 1961 (number 11)—did the South go so high. But it also is a measure of the South's relative position on multilateralism that in only two votes (numbers 8 and 13) was the region's vote disproportionately heavy on the multilateralist side. Put concretely, in only those two cases did the South furnish a percentage of the overall negative vote that was smaller than the 29 per cent of the seats it holds in the House. In twelve of the fourteen votes, the South played more than its just part in opposition.

The table also underscores the significant change in Southern behavior on foreign policy—as well as the new face

TABLE 11

AFFIRMATIVE AND NEGATIVE VOTES ON SELECTED INTERNATIONAL ISSUES,
HOUSE OF REPRESENTATIVES, 1953-1962

VOTE NO.	1	2	3	4	5	6	7
House:	310- 75	221-185	82-322	167-205	295- 58	311- 57	231- 87
% Yea:	80.5	54.4	20.3	44.9	83.6	84.7	72.6
South:	67- 49	11-106	64- 54	66- 42	56- 46	71- 31	61- 43
% Yea:	57.8	9.4	54.2	61.1	54.9	69.6	58.7
Non-South:	242- 26	210- 79	18-268	101-163	230- 12	244- 26	170- 44
% Yea:	90.3	72.7	6.3	38.3	95.2	90.4	79.4
South % of Negative:	65.3	57.3	78.0*	39.5*	79.3	54.3	49.4

VOTE NO.	8	9	10	11	12	13	14
House:	295-114	249-158	328- 83	329- 66	288- 97	290- 54	257-134
% Yea:	72.1	61.2	79.8	83.3	74.8	84.3	65.2
South:	71- 29	42- 72	82- 35	71- 37	74- 33	73- 16	63- 53
% Yea:	71.0	36.8	70.1	65.7	69.1	82.0	54.3
Non-South:	224- 85	207- 86	246- 48	258- 29	214- 64	217- 38	194- 81
% Yea:	72.6	70.6	83.7	89.9	76.9	85.1	70.5
South % of Negative:	25.4	45.6	42.1	56.1	34.1	29.6	39.0

* "Yea" counted as "nay"—in effect, a denial of the multilateralist premise.

of the House as a whole—during the 87th Congress that sat during the first two Kennedy years. Prior to 1961 (numbers 1 through 9) the House as a whole averaged 71 per cent affirmative and fell below 70 per cent on only two occasions. Meanwhile, the South reached 70 per cent only once (number 8—the Health and Medical Research Act), and the divergence between the South and the non-South was clearly shown in the difference in their respective cumulative affirmative percentages. The South managed to vote "yea" only 48.4 per cent of the time, while the non-South compiled an affirmative level of 80.2 per cent.

All this changed perceptibly in 1961. Under President Kennedy's leadership and in the climate of executive pressure and strident urgency in which the New Frontier's legislative proposals were presented to Congress during 1961 and 1962, the general level of House support for the important multilateralist measures that flowed from the White House— already high—increased still further. The House increased its percentage of support from the 71 it had achieved under Eisenhower to the impressive level of 77.5 on the five Kennedy foreign policy proposals included in the table. The South also increased, and by a considerably greater margin than the House in general; its score on the Kennedy bills resulted in an affirmative percentage of 67.6, an increase of over 19 percentage points. The non-South, with relatively less room for improvement and (it must be admitted) with Republicans not sharing the Kennedy euphoria more inclined to resist, was able to move its support level upward only one percentage point to 81.2.

The Kennedy international program, cutting across so many established lines as it did, had an interesting effect on the House in other ways. This can be illustrated by returning to the three-group division of the House that was used in the preceding chapter: the South, the Midwest, and the two-coast bloc. The roll call votes on the five Kennedy

TABLE 12

ROLL CALL VOTES AND PERCENTAGES, FIVE KENNEDY ADMINISTRATION
MEASURES, HOUSE OF REPRESENTATIVES, 1961-1962

VOTE NO.	HOUSE		SOUTH		MIDWEST		TWO COASTS	
	Vote	% Yea	Vote	% Yea	Vote	% Yea	Vote	% Yea
1.	328- 83	79.8	82-35	70.1	81-43	65.3	165- 5	97.1
2.	329- 66	83.3	71-37	65.7	102-10	91.1	156-19	89.1
3.	288- 97	74.8	74-33	69.2	82-38	68.3	132-26	83.5
4.	290- 54	84.3	86-16	84.3	78-21	78.8	139-17	89.1
5.	251-134	65.2	63-53	54.3	61-50	54.9	127-31	80.4

Key to Votes:
1. Alliance for Progress (1961)
2. Mutual Education and Cultural Exchange Act (1961)
3. Peace Corps Act (1961)
4. Creation of United States Arms Control Agency (1961)
5. United States Purchase of United Nations Bonds (1962)

proposals, shown in Table 12, are significant in their similarity to the foreign aid pattern.

These figures tend to confirm the striking similarity in the voting behavior of Southerners and Midwesterners under the Kennedy administration. The two groups were within only a few percentage points of each other on four of the five votes; only the Mutual Education and Cultural Exchange Act shows any significant difference. Although on three of the five the Midwest showed a higher affirmative percentage than the South, this point is virtually without significance since all the 1961 votes were heavily affirmative in any case and cannot be interpreted as revealing any fundamental cleavages of opinion. The 1962 case, however, is quite another matter. The measure to authorize the purchase of United Nations bonds by the United States, complicated as it was by the emotion and confusion that surrounded the action of the United Nations in the Congo at the time, created a political climate reminiscent of the annual crisis over foreign aid. The result was a vote clearly inspired by the same sorts of factors that divide the House on foreign aid, and both the South and the Midwest voted on the United Nations bonds question in symmetrical— if less extreme—terms, much as they did earlier in the year on the aid authorization.

The Kennedy impact on the South, measured in terms of the five bills analyzed here, was already foreshadowed in the previous chapter. New Frontier pressure was able to bring out into the open many hitherto-hidden affirmative votes on foreign-policy proposals; the South's affirmative percentage, it will be remembered, increased nearly 20 points under Kennedy. The number of Southerners actually voting on foreign policy issues (other than foreign aid) was markedly larger under Kennedy than under Eisenhower, and almost all those that turned out stayed to vote "yea." But no significant reduction in the number of negative votes by Southerners can be found; it would appear that the hard-line opposition had been voting each time previously, and few of them appear to have been persuaded to change sides permanently. A Southerner who had come to the point of rejecting multilateralism under Eisenhower seemed to find the concept no more attractive when advanced by Kennedy.

On balance, the figures for all fourteen votes suggest strongly that there was a bloc of some thirty-five votes within the Southern delegation in the House that under almost any circumstances could be counted on to vote against any kind of multilateralist proposal. On only four votes did the Southern negative figure drop below thirty-five, and district-by-district analyses show that these thirty-five votes came heavily from the same set of districts on roll call after roll call. But more discriminating criteria must be applied to the data before any clear relationship between this group and the anti-foreign aid vote can be clarified; it is also obvious that other Southerners than these thirty-five vote against multilateralism with varying frequency. These two inquiries form the next step in the analysis.

THE STATES AND MULTILATERALISM

The first step in reducing the summary figures to manageable and communicative parts is the identification of the states from which the opposition to multilateralism came and those in which the principle remains strong. Table 13 gives this information by arranging the roll call figures for the fourteen votes on a state-by-state basis, in the same fashion as was done for foreign aid.

These data, it should be kept in mind, are intrinsically different from those for foreign aid; the aid votes formed a series of referenda on a single issue across time, while these fourteen proposals were all one-time choices. The wide spread in the results shown here should be less surprising, therefore, than on the aid votes. No state shows the consistency in voting on these issues that several—on both sides—indicated in the latter series.

Two possible reasons for the greater "scatter" effect can be suggested. In the first place, the fourteen issues were extremely varied in their nature and thus any particular Congressman would be more likely to have a less unified range of response to them. But perhaps more important in explaining the inconsistencies is the fact that there was a broad spectrum of public interest and involvement in these

TABLE 13

ROLL CALL VOTES BY STATES ON SELECTED INTERNATIONAL ISSUES,

STATE/VOTE NO.:		1	2	3	4	5
Alabama	(9)	8-1	0-9	5-4	5-3	5-3
Arkansas	(6)	4-2	0-6	3-3	1-5	1-4
Florida	(8)	5-3	0-8	3-5	6-2	1-5
Georgia	(10)	5-4	0-10	8-1	2-4	2-4
Kentucky	(8)	6-0	3-3	0-6	2-5	5-1
Louisiana	(8)	2-5	0-7	4-3	4-1	5-1
Mississippi	(6)	2-4	0-6	6-0	4-1	1-5
North Carolina	(12)	3-8	1-8	9-2	10-1	5-5
Oklahoma	(6)	6-0	0-6	1-5	1-4	5-0
South Carolina	(6)	4-2	0-6	3-3	5-1	1-4
Tennessee	(9)	7-2	1-8	6-3	3-4	5-3
Texas	(22)	7-10	3-16	13-6	10-9	11-6
Virginia	(10)	2-8	0-10	1-9	9-0	4-5
West Virginia	(6)	6-0	3-3	2-4	4-2	5-0
TOTALS		67-49	11-106	64-54*	66-42*	56-46

* All "yea" votes on numbers 3 and 4 indicate an anti-

fourteen proposals. Some were matters of great public moment during their consideration, such as the United Nations bond purchase bill, while others were debated and voted in almost total public ignorance or unconcern. The figures themselves show clearly that several state delegations as well as scores of individual Southern Congressmen vote differently on a multilateralist issue when the public

House of Representatives, 1953-1962

6	7	8	9	10	11	12	13	14
5-2	8-0	8-0	1-8	5-3	8-1	8-1	8-0	3-5
5-1	4-1	4-1	3-1	2-4	5-1	3-3	3-2	2-3
3-4	8-0	6-2	6-2	6-1	6-2	6-2	6-1	3-5
2-3	3-5	4-3	1-7	4-6	4-2	5-2	7-1	5-2
6-1	5-1	5-1	4-4	7-1	7-0	7-0	6-0	7-1
5-0	3-1	3-0	3-2	7-1	2-1	4-1	3-1	5-3
1-5	1-4	2-4	1-5	1-5	1-5	1-5	2-2	1-5
4-6	4-6	2-4	1-11	9-2	4-8	10-1	10-0	9-2
5-0	3-1	3-1	4-0	5-1	4-1	5-1	5-0	4-2
1-3	1-4	4-2	0-6	0-5	1-5	2-3	2-4	0-5
4-1	4-3	4-2	4-4	6-1	3-3	4-3	6-0	5-2
19-2	14-5	17-3	11-10	14-5	14-5	9-7	14-5	11-10
6-3	1-9	4-5	2-8	10-0	6-3	6-3	9-0	3-7
5-0	2-3	5-1	1-4	6-0	6-0	4-1	6-0	5-1
71-31	61-43	71-29	42-72	82-35	71-37	73-33	86-16	63-53

multilateralist position and opposition to the bill in question.

is clamorous than when the voters are uninformed, apathetic, or diverted by other matters.

On a percentage and raw figure basis, the following table can be constructed. It should be kept in mind that in these computations votes 3 and 4 are reversed; that is, a roll call "yea" is counted as a "nay" in the total and *vice versa.*

TABLE 14
AFFIRMATIVE AND NEGATIVE VOTES AND PERCENTAGES,
FOURTEEN INTERNATIONAL ISSUES,
HOUSE OF REPRESENTATIVES, 1953-1962

STATE	YEA	NAY	% YEA
Alabama	74	43	63.3
Arkansas	44	33	57.1
Florida	63	44	58.9
Georgia	47	59	44.3
Kentucky	79	15	84.0
Louisiana	45	31	59.2
Mississippi	15	65	18.8
North Carolina	65	80	44.8
Oklahoma	58	15	79.4
South Carolina	20	57	25.9
Tennessee	60	41	59.4
Texas	159	107	59.8
Virginia	62	71	46.6
West Virginia	60	19	75.9
TOTALS	851	680	55.6

In certain important respects the configuration of these data is much the same as those that correspond on the foreign aid issue. Kentucky, Oklahoma, West Virginia, and Alabama, all with high affirmative percentages on foreign aid, show the highest levels of support as well on these fourteen tests of multilateralist sympathies. On the other hand, Mississippi, South Carolina, Georgia, North Carolina, and Virginia all show a less than 50 per cent affirmative stand; these states are already familiar from the analysis of the foreign aid votes. Thus the connection is established: the same states show up at the top and at the bottom of the column of support, regardless of whether the issue is one of foreign aid or of some otherwise undifferentiated multi-lateralist proposal.

Another striking point about the data in Table 14 is the percentage of participation in these votes by individual Congressmen. There are many reasons why a member of the House might miss a roll call vote, of which several are perfectly legitimate; one of the most frequently relied on—although only seldom verbalized—is, however, a perfectly normal reluctance to put himself on record on a contro-versial issue. No Congressman is anxious to give ammuni-tion to any potential future adversary by casting an un-popular vote. Since the frequency with which Southern Representatives voted on the fourteen multilateralist issues varied so much from state to state, it is interesting to com-pare percentages of participation in the fourteen votes with those on foreign aid (Table 15).

These figures point one moral: when public interest in a question is high and the President actively involves him-self in pushing a measure through Congress, a significantly larger percentage of Southern Congressmen turn out for the roll call, whichever side they may take. This is clearly true in the case of foreign aid; note the appreciably higher per-centage of participation overall on the latter question for the ten years. Ten of the fourteen individual states proved themselves more anxious (or at least more willing) to vote on foreign aid than on the other group of questions, and the four who did not had percentages of participation only fractionally greater for the miscellaneous set of questions than for aid.

Three states, however, show markedly higher percen-tages of participation on the foreign aid votes: Georgia (14.3 percentage points difference), Kentucky (12.4 percentage points), and Louisiana (9.7 percentage points). The differ-ence in the case of Kentucky is perhaps the least meaningful of the three, since the lower figure for that state (83.9 per cent participation on the multilateralist group of measures)

TABLE 15
PERCENTAGE OF PARTICIPATION, FOREIGN AID AUTHORIZATIONS
AND FOURTEEN SELECTED INTERNATIONAL ISSUES,
HOUSE OF REPRESENTATIVES, 1953-1962

STATE	14 ISSUES	FOREIGN AID
Alabama	92.9	88.9
Arkansas	91.7	95.0
Florida	95.5	95.0
Georgia	75.7	93.0
Kentucky	83.9	96.3
Louisiana	67.8	77.5
Mississippi	95.2	98.3
North Carolina	86.3	85.8
Oklahoma	86.9	93.3
South Carolina	91.7	90.0
Tennessee	80.2	88.9
Texas	86.4	86.8
Virginia	95.0	98.0
West Virginia	94.0	93.3
TOTALS	86.8	90.6

is only slightly below the regional average. But Georgia
and Louisiana depart so extensively from the Southern norm
as to merit a closer second look.

These two states had the lowest levels of participation
of all the Southern states, at least on the multilateralist
measures. Georgia's 75.7 per cent was the only state figure
in the seventies, and Louisiana's 67.8 per cent was so out of
phase with the regional trend as scarcely to seem to belong
in the list at all. On foreign aid, however, Georgia's participation was above the overall Southern average and was
the more remarkable because of the state's relatively large
delegation. Louisiana, on the other hand, almost matched

its two percentage levels and took the bottom place in the participation ranking on foreign aid as well. While undoubtedly many of the absentees of both states had perfectly valid reasons for not placing themselves on the record any more frequently than they did (three of Louisiana's roll calls in the multilateralist group of votes showed that only three of its eight-man delegation actually cast votes), one is nevertheless tempted to suspect that there were members of both delegations whose interest in foreign policy in general and in multilateralist legislation in particular was no more than minimal.

The impact of percentage of participation upon the level of support for these measures may be suggested by a comparison of the affirmative percentages given the two types of bills by the several states (Table 16).

With these figures the cross-checking effect of the several tabulations begins to make itself felt. The fourteen states of the South may be divided into three groups, each of a distinctive and meaningful character, simply on the basis of the differences in the level of support they gave to the two types of measures.

Four states (Alabama, Arkansas, Kentucky, and Tennessee) all show affirmative percentages on foreign aid greater than they accumulated for the fourteen multilateralist measures, Alabama by more than 12 percentage points. A second group consisting of five states (Louisiana, Oklahoma, North Carolina, Texas, and West Virginia) shows a differential of between 14 and 28 percentage points in favor of the multilateralist group of bills, and were obviously much more enthusiastic about them than they were about foreign aid. The remaining five states (Florida, Georgia, Mississippi, South Carolina, and Virginia) have only minimal differences in their two percentages (the largest is South Carolina's 5.5 points).

The analysis of the foreign aid votes in Chapter III already has established something of the basic orientation

TABLE 16

AFFIRMATIVE PERCENTAGES, FOREIGN AID AUTHORIZATIONS
AND FOURTEEN SELECTED INTERNATIONAL ISSUES,
HOUSE OF REPRESENTATIVES, 1953-1962

STATE	14 ISSUES	FOREIGN AID	DIFFERENCE IN FAVOR OF AID
Alabama	63.3	75.5	12.2
Arkansas	57.1	58.0	0.9
Florida	58.9	55.2	—3.7
Georgia	44.3	39.8	—4.5
Kentucky	84.0	87.0	3.0
Louisiana	59.2	30.6	—28.6
Mississippi	18.8	16.9	—1.9
North Carolina	44.8	27.2	—17.6
Oklahoma	79.4	60.7	—18.7
South Carolina	25.9	20.4	—5.5
Tennessee	59.4	66.3	6.9
Texas	59.8	45.0	—14.8
Virginia	46.6	45.9	—0.7
West Virginia	75.9	66.0	—9.0
TOTALS	55.6	49.5	—6.1

of each of these groups of states, and their record on the
multilateralist bills considered in this chapter fills in much
of the outline that was developed earlier. The characteristic
that is the easiest to identify in each group is flexibility of
purpose.

The first group is composed entirely of states with a
generally quite favorable record on foreign aid. Kentucky,
Alabama, and Tennessee, it will be recalled, were the three
leaders in support of the aid program, and West Virginia
was beaten out for fourth place by Oklahoma by only a

fraction of a percentage point. Only in the case of Alabama, furthermore, is a really significant difference in support level involved (12.2 percentage points), and it will be noted that Alabama's participation in the foreign aid voting was consistently below the regional average. Only Alabama, furthermore, does not belong to the group of "border states" identified in Chapter III, and it must be admitted that Alabama's record makes it more akin to Kentucky and Tennessee than to its neighbors to the east and west, Georgia and Mississippi. The differences in support given by these four states to the humanitarian measures are perhaps less important than the fact that all four supported both types of bills by comfortable margins. The atypical pattern of their voting would seem to be more a function of accidents of participation and the peculiarities of individual proposals than of any general point of view.

The second group of states, however, includes those whose record of voting on foreign aid shows the widest swings and whose mean percentage of participation in both sets of votes is the lowest of the three groups. From these data one may tentatively generalize that in these states a constant pressure of opposition to a multilateral foreign policy must be reckoned with by individual Congressmen as they face the periodic necessity of placing themselves on one side or the other of a roll call. The nature and extent of the public outcry they confront varies from year to year and measure to measure, and is reflected in rapid changes in the level of support a state's delegation may be moved to give any particular proposal. The very flexibility these states show in their voting, materially greater than that evinced by the first group and several times more impressive than the third, points to a generally active political climate with relatively heavy public involvement in matters of foreign policy. This is the province of the factor of protest— a point that will be examined in detail in later chapters.

The third group is the least elastic of all. It includes

the two states that showed the most implacable opposition to foreign aid (Mississippi and South Carolina), a third whose conversion to an anti-foreign aid position did not occur until 1957 but whose posture then became absolutely hostile (Georgia), a fourth whose split on foreign aid, although almost even, is unyielding on either side (Virginia), and a fifth with a crystallized minority of solid opposition to the aid program (Florida). These five states show in their respective records virtually equal resistance to the foreign aid program as a specific undertaking and to the broader philosophy of a co-operative foreign policy of which the aid program and the various multilateralist measures form constituent parts. In these states the political climate, although often tense, is static; there is little changing of sides and only a barely perceptible trend of evolution in foreign policy attitudes. In many ways this group of states epitomizes the acute form of the Southern political dilemma.

MULTILATERALISM IN THE DISTRICTS

The final step in the process of particularizing the attitudes of Southern Congressmen toward the multilateralist measures included in the sample in this chapter requires that—as in the case of foreign aid—a district-by-district record be prepared. In point of fact, of course, it should be repeated that in reality the process went in the opposite direction: the district figures for individual Congressmen were the first data to be assembled. The results of this compilation are found in the table in Appendix III.

The long list of voting records found in the table includes many variations and inconsistencies in the performance of individual Congressmen, but in general the stands taken may be grouped around the three modal points of extreme hostility, extreme support, and a divided response. Three districts (Kentucky 2, 3, and 5) have perfect records

of never casting a negative vote; three, on the other hand
(Georgia 5, South Carolina 3, and Texas 5), have as clean
a record but on the negative side. None of the latter group
ever voted for any of the fourteen measures, and one
(South Carolina 3) coupled consistency in attendance with
ideological purity: a vote was recorded on every one of the
fourteen measures, and every vote was anti-multilateralist!

Eleven other districts showed themselves almost as
favorably inclined to multilateralism; these compiled records
included only one negative vote—in most cases, furthermore, that one "nay" was cast on the Refugee Act of 1953 on
which the South as a whole voted 11-106 against. Only
three hostile districts had correspondingly negative records
marred by only a single "yea": Mississippi 4 and 5, and
Texas 7.

Beyond these clear cases, it is fairly simple to infer the
general orientation of a district from the pattern formed by
the votes its Congressmen cast during the ten years. A
record of 9-3-2 (9 "yea," 3 "nay," 2 votes missing), for
example, may be fairly judged as a conspicuously favorable
one; one of 3-10-1, on the other hand, would place the
district concerned in the anti-multilateralist camp. What use
is made of this rule of thumb will become apparent in the
chapter that follows.

Before leaving the district-by-district figures, however,
it is worth pointing out once again in these terms how the
Kennedy administration's pressure on Congress resulted in
a general improvement in the South's percentage of affirmative voting. Votes 10 through 14, it will be recalled, all
involve Kennedy proposals of 1961 and 1962. A quick
glance at the table in Appendix III will reveal that a sizeable
number of Representatives with evenly-divided records
prior to 1961—or, as in the case of several from North Carolina, Florida, Tennessee, and Texas, actual indications of
anti-multilateralism—cast "yea" votes on the Kennedy proposals with admirable consistency, even on a measure like

the United Nations bond purchase bill which, had it been advanced under Eisenhower leadership, their records suggest they would have strongly opposed.

By and large, the detailed vote-by-vote performance of individual Congressmen corroborates in many respects the impressions produced by the foreign aid votes, but also contains a number of important and impressive discrepancies. The rationalization and schematization of both similarities and differences will result in the final identification of the several schools of Southern Congressional thought on world affairs.

THE SOUTH AND FOREIGN TRADE

Before proceeding to that discussion, however, it is necessary first to deal with a question that almost everyone concerned with the South comes to sooner or later: the Southern attitude toward trade legislation. Many observers of the contemporary Southern political scene have assumed that the fundamental change in the outlook of the region on world affairs has its roots in and finds its major expression in a changed position on international trade. The South, the argument goes, has abandoned its traditional free-trade (or, more accurately, relatively low-tariff) position and has become a hotbed of protectionism.

The unemotional evidence of the roll call votes on foreign trade legislation during the ten years, however, lends little support to this thesis. The South has unquestionably moved a considerable distance away from its virtually unanimous support of the trade-agreements program that dated from 1934 and that bore (in the person of Cordell Hull) something of a distinctively Southern stamp. But except in a few scattered cases, no direct relation between economic interest expressed in protectionist voting and a generally anti-multilateralist outlook can be found or inferred. The shift in Southern attitudes toward trade has taken place at the same time and in the same general direction as the region's reorientation of international outlook, but whatever coincidence there may be in the two changes, the discovery of any causal relationship remains impossible by any reliable techniques.

Table 17 shows the way the Southern states voted on the several renewals of the Trade Agreements Act in 1953, 1954, 1955, and 1958 and, in the final column, on President Kennedy's Trade Expansion Act in 1962.

TABLE 17

ROLL CALL VOTES ON RENEWALS OF TRADE AGREEMENTS ACT AND TRADE EXPANSION ACT, 1953-1962

STATE	1953	1954	1955	1958	1962	TOTAL
Alabama	8-0	9-0	8-1	8-1	7-1	40-4
Arkansas	6-0	5-0	6-0	6-0	5-0	28-0
Florida	8-0	8-0	8-0	8-0	5-3	37-3
Georgia	9-0	7-0	7-3	6-4	8-0	37-7
Kentucky	5-2	6-2	6-1	6-1	7-1	30-7
Louisiana	7-0	4-0	7-0	7-0	4-2	29-2
Mississippi	4-0	5-0	6-0	1-5	1-5	17-10
North Carolina	12-0	8-0	9-3	7-5	9-3	45-11
Oklahoma	6-0	3-1	5-0	3-2	3-3	20-6
South Carolina	6-0	2-1	2-3	0-6	3-3	13-13
Tennessee	9-0	6-0	7-1	8-1	8-0	38-2
Texas	21-0	19-0	18-3	17-3	15-7	90-13
Virginia	10-0	7-1	9-1	10-0	10-0	46-2
West Virginia	0-5	0-6	0-6	0-6	4-2	4-25
TOTALS	111-7	89-11	98-22	87-34	89-31	474-105
% YEA	94.1	89.0	81.7	71.9	74.3	81.9

The most conspicuous opponent of the several renewals of the Trade Agreements Act across the decade was obviously West Virginia—a state with a normally favorable point of view toward foreign aid and a basic multilateralist bias toward foreign policy questions generally. Mississippi and South Carolina, of course, show their unilateralist colors as unabashedly on trade legislation as they do in other matters, but in the case of both states the time sequence is quite interesting. Mississippi did not become an open opponent of the trade agreements program until the 1958 bill was under consideration, even though the state had been solid in its opposition to multilateralism in foreign policy ever since 1953. In view of the internal economic situation in Mississippi (as well as the trends of its political development), the state's stand on foreign trade bills in 1958 and 1962 may be classified as a deduction from a generalized international outlook; in other words, Mississippians finally applied to trade legislation the same criteria that they were using on other international matters. South Carolina's case, on the other hand, would appear to be less clear in view of its heavy concentration of textile production and the simultaneity of its change on foreign aid and on trade.

But several states follow a pattern on trade voting quite different from their generalized foreign-policy stand. Arkansas, Florida, Georgia, Louisiana, North Carolina, Tennessee, and Virginia—all states with records of opposition to multilateralism that range from a substantial minority to near-unanimity—have held the line on trade legislation with impressive consistency. Whatever the impact of protectionist interest within the state—textiles, cotton, lumber, petroleum, chemicals, food products, and so on—on the general context of public discussion, the record indicates that these attitudes have not spilled over into the actual voting of the delegations. It is self-evident, of course, that Southern protectionists, like their Northern and Western counterparts, play their part in influencing the content of a bill by the insertion of specific provisions that will suit their interests, but they have in only a few instances brought Congressmen to the point of opposing the program *in toto*.

Trade bills, both the renewals of the Trade Agreements Act and the 1962 Trade Expansion Act, usually go through the House of Representatives under very tightly controlled parliamentary conditions. The most common device is a "closed rule" that sharply limits both the length of debate and the offering of amendments from the floor. This restrictive technique has the effect of making the actual roll call somewhat less accurate as a reflection of Congressional attitudes. The members of the House are, in fact, faced with the choice of accepting virtually unchanged a committee-written measure or of rejecting the entire program. The managers of the bill, on their part, maximize their chances of success by placating enough of the opposition in advance by modifying the legislation before it reaches the floor.

Thus the figures given in Table 17 should not be taken as completely expressing the viewpoints held by Southerners. A more accurate picture—or at least one that shows a few additional nuances—may be drawn from Table 18, which covers the roll call votes on a number of preliminary steps in the passage of the several bills, either in the form of a motion to adopt a closed rule or by one of the few modifying amendments that might have been permitted. The sample shows that Southerners really divide more sharply on trade matters than the raw final-passage figures might indicate.

The relatively large minorities accumulated among Southerners against the will of the House on these ancillary motions and amendments indicate that there is more opposition to the trade program than the figures earlier cited would show. Yet the pattern, although blurred, is nevertheless not significantly different from the starker choices forced by the bills themselves. Many Southern Congressmen oppose particular provisions of the proposals, and many

TABLE 18
ROLL CALL VOTES ON PRELIMINARY ISSUES,
TRADE AGREEMENTS AND EXPANSION ACTS, 1953-1962

STATE/VOTE NO.:	1	2	3	4	5
Alabama	7-2	7-1	2-8	2-7	2-9
Arkansas	3-3	4-1	5-0	0-6	0-5
Florida	8-0	8-0	8-0	2-6	3-5
Georgia	8-1	4-3	3-7	8-2	1-8
Kentucky	2-4	5-3	4-2	1-5	1-7
Louisiana	2-4	3-1	5-0	3-4	2-4
Mississippi	5-0	2-2	2-4	2-4	5-1
North Carolina	11-0	8-0	5-7	7-5	6-6
Oklahoma	0-6	2-2	1-5	5-1	3-3
South Carolina	4-1	2-0	2-4	4-1	3-3
Tennessee	7-1	7-0	6-2	2-6	0-8
Texas	9-11	13-6	14-7	11-10	12-10
Virginia	8-2	5-2	6-4	5-5	6-4
West Virginia	0-6	0-6	0-6	6-0	2-4
SOUTH	74-41	70-27	63-56	58-62	46-75
HOUSE	242-161	273-63	193-192	199-206	171-253

Key to Votes:
1. Motion to recommit "Simpson Bill"—a more protectionist version of the renewal of the Trade Agreements Act (1953).
2. Adoption of closed rule for consideration of the bill (1954).
3. Adoption of closed rule for consideration of the bill (1955).
4. Motion to recommit bill with instructions to amend to require the President to comply with the recommendations of the U.S. Tariff Commission, except when national security was involved (1955).
5. Motion to substitute a one-year extension of the Trade Agreements Act for the Trade Expansion Act (1962).

seek to place impediments in the way of the full implementation of the national commitment to a more liberalized flow of international trade. Yet there is no real evidence that the South is on a runaway protectionist surge. Even the considerable vote in defiance of the New Frontier on the Trade Expansion Act of 1962 was, it must not be forgotten, not an attempt to emasculate the entire movement for low tariffs and free trade, but rather a vote in favor of the extension of the Trade Agreements Act itself.

Nor can the case be convincingly made that the South is either trending toward short-sighted protectionism or is especially distinguished in its opposition to free trade. Table 19 provides some basis for comparing Southern support with that of the House as a whole:

TABLE 19
ROLL CALL VOTES ON TRADE BILLS, 1953-1962

YEAR	HOUSE	SOUTH	SOUTH % OF NEGATIVE
1953	363- 34 (91.4% Y)	111- 7 (94.1% Y)	20.6
1954	281- 53 (84.1% Y)	89-11 (89.0% Y)	20.8
1955	295-110 (72.8% Y)	98-22 (81.7% Y)	20.0
1958	217- 98 (76.4% Y)	87-34 (71.9% Y)	34.7
1962	298-125 (70.4% Y)	89-31 (74.3% Y)	24.8

Thus only in 1958 was the South's level of support lower than that of the House as a whole, and only in that year did the South's contribution to the overall negative total surpass its proportionate share of the membership. Even in the 1962 vote on the substitute to the President's Trade Expansion Act, Southern votes made up only 26.3 per cent of its total support—once again less than the region's proportionate share and quite close to the level at which the South eventually supported the Kennedy program.

For what is new in the international outlook of Southern Congressmen as a group, the rise of protectionism cannot be blamed. The votes themselves indicate that the increase in opposition to trade legislation set in well after the appearance of unilateralism on general foreign-policy matters, that protectionism never spread to as many states as did the political unilateralism implicit in the rejection of foreign aid, and that protectionism never had as large an effect on the overall record of the House. The evolving Southern outlook on foreign trade legislation is a phenomenon in itself, important and possibly portentous for the future, but it has no discernible relationship with the broader issue except in the case of a handful of Congressmen—and then often in unexpected ways.

V

THE RANGE OF
SOUTHERN ATTITUDES

UP TO THIS POINT in the analysis, it has been abundantly demonstrated that many Southern members of the House of Representatives—between sixty and seventy, or approximately half the Southern delegation—can be counted on to vote against foreign aid on the basis of their performance between 1953 and 1962. A somewhat smaller number—between thirty-five and sixty—usually also voted against most multilateralist foreign policy ventures. What do these two sets of figures mean with regard to the general international outlook of Southerners?

Initially, of course, they confirm the validity of the thesis that a major change in Southern attitudes toward world affairs has actually taken place, reaching its peak sometime in the mid-1950's and receding only minimally since. But the figures as advanced in the two preceding chapters can do no more than suggest the magnitude of the change in the South as a whole and to a lesser extent within particular states. Before the Southern phenomenon can be fully grasped, the problem of foreign-policy attitudes must be grappled with on the politician's favorite stamping ground —the grass roots of the individual districts—and in the personalities and characters of the men who represent Southern constituencies.

It is, in a word, necessary to give the Southern metamorphosis some concrete dimensions of breadth and depth, to point out the range of opinion on international affairs that characterizes Congressmen from the South, to locate the extreme positions and then to plot the intermediate positions. Only by segregating the 126 Congressmen into attitude groups and by comparing these groups with each other can generalizations, insight, understanding, and at least a low level of prediction be hoped for.

In this effort the district-by-district tabulations of the roll call votes on foreign aid (Appendix II) and on the multilateralist issues (Appendix III) are the necessary instruments. Each of the Congressmen has two voting records, one drawn from each table. If these two are compared with each other, the degree of coincidence or divergence in the records provides the basis for a useful and meaningful scheme of classification. It is on this principle that the groupings used in this chapter are grounded.

There is no attempt made here to argue that this device is immune from all methodological criticism, but in its defense a few important points may be made. It is founded on the hard evidence of the official record on each case; its purpose is only to group Congressmen who—for whatever reasons—voted on international issues in rather much the same way; it provides, finally, a base for hypotheses that will themselves be subject to further testing. One final point might also be made: when applied to the 126 Southern districts, it divides these seats into a number of quite distinct and certainly differently-behaving categories. Whether the criteria measure the relevant variables, in other words, may be seriously (if inconclusively) debated; that they do measure something, however, would seem beyond doubt.

SCHOOLS OF SOUTHERN THOUGHT

To sum up a rather tedious task quickly, it can be simply stated that the voting-record comparison of all 126 Congressional districts in the South revealed a very broad range of attitudes. The extreme positions, being unequivocal—and being occupied by fairly large numbers of very consistently voting seats—were not especially difficult to identify and define; the intermediate points of view, however, were both less cohesive internally and more difficult to distinguish from one another. Ultimately, however, a range of attitudes was formulated that comprehended six different positions, each incorporating a distinct point of view toward American co-operative foreign policy during the decade. In the description that follows here, the six are arranged roughly in decreasing order of identification with the dominant line of American policy during the 1950's and early 1960's.

The *first*—and the largest—group of Southerners includes those who voted consistently in favor of both foreign aid and the multilateralist measures used in the analysis. No more than three anti-foreign aid votes were cast by any of this group during the ten years, nor more than four "nays" on the multilateralist measures. The level and type of support given American foreign policy by these Congressmen differed in no important degree from dominant attitudes in the Northeast, the West, and the Midwest. Forty-three districts were found to be qualified on those grounds:

Alabama:	4,5,7,8,9
Arkansas:	2,3
Florida:	1,2,4
Georgia:	6
Kentucky:	1,2
Louisiana:	1,2,3,4,5,6,7
Mississippi:	3

North Carolina:	4,6
Oklahoma:	2,3,5
Tennessee:	3,4,9
Texas:	1,2,3,4,9,10,12,13,19,20
Virginia:	2
West Virginia:	2,4,5

Without going into an elaborate analysis at this point, certain aspects of this list are striking. In the first place, every Southern state except South Carolina was represented during the decade by at least one multilateralist Congressman. Second, Kentucky's powerful support of the major lines of United States foreign policy is demonstrated by the fact that seven of its eight Representatives earned places. The only other states that put approximately half their delegations in this group were Texas (ten of twenty-two) and Florida (three of eight).

The *second* Southern point of view is oddly at variance both with the first and with those to follow. Ten districts showed themselves to be consistent supporters of foreign aid, but gave only lukewarm adherence (or even actual overall opposition) to the multilateral measures. The figures advanced in Chapter IV underscore that this is a distinctly atypical position among Southerners. The districts that adopted it were:

Alabama:	1,6
Arkansas:	1
Florida:	8
Tennessee:	2,5,8
Virginia:	3,10
West Virginia:	6

This list is too short to permit any generalizations, but it is worth remarking in passing that Tennessee furnished three of the ten examples of this eccentric voting pattern, and that Virginia produced two (both, incidentally, highly urbanized and—at least by Southern standards—sophisticated districts). Also, interestingly enough, there are no Texas districts included.

The *third* position, so neatly a mid-point, was occupied by only a handful of Congressmen. Six showed themselves (or their districts) to be either relatively unconcerned or else deeply split over the issues implicit in a multilateralist foreign policy, for their records are almost evenly divided on both sets of votes. Several, however, were brought up to a 50 per cent affirmative level only during 1961 and 1962 as a result of the Kennedy Administration's get-out-the-House-vote campaign on foreign policy issues. The six divided districts were:

Arkansas:	4
Florida:	5
North Carolina:	5
Oklahoma:	4
South Carolina:	5
Virginia:	6

It must be said in further elaboration of this brief list that two districts among the six are in some measure deceptive. On foreign aid in particular, the final two on the list (South Carolina 5 and Virginia 6) are at the half-and-half level only because of a consistent record of "yeas" early in the decade. Both swung to consistent opposition after 1957 and show no signs of returning; both will cease to be evenly divided in a few years if their present patterns persist.

The first three positions identified have one element in common, if only a negative one: in none is strong opposition to foreign aid over the bulk of the ten years a determining factor. Even the divided districts show a willingness to go along with the aid program at least part of the time, and the first two groups are heavily in support. The three groups that remain to be examined, however, make up the anti-foreign aid camp among Southerners in the House and are distinguishable from each other primarily by the differing responses they make to the multilateralist challenge.

The first of these anti-foreign aid groups—the *fourth* position overall on the scale being developed here—is the closest to the center and the least removed from the multi-lateralist approach. In many ways these districts behaved much more like the old-line multilateralists than did their fellows on their side of the line. In several respects they form the most interesting and provocative cluster of all, consisting of the eighteen districts whose Congressmen were heavily against foreign aid—several were unwavering in their opposition—and yet were as a rule strongly in favor of the multilateralist measures, usually by as large a margin as they were hostile to aid.

This voting pattern reflected a set of highly pragmatic political judgments by the Congressmen concerned. By most indices more identifiable with the pro-internationalist side of the foreign policy debate, they nevertheless voted against foreign aid (and on occasion against other multilateralist projects as well) apparently in response to their calculation of the state of mass resistance to this sort of policy in their districts. Where public opposition existed in their con-stituencies, the "pragmatists" voted against the measure; where apathy—or, more rarely, positive support—prevailed in the domestic political climate, they tended rather to follow their normal instincts and to go along with majority and leadership opinion in the House.

These challenging districts made the following list:

Florida:	3,6
Georgia:	1,7,10
Louisiana:	6
North Carolina:	2,10
Oklahoma:	6

Tennessee:	1,6
Texas:	8,11,14
Virginia:	1,9
West Virginia:	1,3

The pragmatic districts could thus be found in nine different states, and only Georgia and Texas had more than two. There were none from Alabama, Arkansas, Kentucky, Mississippi, or South Carolina—the first three being leaders in support of foreign aid, the latter two leaders in opposition. These five states had perhaps the most rigid international outlooks of the entire South and would have been most unlikely to permit, let alone demand, such a schizoid voting pattern in their Congressmen.

The *fifth* position is marked by an anti-foreign aid posture and a divided record—leaning toward the hostile—on multilateralism. These nineteen districts were saved from classification as total opponents of the main lines of American policy only by the fact that all of them voted in favor of between five and nine of the multilateralist bills. In spite of their avoiding identification as extremists by their pro-multilateral votes, the actual difference between them and the group that follows was small, while a broad gulf separated them from the pragmatists. They may be called the "waverers":

Alabama:	2,3
Georgia:	2
Louisiana:	3,4,7,8
North Carolina:	1,3,7,8
Oklahoma:	1
South Carolina:	2
Texas:	15,16,21,22
Virginia:	7,8

These wavering districts, it will be noted, came from only eight states, with three (Louisiana, North Carolina, and Texas) producing four each. Louisiana again showed up as it did in Chapter IV as unique, placing half its delegation in a category marked by the lack of a clear orientation. The relatively high numbers borne by the four Texas districts are also interesting.

Finally, the *sixth* position is reached and the scale is complete. At the opposite extreme from the solid multilateralists that were identified first is the group of hardcore opponents of the entire concept of co-operation in American foreign policy. These thirty districts are classified here as "ideological" because of the almost mechanical consistency with which their Representatives voted against foreign aid or almost any other multilateralist proposal. No Congressman could be so free of inner conflict on the many-formed and frustratingly complex issues of foreign policy unless he enjoyed the serenity and simplistic worldview provided by a full-fledged ideological approach to the problems. And the single-mindedness of the ideological districts was truly remarkable.

The ideological districts formed the source of the Southern militants, on foreign policy and on many domestic issues as well. Implicit in much of their political maneuvering was their faith in the self-conscious "old South," in spite of the fact that only a very few really spoke for socio-political-economic systems that related in any meaningful way to the symbolism of either antebellum or late-nineteenth-century Southern folkways. To an ideologist the myth is everything, and in many of these self-appointed crusaders (and in the movements they headed) the myth of the South was very much alive.

The ideological districts were distributed rather widely throughout the South:

Arkansas:	5,6
Florida:	7
Georgia:	3,4,5,8,9
Kentucky:	8
Louisiana:	5

Mississippi:	1,2,4,5,6
North Carolina:	9,11,12
South Carolina:	1,3,4,6
Tennessee:	7
Texas:	5,6,7,17,18
Virginia:	4,5

Thus Georgia, Mississippi, and Texas each contributed five districts to the list, and South Carolina four; almost two-thirds of the group, in other words, came from four states. It is also noteworthy that North Carolina's pronounced antipathy to foreign aid (surpassed only by Mississippi and South Carolina) was not translated into very many places on the list. Only three states—Alabama, Oklahoma, and West Virginia—produced no ideologists at all. The latter three states, however, were all members of the "border" group, and Alabama's consistent atypicality has been a constant through the entire analysis.

To recapitulate: six positions on foreign affairs can be detected among Southern Congressmen. The two extremes together claimed, in 1962, nearly 60 per cent (73 of 126) of the total: the *multilateralist* point of view with 43 adherents and the *ideological* outlook with 30 disciples. The four intermediate postures, running the scale from multilateralist to ideological, may be classified as *reversed* (10 districts), *divided* (6), *pragmatic* (18), and *wavering* (19). The pragmatic position involved opposition to foreign aid but support of other multilateral measures, the wavering opposition to foreign aid and a split on multilateralism, the divided an even split on both types of measures, and the reversed support of foreign aid but a split on multilateralism.

Since this study is basically more concerned with the general problem of anti-multilateralism among Southerners, only four of these six positions will be analyzed in detail below: the ideological, the wavering, the pragmatic (these three all anti-multilateral or tending toward it) and the multilateral. The two smaller groups can indeed be disposed of here with much less ceremony, although they will reappear later in the book.

THE IDEOLOGICAL DISTRICTS

What are the common characteristics of the ideological districts? What are the components of their political dynamics that lead their Representatives to adopt such a firm position on international affairs, especially one that sets them apart so sharply from the nation at large as well as from the remainder of their Southern brethren? What, in other words, are the distinguishing marks of the ideological districts?

The most obvious and pervasive characteristic of the group, looked at in the round, is their relative and, in many cases, absolute sluggishness in economic, social, and political life. By and large almost all of these thirty districts lag behind the rest of the South in nearly every index of growth and modernization. The handful of exceptions to this generalization can show other factors that explain their ideological stand.

The districts are generally on the small side in terms of the sheer number of human beings involved. The average constituency of a Southern Congressman during the decade was 402,081 people, but for the ideological districts the mean figure was only 373,619. The overall rate of population growth for the South during the 1950's was 16.5 per cent, while the ideological districts increased their total over 1950 by only 10.7 per cent. They simply failed to keep pace with the rest of the region, let alone with the remainder of the nation.

To put the matter another way, the 126 districts of the South can be divided into three categories in terms of their rate of population growth betwen 1950 and 1960. Fortyfour (or 34.9 per cent of the whole) grew more rapidly than the regional average, fifty-one (40.5 per cent) increased in population but by a lower rate than the average, and thirty-one (24.6 per cent) suffered a net decrease. How did the ideological districts distribute themselves within these categories?

Six of them grew more rapidly than the Southern average: Florida 7 (Sarasota), Georgia 5 (Atlanta), Mississippi 6 (Gulfport), South Carolina 1 (Charleston), Texas 5 (Dallas), and Texas 18 (Amarillo). These six formed 13.6 per cent of the rapidly-growing districts of the South. The fact that these metropolitan centers were included in a group with an overall growth rate of only 10.7 per cent for the decade speaks volumes about the slow pace of development of the remaining twenty-four districts.

Sixteen of the thirty fell into the slow-growing category, with percentages between zero and 16.4 per cent. This was 31.3 per cent of the South's fifty-one slow-growing districts, appreciably in excess of the ideological group's 23.8 per cent of all Southern seats. The fact that more than half the ideological districts are of the slow-growing type is itself suggestive.

Finally, eight were included in the list of the districts that lost population: Arkansas 6, Kentucky 8, Mississippi 1 and 5, Tennessee 7, and Texas 6 and 7. In spite of this relatively large representation of shrinking districts, however, the ideological group has only a fraction more than its proportional share of this type; the eight constitute 25.8 per cent of the total of thirty-one, in close proximity to the roughly one-quarter of all Southern seats held by ideologists.

In sum, the overall curve of population distribution of the ideological districts weights heavily the second category of slow growth, gives them substantially less than their share of the rapidly growing districts, and almost exactly a fair share of those losing population. This 6-16-8 pattern is quite distinctive; no other group of the six identified among Southerners presents a picture anything like it.

In the same way, the ideological districts fall behind

the South in the predominant criteria of modern American
life, urbanization and industrialization. The urban revolution in the South as a whole during the 1950's was impressive; the region was less than half urban in 1950—the
precise percentage was 49.1—but by 1960 the percentage
had increased to 58.5. Since the fourteen states used in this
study make up less than the Census Bureau's regional concept of "the South," a different overall percentage of
urbanization for the fourteen than for the larger group
obtains. This is, however, not significantly different, being
slightly lower at 57 per cent.

Here again the ideological districts separate themselves
from broader Southern patterns. Their combined urban
percentage in 1960 was only 48.9—not even equalling the
regional average of a decade earlier. Only five of the thirty—
the districts containing Little Rock, Sarasota, Atlanta, Dallas, and Amarillo—surpassed the regional urban average
and no less than eight were less than 30 per cent urbanized.

A correlative—if not indeed a causative—element in
the slow growth and under-urbanization of the ideological
districts is the nature of their economic life. Although there
are many statistical yardsticks by which patterns of economic
activity may be measured and compared, two criteria would
seem to be as basic and as revealing as any: value added by
manufacturing (the difference between cost of raw ma-
terials, etc., and the final sales price of commodities) and
per capita income. The two together not only suggest the
magnitude of the manufacturing activity in a district but
also discriminate between "soft goods" production, which
tends to low wages and cyclic ups and downs, and heavy
and "hard goods" production, with higher wage rates and
a more stable economic effect. The classic contrast, particularly in the South, is between metal fabrication as a
high-quality economic activity and textile manufacture or
food processing as low-quality.

For the United States as a whole, the average value

added by manufacturing per Congressional district in 1958 (the latest year for which the Bureau of the Census has complete figures) was $323,526,000. The average for the 126 districts of the South was much lower, at $201,963,000. For the thirty ideological districts, however, the average was only $186,214,000—and if the great manufacturing centers of Atlanta and Dallas were eliminated, the average figure would drop to less than half the national average, $142,-625,000. Truly these districts lag behind the Southern and national patterns of growth; the "Southern boom" has passed most of them by.

The per capita income averages tell much the same story. The national per capita income in 1959-1960 was approximately $1,850, while for the fourteen Southern states it was $1,419. But the ideological districts' average was only $1,265. In only four of the thirty districts was the per capita income above the Southern average; these were Arkansas 5 (Little Rock), Florida 7 (Sarasota), Texas 5 (Dallas), and Texas 18 (Amarillo). Only the latter two, furthermore, were also above the national figure.

With the image of turgidity and potential decline so clearly a part of the ideological position on foreign affairs, how can one account for the appearance of even the relatively few metropolitan and prosperous districts on the list? These, it would seem, are exceptions to the generalization forming here about the kind of district that tends toward an ideological response to international questions, and a word should be said about each of them.

Little Rock's reorientation that followed the defeat of its multilateralist Congressman by a unilateralist in 1958 would appear to be no more than a function of the racial crisis through which Arkansas and its capital city passed in 1957. With the readjustment of district lines made necessary by the reduction of the Arkansas delegation from six to four after the 1960 census, this particular seat disappeared (as well as its incumbent); the district's feelings will now be somewhat diluted in a larger constituency, which may well not be entirely of the same opinion.

Atlanta's Congressman (until his defeat in 1962) was an almost perfect stereotype of the ideological Southerner. He went into total opposition to foreign aid only in company with his state's delegation, making the shift as part of the 1957 bolt. In the meantime, however, he had been voting a steady unilateralist line on all other issues, accumulating a perfect negative score for the ten years.

Dallas has been represented by a Republican since 1954, and is the only Republican district to appear on the list except for Kentucky 8. The change in party affiliation of the incumbent Congressman that year did not bring about any change in the record of the district on foreign policy. Texas politics generally, and Dallas politics particularly, are so distinctive that party labels mean little. Dallas would appear to be dominated by an ideological construct of foreign affairs, and simple survival for a Congressman, regardless of party, demands that he accede to the insistent demands of the organized and articulate segment of his constituency.

The others may be dismissed more briefly. Florida 7 is a special case with a special constituency that is not particularly Southern. This Congressman shifted in 1954 from multilateralism to unilateralism, and he apparently satisfied his public. Mississippi 6 is quite different in social and economic ways from the rest of the state, but the near-paranoid character of contemporary Mississippi politics effectively inhibits any expression of different points of view. At that, however, this Congressman's record on the fourteen-vote test of multilateralism reveals him to be distinctly less militant than his fellows from Mississippi. Charleston and Amarillo, the final two, have each been the scenes of heavy doses of right-wing political agitation.

THE WAVERING DISTRICTS

The wavering districts, it will be remembered, are marked by a strong anti-foreign aid orientation and only a limited commitment—usually no more than halfway—to the other multilateral measures. They thus represent a middle of the road position between the ideologists on the one side and the pragmatists on the other. The issue of their basic orientation, however, is yet to be decided. Is the bottle, in other words, half full or half empty; are the waverers ideologists with a pragmatic dash or pragmatists with a special type of constituency?

When one applies the same set of criteria to the wavering group that was used to measure the ideologists, the evidence points emphatically to the ideological side of the choice. The districts are neither completely akin to the ideological group nor entirely alien to them, for there are statistics that point both ways. The preponderance of the data, however, argues that left to their own devices most waverers would be ideologists; only strong leadership in Washington or recurrent pressure from home can persuade them, on occasion, to vote a multilateralist position. Confirming this conclusion is the evidence that no less than nine of the nineteen had their score on the multilateral issues materially improved during 1961 and 1962 under the extensive and open pressure exerted by the Kennedy leadership. These would-be, but less committed, ideologists represented the following districts: Alabama 2 and 3, Louisiana 3 and 8, South Carolina 2, Texas 16, 21, and 22, and Virginia 7.

Just how much the wavering group actually does waver may be briefly illustrated by two votes in 1960. The International Health and Medical Research Act, it will be remembered, passed the House that year by better than two to one, with the South dividing 71-29 in favor. On this obviously popular but relatively unpublicized measure, the wavering districts voted 9-5 in favor of the bill, with five absentees; thus on this pressure-free vote more than a quarter of the group voted alongside the majority of the ideologists (who split 6-18 against the measure). On the proposal to authorize the appointment of a private citizen commission on NATO—which would seem to be, on its face, a relatively inoffensive measure—the wavering districts voted 7-8 *against* the bill, thus aligning themselves with the ideologists (albeit by a much smaller margin; the latter turned in their usual overwhelming negative vote, this time 5-24).

As was suggested above, the statistical picture of these nineteen districts is to a great extent ambivalent. As a group they are much larger than the ideologists in population, averaging 411,077 inhabitants—well above the Southern mean. Their urban percentage, on the other hand, is astonishingly low at 40.3.

Economically, however, the wavering districts do not match their raw rate of population growth. The mean value added by manufacture per district was only $136,294,000, and their per capita income was only $1,278. Both figures are far below the regional averages; the manufacturing figure, as a matter of fact, is even lower than that of the ideological group without Dallas and Atlanta.

Other indices strengthen the impression of ambiguity. The combined growth rate of the nineteen districts between 1950 and 1960 was extremely high at 22 per cent; the pattern of distribution among rapid growth, slow growth, and decreasing districts was astonishingly symmetrical. Nine of the total increased more than 16.5 per cent, nine were slow-growing, and only one declined in population.

This 9-9-1 growth rate pattern suggests the bifurcated character of the group as a whole. The phenomenon of slow growth, which correlates so significantly with the evolution of ideological international attitudes, contributes to the resistance to multilateral humanitarianism these districts show; the relatively high incidence of rapid-growth districts, on the other hand, strengthens whatever tendency may be present toward support of any of these measures and also makes the Congressman (since the stakes of political action are higher in a dynamic constituency) somewhat more amenable to strong executive leadership in behalf of a particular bill.

The two-sided approach of these wavering districts may be highlighted by reference to a quirk of the rapid movement of population in the South during the 1950's. Almost exactly one-third of the South's districts—41 out of 126—experienced a particular growth pattern in which rapid urbanization and rural depopulation went on within the same constituency so speedily that the growth of one or a few metropolitan centers in the district was greater than the total increase in population of the district. In thirteen of these, the district actually lost population overall, although the raw figures tended to conceal significant growth in the district's major city. One of the most extreme examples of this sudden migration is the sixth district of West Virginia. The district suffered a net population decrease of 25,000 people; at the same time, the city of Charleston increased in population by over 12,000, or 16.7 per cent.

Of the thirty ideological districts, nineteen fell into this group of forty-one, or 46.7 per cent of all the ideological districts; of the nineteen waverers, seven showed these urban-rural characteristics, or 36.8 per cent of the nineteen. Since districts with this characteristic constitute only 32.5 per cent of the South's total number, there would seem to be a heavy over-supply of them among the ideological group, but only a slight excess in the waverers. Rural and small-town depopulation, obviously a factor in both groups of districts, cannot help but have some kind of political consequences, particularly when juxtaposed to rapid urban growth within the same political units.

It is possible, however, to reconcile the rapid growth rate of the split districts with their low level of urbanization and manufacturing activity. Most of the cities in this group were fairly small to begin with; the metropolitan centers of the nine districts exceeding the regional growth rate were Lafayette (Louisiana 3), Shreveport (Louisiana 4), Lake Charles (Louisiana 5), Goldsboro (North Carolina 3), Tulsa (Oklahoma 1), Columbia (South Carolina 2), El Paso (Texas 16), Houston (Texas 22), and Charlottesville (Virginia 8). Of these only Houston was included in the list of the forty-five largest cities in the United States, and the district, it must be remembered, included only half the city. Otherwise, El Paso and Tulsa were the largest cities in the group.

Thus, in spite of the high growth rate of the group as a whole, in 1960 only five districts among the nineteen surpassed the South's overall urbanization level: Alabama 2 (Montgomery), Oklahoma 1 (Tulsa), Texas 15 (Brownsville), Texas 21 (San Angelo), and Texas 22 (Houston). Of these, all except Houston were included in the group suffering the urban-rural spiral pointed out above. The growth rates of Alabama 1, Texas 15, and Texas 21, furthermore, were all below the regional average, and Texas 21 was the only district in the entire group to suffer a net population loss for the decade.

A high rate of population growth cannot produce dramatic results in a district if the orginal base was so low as to inhibit the absolute figures. If the trends of growth of this group of districts were to be projected through the 1960's and beyond, at least some would then acquire a different demographic and economic structure—with possible consequences for their outlook on world affairs. In the meantime, the record of the 1953-1962 decade stands; the wavering districts show by their votes and their makeup their intrinsically ideological orientation and only occasionally, unpredictably, and reluctantly will their Representatives vote for the multilateral solution of international problems.

THE PRAGMATIC DISTRICTS

The pragmatic districts, it will be remembered, are marked by a heavy preponderance of anti-foreign aid votes by their Congressmen but an equally overpowering majority in favor of the other multilateral measures. This simple characterization of their posture suggests strongly an exactly opposite orientation from the wavering group; where the latter were at bottom ideological and were pressed to adopt multilateral positions, the pragmatists are fundamentally multilateralists who respond to the necessary minimum extent to stirrings of foreign-policy protest in their districts. The waverers are hostile toward—or at least doubtful of—the multilateralist premise in foreign policy; the pragmatists accept it in principle but are forced to modify it in practice.

One might suspect, therefore, that pragmatists vote against foreign aid primarily because they fear constituent reprisals. They could logically be expected also to vote against any other multilateralist proposal against which crystallized opinion at home has passed the critical mass. Although instinctively multilateralists, in other words, the pragmatists never permit principle to override political expediency.

Such a judgment of course presupposes a fairly high level of political awareness and commitment within the pragmatists' constituencies—although it implies nothing about the sophistication or the level of information of the voting public. Only such an activist and involved populace could persuade intrinsically internationally-minded Congressmen to vote against programs with which they would be otherwise inclined to agree. Do the eighteen districts that enforce such behavior on their Representatives show such characteristics as to make this hypothesis tenable?

In almost every respect, the pragmatic districts differ sharply from the ideological group and to a major extent with the waverers as well. Where the ideologists generally represented districts marked by slow growth and economic sluggishness, rapid growth and relatively advanced economic patterns are common characteristics of the pragmatic districts. This generalization is verified in almost every statistic used for comparison.

The overall growth rate of these eighteen districts for the 1950-1960 decade was 21 per cent—more than double the ideological group. Eight of the eighteen had growth rates in excess of the Southern average (led by the sixth district of Florida, whose increase of 161.6 per cent was the largest in the nation). Only three showed a net loss, and only seven fell into the slow-growth category. This 8-7-3 classification of the districts by rate of growth contrasted sharply with the 6-16-8 grouping of the ideological group.

But, although overall growth rate figures and the distribution of districts by type of growth pattern sharply distinguished the pragmatic districts from the ideological ones, the former group was almost exactly even with the waverers on these two counts. On the matter of average population per district, the same similarity between pragmatic and waverer is noticeable; the pragmatics averaged 429,892 people per Congressman, the waverers 411,077. The near-identity of the figures is striking.

But the pragmatic group parts company with both the ideological and the wavering districts when additional data are examined. One of the most striking differences is in urbanization, where the pragmatic districts averaged 58.1 per cent urban, far above both of the other groups and slightly above the overall Southern average. Major cities included in this group of districts were Tallahassee and Fort Myers, Florida; Rome, Georgia; Baton Rouge, Louisiana; Charlotte, North Carolina; Houston and Corpus Christi, Texas; and Newport News, Virginia. The most highly urbanized district of all eighteen was the eighth of Texas, comprising half of Houston; the most rural, the ninth of Virginia, including the mountainous far southwest of the state.

The impact of these population figures becomes apparent when the economic indices being used here are applied. The eighteen pragmatic districts averaged $250,-719,000 per district in value added by manufacturing, almost 50 million dollars above the region's average and outstripping the ideological districts by almost 65 million dollars per district. If the three pragmatic districts with the lowest percentage of urbanization (Virginia 9, 16.4 per cent; West Virginia 3, 22.8 per cent; Tennessee 6, 25.8 per cent) are eliminated from the figures, the average for the remaining fifteen jumps sharply to $276,225,000—a figure coming reasonably close to equalling the national average of something over 320 million dollars.

The intense economic activity suggested by these manufacturing figures is confirmed by the second economic index, that of per capita income. The pragmatic districts far outstripped both the ideological and the wavering groups in this important comparison. The per capita income in the eighteen districts was $1,435—a figure sufficiently in excess of the overall Southern average to indicate a significantly higher standard of living than in those areas represented by ideologists. This is corroborated by the more meaningful criterion of the median per capita income per district. The pragmatic median of $1,333 was almost exactly $200 higher than the ideological group's $1,134 and more than $150 above the waverers' $1,179.

What do these data suggest with regard to the hypothesis of political activism? Initially, for all but two or three of the eighteen districts, a high rate of population increase, a higher per capita income, and a high level of manufacturing activity all strongly suggest the entry of non-Southern influences and values into the social and economic life of the communities. The in-migration of labor from surrounding rural areas, the importation of Northern managerial and technical personnel, and the substantial investment of out-side capital in manufacturing enterprises all contribute a sizeable measure of movement and change. All these factors —without even bringing into the equation other dynamic factors with a peculiarly Southern twist, such as the race issue—would conduce a heightened political sensitivity in the population, however little it might augment their level of political maturity. It is also worth noting here in passing (as possibly throwing some light on the voting behavior of these Congressmen) that none of the large cities included in this group suffered any serious racial disturbances during the decade, a claim that cannot be made with regard to most of the major centers of the first two groups.

Also illustrating the inherently pro-multilateralist orientation of the Congressmen and possibly the relatively weaker unilateralist pressures in their districts is the marked reversal of the anti-foreign aid stand of four of the districts involved here. The first district of Virginia reversed its position completely after 1958 when the long-term incumbent retired and was replaced by one whose record for the next four years was that of a solid multilateralist. Three others (Louisiana 6, Tennessee 6, and West Virginia 3) voted in favor of foreign aid in 1961 and 1962 under the impetus of President Kennedy's leadership. If these changes are the result of major reorientation in attitude rather than the short-term rewards of executive pressure, these three constituencies may well soon be shifted from the pragmatic column to that of the multilateralists.

THE SOLID MULTILATERAL DISTRICTS

As a check on the characterizations of the several types of anti-multilateralist positions pointed out in the three preceding sections, it is useful to return to the list of multilateral districts advanced early in the chapter. From this group of forty-three districts with a generally favorable orientation both to foreign aid and to the other multilateralist measures, a somewhat more selective choice can be made of only those districts whose Representatives have been virtually solid in their support of both categories of legislation. This elite group of twenty-eight districts consists only of those whose Representatives cast no more than two negative votes against foreign aid during the decade (none in 1961 and 1962) and no more than three negative votes on the group of multilateral measures. Such a one-sided record would seem easily to minimize (if not entirely to eliminate) the possibility of accidental factors distorting any Congressman's record.

This core group of twenty-eight stalwart multilateralist districts is made up as follows:

Alabama:	4,5,7,8
Arkansas:	3
Florida:	4
Georgia:	6
Kentucky:	1,2,3,4,5,6,7
Louisiana:	1,2
Mississippi:	3
Oklahoma:	2,3
Tennessee:	4,9
Texas:	2,10,12,19,20
West Virginia:	2,5

The twenty-eight districts thus come from eleven states, with only Virginia, North Carolina, and South Carolina not providing any at all. All of Kentucky's seven on the larger list earned places in this inner group, and the five from Texas and the four from Alabama make up the other large state delegations.

The basic statistics of this group of districts are, somewhat surprisingly, not especially impressive. Their overall growth rate was below the Southern average at 13.9 per cent; their average population per district was only minimally greater than the average of 409,888. The percentage of urbanization was likewise no more than average, while the per district mean value added by manufacture was significantly lower, at $183,551,000. Only on the matter of per capita income did the stalwarts stand out; their $1,465 was the highest of all four groups of districts.

Not until the trends of growth within the group itself are examined do patterns begin to become noticeable. Ten of the twenty-eight grew at a rate above the Southern average: Alabama 8, Florida 4, Kentucky 3, Louisiana 1 and 2, Tennessee 9, and Texas 2, 12, 19, and 20. Ten, on the other hand, suffered population losses—almost a third of the total of such districts in the South. Only eight were in the slow-growing category.

Included in the rapidly-growing districts were some of the South's major cities: Miami, Louisville, New Orleans, Memphis, and the four Texas centers of Beaumont, Fort Worth, Lubbock, and San Antonio. The tenth rapidly-growing district in the group (with, however, the lowest percentage of increase of all ten) was Alabama 8, whose metropolis of Huntsville benefited significantly from the extensive federal investment in rocketry made there.

These ten had a combined average value added by manufacture of $332,745,000, a combined growth rate of 37.7 per cent, and a per capita income of $1,585. The ten districts in the group that decreased in population, however, had a combined rate of decrease of 9.2 per cent, an average value added by manufacturing of only $89,642,000, and a per capita income of only $1,073. It would be difficult to imagine two more dramatically different groups of districts; two completely different ways of life are summed up in these statistics. Yet their figures are combined into a single total, thus tending largely to cancel each other out. This effect leaves the corresponding statistics for the eight slow-growing districts (7.2 per cent growth, average value added by manufacturing $115,243,000, per capita income $1,223) to come closer to the mean levels for the group as a whole than does either of the larger and more cohesive samples.

This is doubly deceptive because of the eight slow-growing stalwart districts, no less than five are found in Kentucky (Districts 1, 2, 4, 5, and 6). The remaining three are Alabama 4, Georgia 6, and Texas 10. Such a concentration of statistics from a single state tends more to reflect conditions in rural Kentucky than to characterize any broadly-based sample.

The 10-8-10 growth rate pattern of these districts is extremely suggestive. It is difficult to avoid the conclusion that there are probably several different reasons for multilateralism hidden behind the uniform facade of roll call "yeas." The pattern of political life in a rapidly-growing and highly-urbanized district is obviously quite different from that in one which industrialization has passed by, in which agriculture is losing its grip on the economy, and in which population is being drained away. A Congressman representing a dynamic metropolis such as Miami or Fort Worth will support foreign aid for entirely different political reasons and in an entirely different context than will one representing a stagnant mountain district in Kentucky or a declining cotton-growing society in Arkansas or Alabama.

Although this study is more concerned with the majority of Southern Congressmen who have drifted away from this historical multilateralist orthodoxy of the region than it is with the factors that contribute to a continued commitment to the internationalist myth of the South, the bifurcation in the ranks of the multilateralist districts retains considerable interest to the thoughtful. The big-city Congressmen in this group, for example, appear so solidly entrenched in their positions and so unshakeably in control of their own political destinies that it would seem most unlikely that any marked change in their voting records would come about in the foreseeable future. It is also apposite to point out that of the major centers included in this list, only Memphis is in any sense a "traditional" Southern city; the Texas metropolises are all more Western than Southern, New Orleans was never a party to the myth of the "old South" (having a perfectly serviceable myth of its own), Louisville is, as it has always been, a border city, and Miami is not Southern at all in any respect except climatic.

The multilateralists who represent declining districts, on the other hand, incorporate in their persons much of the historic Southern tradition of the gentleman-politician who serves his constituents' best interests as he sees them, never feeling himself beholden to short-term currents of mass opinion at home. The point of view expressed in these votes grows from the outlook of the Congressmen themselves, their own traditionalist view of national and regional interest, the nature of the representative function, and the implications of executive leadership. Blessed more by historic accident than by their own skill with a broad grant of discretion from their constituents, and free to deal with leadership in Washington as they see fit, they are probably the freest agents to be found in the entire Congress.

The big-city Congressmen in the multilateralist group, in other words, come closer than do any other Southerners to accepting the standard liberal-multilateralist posture common among Representatives from the Northeast, the urban centers of the Midwest and the Far West. The spokesmen for the declining areas, however, are occupying the last stand (at least in this generation) of the old-line "Southern internationalist" position that flourished two or more decades ago.

Less need be said in summary about the eight slow-growing districts in the group. The centrality of the five from Kentucky has already been noted, and in at least three of

the eight cases the influence of the occupancy of a committee chairmanship on the party orthodoxy of a Congressman
is clearly a factor. Otherwise, many of the observations made
about the free-agent nature of the Representatives of declining districts apply to these eight as well; after all, the
difference in the internal dynamics of a district that loses
9 per cent of its population and one that gains 3 per cent is
not really so great.

THE IMPACT OF THE NEGRO

One element that has been deliberately omitted from the
preceding discussion of the several points of view on international affairs held by Southern Congressmen has been any
mention of the race question. The Negro, whether as an
abstract "issue" or as an immediate and real problem, is a
ubiquitous consideration in all political judgments made by
Southern Congressmen, and to expect questions of foreign
policy to be exempted from this general rule would be un-
realistic. But there is no point to be served here by a review
of the mythology of race in Southern politics. The focus of
the present discussion is statistical, and only such quantitative data will be used as are relevant.

Probably the most immediate and significant fact to be
ascertained about the Negro in this context is his distribution throughout the Southern landscape. A simple comparison of the four major groups of districts discussed here in
terms of the percentage of Negroes in the population produces clear and suggestive results that fill in another detail
of the picture that has been drawn.

Two of the four groups of districts—the ideological and
the waverers—each have a population that is more than one-
fourth Negro; the precise percentages in 1960 were 25.3 for
the ideologists and 26.3 for the waverers. On the other hand,
the remaining two—the pragmatic and the multilateralist—
both have Negro percentages well below those of the first

two and very much like each other; the pragmatists in 1960 represented constituencies averaging only 17.1 per cent Negro, the multilateralists only 16.3 per cent.

This set of percentages tends again to strengthen the thesis advanced earlier that the wavering districts are all incipiently ideological in their basic outlook but are forced to accept a moderately pragmatic position by political necessity. The coincidence in percentages is too striking to dismiss as accidental; at the very least it seems a safe conjecture that the higher the percentage of Negroes in a district's population during the 1950's, the more likely the district was to be or to tend toward becoming ideological. Contrariwise, the lower percentages evinced by the pragmatists and the multilateralists would suggest that—whatever the causal relationship—a district with less than 20 per cent Negroes in its population was more likely than not to be multilateralist on all measures except foreign aid, and then to split fairly evenly on that issue.

Of course, with the ideological group drawing so many of its members from states like Georgia, Mississippi, and South Carolina—all with high Negro population percentages and all with a history of racial militancy during the decade—the prophesy is in one sense self-fulfilling. In like fashion the waverers draw four districts from Louisiana, four from North Carolina, and two from Alabama (all ten, incidentally, from the areas of their respective states with the greatest concentration of Negroes), again automatically weighting the figures in favor of relatively high concentrations of Negroes. Yet, it is interesting that the most heavily Negro district in the entire South—the third district of Mississippi (the "Delta") with a population 65.4 per cent Negro—was represented during the decade by a Congressman with one of the very highest averages of consistent multilateralist voting.

Nevertheless, the human geography of the Negro in the South comported so remarkably well with the way votes in

Congress were cast that there was obviously some kind of interaction pattern at work. It would be at least arguable that a multilateralist district in which the Negro population is relatively large will bear close watching for signs of a reversal of its position, particularly if the other characteristic indices of ideological international attitudes—low urbanization, slow growth, low per capita income, and a low level of manufacturing—are also present.

PRESIDENTIAL VOTING AND THE GROUPS

Implicit in much of the discussion of the several groups into which the South's Congressional districts can be divided is an assumption that there is a difference in the temper of political life from one group to another. One way of checking the validity of this premise is by comparing their several patterns of voting in recent presidential elections.

The election of 1960, coming as it did near the end of the decade and clearly marking the liquidation of the Eisenhower era, provides a useful first bench mark. In that momentous election Vice-President Richard Nixon confounded the experts by performing much better than anyone had thought he (or anyone else but President Eisenhower himself) could do throughout the South. Of the 126 Congressional districts in the region, Mr. Nixon won 52, or 41.3 per cent. The distribution of his winning districts among the four groups being examined here, however, was rather uneven.

The ideological districts split 18-12 in favor of Mr. Kennedy. Of Mr. Nixon's twelve districts, four were rapid growers, six slow growers, and two were among those losing population. Mr. Kennedy's pattern was quite different; only two of his districts were rapid growers, no less than ten were slow growers, and six were in the declining group. Thus it would seem that a growing ideological district showed a tendency to vote Republican, while slow growers or losers tended to cling to their traditional Democratic allegiance.

The pragmatic districts with a more active political life on which to build voted 12-6 for Kennedy. The eight rapidly growing districts in this group divided 4-4; the slow growers split 4-2 for Kennedy; all three declining districts also stayed in the Democratic column. Here there are fewer meaningful signs, due perhaps to the smaller sample; it is still noticeable, however, that slow-growing and declining districts tended to remain Democratic while the chief Republican strength was in the rapidly developing group.

The waverers provided the scene of Mr. Nixon's best showing. Here Mr. Kennedy had a majority of only one district by a 10-9 margin. Mr. Nixon won six of the nine rapidly growing districts but only two of the eight slow growers. The single losing district in the group also voted in favor of Mr. Nixon. Again, since the wavering group is so much like the ideological cluster, the similarity in the patterns of the two is remarkable: rapidly-growing districts tend to vote Republican, slow-growing ones Democratic.

The stalwart multilateralists—as they tend to do on other statistical yardsticks—fell between the other groups. They divided 16-12 for Mr. Kennedy; the ten rapid growers split 6-4, the eight slow growers divided evenly at 4-4, and the ten losing districts also split 6-4. The twelve Nixon districts were thus drawn equally from all three groups; Mr. Kennedy was stronger with the two extremes than with the slow-growers—thus reversing a pattern that prevailed within the other three groups.

The multilateralist districts formed the only group in which Mr. Kennedy won a majority of the rapidly-growing category, and the only one in which he did not win a majority of the slow-growers. Again it is possible to see the dual bases of multilateralism among Southerners, one representing a vigorous urban district with a political rhythm much like that of the North, in which "liberalism" is a valuable political asset, and the other speaking for a relatively quiescent district in which the Congressman is given virtual *carte blanche* by his constituents.

A further elaboration of the role of presidential voting can be arrived at by comparing the 1960 breakdown with the results of the two Eisenhower-Stevenson elections in 1952 and 1956. These data are given in the table:

TABLE 20
PRESIDENTIAL ELECTION RESULTS,
126 SOUTHERN DISTRICTS, 1952, 1956 AND 1960

(Democratic total is given first in every case)

	1960	*1956*	*1952*
Ideological Districts	18-12	18-12	18-12
Wavering Districts	10- 9	7-12	9-10
Pragmatic Districts	12- 6	8-10	9- 9
Multilateralist Districts	16-12	11-17	18-10

These data corroborate the initial hypothesis of political inflexibility as a characteristic of the ideological districts. Not only does the 18-12 pattern repeat itself each time, but close examination indicates that there was remarkably little migration of individual districts from one side to the other in all three elections.

The intrinsic Republican strength of the wavering group shows in all three elections—perhaps a factor in keeping the group away from full ideological membership. In 1952 the only group to favor Eisenhower, in 1956 almost two-to-one in favor, and in 1960 giving Kennedy only a one-district margin, the wavering group of districts—particularly those characterized by rapid growth in which Nixon had a two-to-one margin in 1960—provides a powerful Republican springboard.

The range of choice in the pragmatic group, on the other hand, was not as great. It divided evenly in 1952, favored Mr. Eisenhower in 1956, and gave Mr. Kennedy his only two-to-one margin in 1960. Despite the relatively narrow range of change, however, there is considerable back-and-forth movement by individual districts concealed in the figures.

The multilateralists showed in their presidential voting the pattern already discovered in other ways. Strongly in favor of Mr. Stevenson in 1952 (here the traditional factor was at work), they almost reversed themselves in favor of Eisenhower in 1956 (here it is tempting to conjecture that the Southern boom—at its height during these years—was having its effect). Then in 1960, the traditional rural districts and the liberal city organizations combined to swing the pendulum back again to the Democrats, if by a smaller margin than in 1952. Obviously, many districts in this group move back and forth, and the mean average of victory margins is growing smaller each time.

In general the patterns of presidential voting strengthen the broad impressions derived from the other data. The typology of Southern attitudes toward international affairs correlates certain types of districts with certain outlooks, particularly in the cases of the extremes. That these have some validity is confirmed by the way the districts vote in presidential elections.

VI

THE POLITICS
OF FOREIGN POLICY

THROUGHOUT this study one basic assumption has been ubiquitous: to a member of the House of Representatives facing the moment of truth of a roll call vote on an important issue, "politics" is a constant concern. The Congressman is a political animal who owes his position of power and renown to his ability to capitalize upon the nuances of electoral dynamics within his constituency. One major purpose guiding the conduct of his duties is always to maximize the prospects of his being returned to office; he is most solicitous of the "record" he will some day be called upon to defend. In the American system of government, therefore, Congressmen feel free to exercise independent judgment and reach their own decisions only to the extent that they are permitted by their constituents.

Many scholars, journalists, and politicians have complained about this almost mechanical theory of representation, arguing with cogency (and often with no little heat) that Congress can under these conditions never do any more than reflect the least common denominator of mass

opinion. For decades suggestions looking toward the inculcation and enforcement of strong party discipline, the acceptance of vigorous leadership on the part of the President,
and the divorce of a seat in Congress from short-term and
local tides of opinion have been common, but none has ever
had the slightest prospect of being accepted. The voting
public throughout the nation demands that each Representative in Congress actually "represent" the opinions (or at
least the predominant opinion) in his district and instinctively rejects the broader idea that in pursuing a generalized
concept of national or public interest the "true" interests of
each constituency are best guarded.

From this generalization, however, most of the Congressmen from the South have historically been exempted.
Public opinion has long been much less of an immediate
factor influencing the conduct of Representatives from the
Southern states than it was for men from other parts of the
United States. The South's one-party system meant that a
Southern incumbent had nothing to fear from Republican
opponents. In practice, therefore, assuring his own renomination was—in the words of the newspaper cliché—
"tantamount to election." To win renomination, furthermore,
required usually only that he retain the support (if not
indeed the control) of the Democratic party organization
in his district.

Widespread voter apathy, the normal condition of one-
party Southern politics, in turn reinforced the role of organization support in prolonging the Congressional career of
almost any incumbent. The solidly Democratic delegations
from most Southern states tended to group around the leadership of the state party and particularly in the shadow of
the dominant Democrat of the state, be he United States
Senator, the governor of the state, or merely a party boss
who exercised his power through the state central committee. The rough rule of thumb indicating the extent to which
a state's delegation to Congress was under central control

was the degree of cohesiveness it showed: the more it was boss-controlled, the more it voted as a single bloc.

Only when major tides of change unleashed the un-Southern phenomenon of voter protest on a sizeable scale did either the state party leadership or incumbent Southern Congressmen take account of mass opinion. Ordinarily, Representatives from at least the more "typical" Southern districts were given virtual *carte blanche* by their constituents and were called to account only if and when they violated the political code to which all Southern Congressmen automatically subscribed. Protest, however, threw the delicately poised mechanism out of balance and often forced many Congressmen into new and frequently uncomfortable positions. The capture of a state party organization by a rebel group was normally the signal for wide-spread reversals of position by the Congressmen in office at the time, as each sought to establish his *bona fides* with his new leaders and their highly sensitized followers.

This factor, of course, goes far to explain the new behavior of the Southern bloc on international questions during the ten years under review here. The break away from the support of foreign aid in several states was so sudden and complete that the effect of central decision is obvious: North Carolina's bolt in 1954 and Georgia's in 1957 were both of this type. Other less durable reversals show up in the same light, such as Oklahoma's 0-6 vote in 1957 and West Virginia's 1-5 split in 1958. Similar indices can be discovered in the set of roll calls on other multilateralist measures that were analyzed in Chapter IV.

All this leads quickly to an obvious conclusion: some appreciation of the political significance of international issues to Southern Congressmen is necessary to an understanding of the overall picture. Foreign affairs is important business at any time in history, and is especially so to contemporary Americans, whether Southern or not. A significant part of the record each Southern Congressman makes for his constituents must be based on his performance on international issues, and the analyst must be as sensitive to the political implications of international affairs as is the Congressman himself.

But, by the same token, the weathervane theory of representation must not be taken too seriously or literally. Politics is still a form of interpersonal relations, and personal and personality factors bulk large in its conduct. Much can be learned from objectively cataloguing and comparing certain sets of data about the several Southern Congressional districts, but by no means everything. Politics is more an art than a science, calls much more insistently and more often for evaluation than for measurement, and cannot transcend the intuitive and seat-of-the-pants judgment that has always been of its essence. No two Congressmen read the same statistical datum in the same way; to arrive at a sense of how Southern Congressmen react to change, in other words, it is as important to know what kind of men vote the several different positions as it is to know about the districts each of them represents.

AGE AND SERVICE

A natural starting place for the inquiry into Southern Congressmen as political animals is with certain obvious and important data. How old are they? How long have they served in Congress? How much change has there been in their ranks over the years? The data that follow and give answers to these and other questions are based on the incumbents of the 126 Southern seats at the end of the 87th Congress in the autumn of 1962.

Probably the most striking aspect of the comparison of the several attitude groups in terms of their average age was the relatively small differences among them. The thirty ideologists identified in the preceding chapter were the oldest, averaging 54.9 years of age. The waverers came next, more than three years younger on the average, at 51.8 years. The pragmatists were still younger, but only slightly so, averaging 50.6 years. The twenty-eight stalwart multilateralists fell in between with an overall average of 52.3 years. Thus, although the ideologists were the eldest group by a perceptible margin, the range of average ages was not sufficiently wide to provide any basis for judgment.

A second look at the multilateralists, however, elicits more meaningful figures. It will be recalled that these twenty-eight districts included ten with a high rate of population growth, eight with a low rate, and ten with a net decrease between 1950 and 1960. If the average age of the members of these three smaller groups is calculated, some interesting differentials can be found.

The ten Congressmen from the rapid-growth districts formed the youngest identifiable group of all, with an average of 49.1 years. The ten from the declining districts averaged 52.7 years, only slightly above the average for all multilateralists. The eight from the slow-growth districts, however, averaged 60.1 years, with their average brought well up by the presence in their number of such relatively elderly Congressmen as Carl Vinson of Georgia, Brent Spence of Kentucky, and James Trimble of Arkansas.

But even these differences fail to show any ground for suggesting a correlation between average age and the international outlook of any of these Congressmen. Nor, for that matter, were the data on length of service especially enlightening.

The ideologists, as of the close of business in 1962, had served an average of 12.9 years in the House. The waverers, on this as on so many other points in relative harmony with the ideologists, had an average of 12.1 years. The pragmatists had the lowest average of all four groups, 10.6 years. The multilateralists had the highest of all: 15.1 years of service.

Breaking down the multilateralist group into the same

three smaller categories as above shows some differences. The ten rapid-growth districts had permitted their Congressmen exactly the same average tenure as had the ideological group, 12.9 years. The ten declining districts had an average of 15.4 years, while the eight slow-growth districts had the highest figure on this index as well, averaging 18.7 years of service for each Representative.

In view of the high rate of population growth that is so characteristic of the pragmatic districts, and the other indices of relatively active and dynamic political and social life that they boast, it is not surprising that this group of Congressmen should show a significantly shorter average term of service than do the others. There are simply more reasons for a higher replacement rate among the Congressmen from pragmatic districts, among the most pressing of which are the relatively higher level of voter interest and the greater likelihood of opposition, either primary or Republican. The figures above, however, are arithmetic means; they conceal an even more significant relationship among the several groups. This is the rate of turnover within each of the four sets of districts, and here finally some clear patterns begin to form.

Of the thirty ideological districts, twenty-two had the same Congressmen at the close of the 87th Congress as they had had at the opening of the 83rd; that is, only eight of the thirty seats had changed hands during the decade, for a turnover rate of 26.7 per cent. Eight of the wavering districts had also changed Congressmen; since the total of these is only nineteen, therefore, the turnover rate was much higher at 42.1 per cent. The pragmatic group, however, showed an entirely different pattern. Twelve of its eighteen districts had different Congressmen in 1962 than they had had in 1953, or 66.6 per cent turnover.

The twenty-eight stalwart multilateralists showed overall the lowest turnover rate: six changes in twenty-eight districts, for 21.4 per cent. But here crude averages are truly deceptive. The ten rapid-growth districts in the group showed a turnover rate of exactly 50 per cent, as five of the ten changed Congressmen during the decade. On the other hand, both the declining districts and the slow-growth districts had a turnover rate of zero, as none of the eighteen suffered any change at all.

These data suggest an important classification of the districts under consideration. By and large, both the ideological districts and the slow-growth and declining multilateralist districts (which resemble each other in any case in a number of ways, and differ significantly only in the stands their Congressmen take) are districts of relative political tranquility. These Congressmen, in other words, generally represent "safe" districts in which opposition is negligible and over which the incumbent (or at least the local political party organization) exercises almost complete control. On the other hand, the pragmatic districts and the rapid-growth multilateralist districts, with their relatively high rate of turnover and the comparative youth of their Congressmen (at least in 1962), constitute the list of Southern districts which incorporate the most active political life of which the contemporary South can boast.

This division is reinforced by the evidence of committee chairmanships. Nine standing committees of the House were chaired in 1962 by Southerners whose districts are included in the four groups discussed here (two other chairmen showed divided or reversed positions on foreign policy, and their districts do not appear in these analyses). Of these nine, five chairmen represented ideological districts, one a wavering district, and three multilateralist districts. All three of the latter, incidentally but not surprisingly, were either slow-growth or declining in population. Since unbroken tenure and seniority bulk so large in the acquisition of coveted chairmanships, their concentration in the hands of low-turnover groups is only to be expected. It is ironic that one price Southerners must pay as they come to accept a more modernized political structure with a two-party system is a diminution in the extensive role their long-tenure Congressmen have played in the real deliberations of the House.

ELECTORAL OPPOSITION

Another factor that bears directly upon the way Southern Congressmen structure their representational roles is the importance in their political careers of opposition candidates in a general election. Since all but a handful of the Congressmen being considered here are Democrats, what this comes down to in practice is the extent to which the Republican party enters candidates in Congressional elections and seeks seriously to achieve victory.

Were the South's one-party system literally a reality, no Republican opposition would appear at all in any district and the Democratic nominee would always be unopposed in the general election. The figures, however, indicate that during the decade under analysis this ideal state was enjoyed by less than three-fifths of the Congressmen in the four groups; only in 56.8 per cent of all Congressional electoral campaigns from 1952 through 1960 did the Democratic candidate run unopposed. In 203 of the 269 possible situations of opposition, an opposing candidate actually did appear.

The four attitude groups differed markedly from one another in the frequency and the severity of the opposition met by its members. The thirty ideological Congressmen enjoyed the greatest freedom from Republican competition (although, in the case of the two Republicans in the group, Democratic opposition was unfailing if unsuccessful). Only in 49 instances of a possible 150 (including ten of ten possible cases involving Republican incumbents), did an ideological Congressman face opposition, or in 32.7 per cent of the total cases. The waverers were next in line in their freedom from opposition in 36 of 87 possible cases, for

41.4 per cent. The pragmatists, with only three-fifths as many elections, had precisely the same number of instances of opposition as the ideologists—49. Their percentage of opposition, however, was much higher at 48.9. The multilateralists were a few fractions of a percentage point still higher, with 69 cases of opposition of 140 possible, for 49.3 per cent. An oddity occurred in the case of the three multilateralist sub-groups: the ten rapid-growth districts showed only 44 per cent opposed elections, the ten decreasing districts 60 per cent, and the eight slow-growth districts 42.5 per cent.

These data tend to confirm some of the impressions formed earlier, but to distort certain others. The political safety enjoyed by most ideologists is underscored by their much greater relative freedom from Republican criticism and opposition, and the close affinity of the wavering districts with their ideological mentors is once again demonstrated. The much greater activist complexion of politics in the pragmatic districts that appears here also repeats the judgment reached in other ways earlier.

The record of the multilateralists on electoral opposition, however, tends to reverse the trend to which the other figures point. The high-growth districts, for all their up-to-date appearance on other indices, tend to be more traditionally Southern in this single regard than do many others with a greater external conformity to the familiar Southern image. Easier to explain is the high incidence of competitive politics in the declining districts. The clue is in their geographic location: of the ten, two are in Alabama, one in northwest Arkansas, one in Kentucky, one in Mississippi, two in Oklahoma, one in Tennessee, and two in West Virginia. Of these, five—those in Kentucky, Oklahoma, and West Virginia—contained considerable Republican strength that showed itself in active candidacies in almost every election and a considerable total of Republican votes. The relatively high figure for the slow-growth districts is again explicable by the fact that no less than five of the eight were located in Kentucky, which throughout the decade was virtually a two-party state; the remaining three (in Alabama, Georgia, and Texas) produced only one contested election in their combined total of fifteen for the decade.

So much for the figures showing the number of contested elections. A next—and equally important—consideration is the seriousness of what opposition there was. It may be safely assumed that a Republican total of less than 5 per cent of the vote is in all important respects the same as no contest at all. In these terms, which group of Congressmen faced the most serious threats from the opposition they encountered?

In the calculations that follow, only the number of contested elections was used as a base, and these relationships should be interpreted in the light of the percentages of unopposed elections that each group also showed. But more interesting and possibly significant differentials appeared when the contested elections were analyzed to determine degrees of opposition.

Of the ideological group's forty-nine contests, in eighteen the Republican candidate polled 20 per cent or less of the popular vote, while in twenty-eight the Republican received between 31 and 49 per cent. In other words, ideologists tended to have either negligible and token opposition (in twelve of the eighteen cases, the Republican received less than 5 per cent of the vote) or else to face real and serious threats. By and large the negligible opposition occurred in districts in most respects similar to those in which unopposed elections were the norm—that is, slow-growth and low urbanization—while real contests tended to take place in the rapid-growth and high-urbanization districts.

The waverers showed a different pattern. It was unfortunately so ambivalent and amorphous that not even tentative correlations could be extracted from the frequency and severity of contests in Congressional elections. There is a slight cluster (eight cases of thirty-six) between 21 and 25 per cent Republican votes and another (six of thirty-six) between 36 and 40 per cent, but the remainder scatter widely from less than 5 per cent Republican to over 49 per cent in one instance.

The pragmatic districts, however, again fit their progressively clearer model; not only is opposition more frequent in these districts, but it is also likely to be stronger when it occurs. Of the forty-nine contested elections in these districts, almost half (twenty-three cases) produced opposition figures between 36 and 49 per cent, and in three the opposition party actually won elections. Six of the pragmatists enjoyed safe districts, however, in which no Republican won more than 5 per cent of the vote in any election.

The multilateralist districts show the same tendency toward bifurcation on these figures as they have already on several others. Of the sixty-nine contested elections in which these twenty-eight Congressmen were involved, in thirty-one the opposition candidate polled between 36 and 49 per cent of the vote, and in three the opponent won. There is another cluster much lower on the scale, however, for in seventeen elections the opposition candidate received only between 11 and 15 per cent.

The consistency of the severity-of-opposition figures with those for frequency of opposition continues to be apparent when the three multilateralist sub-groups are analyzed. The ten rapid-growth districts concentrate at the low-opposition end of the scale; of the twenty-two contests involving these districts, in ten the opposition received less than 20 per cent of the vote. The declining districts, however, had more real contests; in sixteen of the thirty cases, the opposition percentage was more than 35. Thanks again to the two-party orientation of the five Kentucky districts included in the slow-growth category, these showed ten of their eighteen contests in the above-40-per-cent-opposition column.

Thus the factor of opposition candidacies cannot be considered a major determinant of the position of the ideologists and the waverers—nor can it really be judged to be important in connection with the rapid-growth multilateralist districts. For reasons probably unique to each case and certainly falling into many categories of detail, these fifty-eight districts provide little ground for arguing that their Representatives assume positions on international questions primarily in response to any urge to win elections. Primary elections are, of course, a completely different matter, but the low turnover rate in all these three groups suggests that few of their number concern themselves overmuch with any dangers from this source as well.

Only the pragmatists and the slow-growth and declining districts among the multilateralists would appear to have sufficient opposition to create a constant worry; less "Southern" in many ways than are the first three groups, a two-party system is a stark reality rather than a meaningless shibboleth for many of them. Their political approach is therefore much different. Note, for example, the frequency with which border-state Congressmen either tended to be pragmatists or clustered in the latter two categories of the multilateralists.

LIBERALISM AND INTERNATIONAL ATTITUDES

Up to this point, the political data which have been advanced to characterize the several schools of thought among Southern Congressmen on international questions have been quite specific and concrete: age, tenure, frequency and magnitude of opposition. No analysis of the Southern bloc, however, could pretend to completeness without some attention to a question never far from the center of any discussion of American politics in general or Southern politics in particular: "liberalism"—or its lack—among Southerners.

Here probably the crucial consideration is that of a

criterion, for what is one man's liberalism is another's socialism, and what is a third man's liberalism may be a fourth's
extreme conservatism. No word in recent and contemporary
political discourse has been more abused, and on none is
opinion more divided. Is liberalism, for example, an attitude,
a way of solving problems, or a platform on specific issues?
Or is it perhaps all three, or perhaps none? Is a liberal one
who generally favors the expansion of government authority
at the expense of private interests, or is he instead one who
emphasizes individual liberty at the expense of any form
of collective control? Is the Democratic party the liberal
party in the United States and the Republican the conservative party; are conservative Democrats therefore
"really" Republicans and liberal Republicans "really" Democrats? These—and many even less specific—questions have
clustered about this vague but energizing concept in the
past three decades.

   This study has no aspirations toward attempting to
settle this particular semantic quarrel nor toward resolving
the ambiguities intrinsic to the discussion. All that is necessary for the purpose sought here is *some* standard of liberalism which has adequate empiric referents to serve as a
way of classifying the several Southern schools of thought.

   The one selected for use in this discussion emanates
from a source unimpeachable in self-conscious liberal circles and widely accepted outside them as epitomizing the
authoritative liberal doctrine: the Americans for Democratic
Action. This relatively small, very articulate, and well-known
organization undertakes each year to conduct a Voting
Survey on Congress, and gives each member a percentage
figure of performance on liberal issues. The particular questions chosen for inclusion in the group on which the overall
percentage is based vary from year to year depending upon
what matters actually come up and upon the ADA's judgment
as to what the liberal side of each question might be. They
almost always include foreign policy issues as well as the

more familiar liberal concerns with economic regulation and civil rights. In one sense the contrast might be sharper if the liberal factor were computed on domestic affairs alone, but even with the partial inclusion of foreign questions the yardstick is sufficiently accurate to distinguish the several schools quite clearly.

Each of the 126 Southern Congressmen received a percentage from the ADA for each session under consideration. In order to reduce the data to manageable size, the two percentages for each member for any Congress were consolidated into a single figure, thus resulting in five entries for each man. Thus for the ideological group there was a total of 150 ratings, for the waverers 95, for the pragmatists 90, and for the multilateralists 140. Separate scales were constructed for the four groups, listing all ratings within blocks of 10 percentage points.

On this basis, for the ideological Congressmen the median percentage rating of liberalism given by the ADA for the five Congresses was 15 per cent. The waverers were modestly higher but still low overall at 24.5 per cent. The median for the pragmatists was some 13.5 percentage points still higher at 38 per cent. The multilateralists, however, were at the opposite end of the scale entirely, with a median liberal percentage rating of 71.

The breakdown of the multilateralists into the three sub-groups provided some further surprises. The ten rapid-growth districts showed a median liberal percentage of 64.5. The ten declining districts showed the highest liberal percentage of any group, with a median figure of 76 per cent. The eight slow-growth districts, on this point as on so many others, closely approximated the level of the multilateralist group as a whole with a median figure of 72 per cent.

The median percentages give a fair idea of the general distribution of the ratings since as many lie above that figure in each case as fall below it. But it is interesting as well to note the way the ratings tended to group around certain points. For the ideologists, for example, exactly one-third of all their ratings were between zero and 9 per cent liberal, and 74.6 per cent of the 150 were between zero and 29 per cent. Only 5.3 per cent of their ratings were 50 per cent or higher.

The waverers did not crowd together quite so much at the zero end of the scale, but were predominantly very low nevertheless. Sixty-seven point four per cent of all their ratings were between zero and 29 per cent, with the largest single cluster in the 20 to 29 per cent bracket, while only 9.5 per cent were above the 50 per cent level.

The pragmatists tended to group toward the middle of the scale, although their ratings were probably the most scattered of all four groups. The largest single cluster was between 30 and 39 per cent, but only slightly more than one rating in four was located there. The middle group of ratings, covering the range between 30 and 59 per cent, included 52.2 per cent of all the pragmatists' ratings, while 34.2 per cent of all their ratings were above 50 per cent. It would seem that the pragmatists generally represented—at least to the ADA—the middle-of-the-road position among Southerners and that these eighteen districts provide the greatest flexibility of views of any of the groups—a point already demonstrated in the votes these Congressmen cast on the broad range of foreign policy issues.

The multilateralists occupy an entirely different place on the scale. The greatest concentration of their ratings is between 70 and 79 per cent, while 65.7 per cent of all their ratings are between 60 and 89 per cent. Only 12.8 of all their ratings fall below the 50 per cent mark. As a group, therefore, the twenty-eight multilateralists compare quite well on liberalism with samplings of equal size that might be chosen from other sections of the country. Were the special questions of civil rights left out of the calculations, it is probable that these Southerners would be very near the top in any rating of liberal attitudes and tendencies.

The stereotype of multilateralist-liberal politics, how-ever, is again ruptured by the disparate performances of the three smaller sub-groups. The ten rapid-growth districts are on balance only slightly above the middle of the scale; 64 per cent of their ratings were between 50 and 79 per cent liberal, but still 24 per cent fell below 50 per cent. Included in this group of ten stalwart multilateralists, in other words, are several Congressmen who are less than totally convinced of the validity of the liberal ethos in domestic affairs. The ten declining districts, however, set the standard of liberal-ism for the entire South; no less than 72 per cent of all their ratings are between 60 and 89 per cent, and only 2 per cent were below 50 (this last small figure represents one rating for one man for one Congress). The eight slow-growth districts show a much wider spread. Although there is an exceptionally high concentration—almost half—of their ratings between 70 and 79 per cent, their median is a bit lower than the declining districts because of several ex-tremely low ratings. Three-fourths of their ratings are be-tween 60 and 89 per cent, but still 12.5 per cent are below 50.

What do these data on liberalism indicate? In the first place, there is a clear rank order of liberal leanings within the four groups that corresponds exactly to their relative commitment to multilateralism. The difference between the stalwart multilateralists and all others is truly remarkable, while the extent to which the ideologists and the waverers huddle together at the very lowest extreme of the scale also confirms both the close connection between the two groups and the link between unilateralism in foreign policy and an overall non-liberal position. The pragmatists, already difficult to classify neatly on purely international issues, again show great diversity and flexibility; although not brought out in the figures cited above, the range of ratings acquired by several individual members of the pragmatic group was astonishing. One, for example, was rated at 16 per cent liberal in the 85th Congress but 88 per cent liberal in the 87th; several went from low ratings (in the 30's) to highs somewhere in the 80's during the five Congresses.

HOW THE CONGRESSMEN SEE IT

Since Congressmen are realistic and intelligent men, obviously they know better than anyone else what has happened to the South and its representatives during the last decade and a half. Although not especially anxious to have the new international outlook of the Southern bloc made a matter of wide discussion, Congressmen from the South make little attempt to deny that the region has developed a newly restrictive position on international questions and are not reluctant to give their own explanations for the change. In articles in general media, in news interviews, in speeches in public and on the floor of the House, and in interviews directly concerned with the problem, the Southern Congressman draws a surprisingly clear picture of how he sees himself and his region.

The Congressmen themselves advance two different sets of reasons for what has happened. One large category of explanations and rationalizations is phrased in terms drawn from the apparently inexhaustible mother lode of Southern political rhetoric; the other is couched in the most immediate and practical political terms. It is probably no coincidence that the Southerners who enjoy virtually complete freedom from electoral opposition tend heavily toward the romantic interpretation of recent Southern votes on foreign policy matters, while those who contend with or face the early emergence of real two-party politics in their constituencies cling more to analyses rooted in realistic and often cynical considerations of electoral maneuvering. But no one dealing with the South and its politics dare disregard the romantic in cataloguing the motivational roots of political action.

The South, so long outside the main stream of American

history, many years ago developed its distinctive and unique code of political behavior. Emotion, passion, impracticality, idealism, and quixotic commitment to abstract causes are natural inheritances from the myth of the ante bellum Old South, the symbolism of the Lost Cause, and the Southern renaissance. Southerners generally take themselves and "the South" quite seriously; they see themselves still as "different" in many important ways, to a great extent in their greater capacity for deep feelings and selfless dedication. As a result, the romantic explanation of a Southern political phenomenon may frequently be as accurate a guide to the real motivations of the participants as the most scrupulously scientific and quantitative exegesis, since the actors themselves consider their roles to be those of participants in a drama that in grandeur and portentousness far transcends the mere human beings who move in response to absolute and awful historic forces.

Southern Congressmen, when pressed for an explanation of the conduct of their group over the five Congresses involved here, therefore frequently base their answers upon an idealized image of the contemporary South and its people. This way of attacking the problem is, as was suggested above, much more common among Congressmen whose own districts retain enough of the Old-South flavor to make the construct believable. This type of response is accordingly much more easily accepted in slow-growing and under-industrialized districts—those, in other words, that are more likely than not to be represented either by ideologists or by unshakeable multilateralists.

What are the ingredients in this formula? Probably the most common explanation for the substantial change in Southern attitudes and votes, widely accepted by ideologists and multilateralists alike (and surprisingly well received by ostensibly sophisticated analysts in the North), is the basic "conservatism" of the Southern people. This particular evocation of the myth of conservatism is heavily small-town and rural in its orientation and nothing so much as genteel in its emphasis, a far cry indeed from the stream-lined "radical right" doctrines growing so popular in certain rapidly growing and industrializing Southern cities. The conservatism that is held to explain so much of the South's response to foreign policy also serves as a rationalization for many votes on domestic issues as well—at least for the ideologists who advance the thesis.

The most frequently cited component of this conserv-ative attitude is that old favorite, "fiscal responsibility." There would appear to be solid grounds for arguing that Southerners generally are more directly moved by this classic shibboleth than are people in other regions of the nation. After all, among Americans only the defeated South has an actual history of total financial collapse and the awful realization that the society is entirely at the mercy of outside economic forces. The Southerner, it has often been suggested, is so idealistic in the myth he adopts largely because he is a pessimist in his approach to the real world. Whatever the value of this thesis, it is undeniable that many Southern Congressmen take the danger of national bankruptcy very seriously indeed and feel that the dollar cost of foreign policy is a massive risk that can no longer be taken lightly.

Also part of the Southern myth is the nature of po-litical leadership. Southern Congressmen whose constituents permit them the luxury still retain the image of the "country squire" theory of representation and argue that "their peo-ple" give them substantially a free hand in voting and trust their judgment implicitly. Again, it must be admitted that many Southerners do indeed act in just this way; the corre-lation between this point of view and the lack of Republican opposition in the corresponding districts, however, is quite striking.

The point to this formulation is, of course, the establish-ment of the principle that a Southern Congressman, in turning away from the national foreign policy consensus, is exercising his riper and more statesmanlike judgment instead of merely following the crowd. Thus the sense of non-identification with the rest of the United States, widely shared throughout the South, is pressed into the service of the regional myth. Far from being a pecadillo requiring explanation, a Congressman's break from the majority on these questions is interpreted as deserving the plaudits of his constituents—and he frequently receives them in full measure.

Finally, the romantic theory of Southern motivation places great emphasis on the symbolism of patriotism. Many ideologists, for example, rely heavily on the cold war as a springboard for patriotic flights that combine panegyrics on the virtues of America with invidious contrasts with the lesser stature of foreigners. From here it is an easy step to discredit multilateralist ventures as futile ("you can't buy friends"), wasteful ("boondoggling"), and ideologically suspect ("spreading socialism"). Patriotism in this argument is a quality that does not calculate, does not compromise, and does not equivocate; instead it feels, it wills, and it acts.

Thus many Southern Congressmen insist that their foreign policy outlook is nothing requiring justification, but is rather a form of dedicated service to the true interests of the United States and a faithful reflection of the feelings and wishes of the people of the South. As a culture that sees itself less indebted to the continent of Europe (as opposed, of course, to the British Isles) than the rest of America, and with no real interest except a vaguely discreditable economic concern with the non-western part of the world, the South considers itself the custodian of the true values of the United States. Particularly among ideologist Congressmen—although to a lesser extent among their mirror-image counterparts, the small-city and rural multilateralists—any discussion of foreign policy tends quickly to acquire overtones of a call to a crusade for the final vindication of the true, the pure, the good, and the beautiful in American life as interpreted by the modern version of the political vestal virgin, the Southern orator.

The other and more realistic explanation for change in Southern attitudes stems more frequently from Congressmen who represent large, growing, urbanized, and industrialized districts in which the patterns of political life are more reminiscent of national norms. These men—although many still retain a strong faith in the myth of the South as a distinctive force in American political life—show their greater preoccupation with contemporary political processes by their emphasis upon the actual imperatives of political action rather than upon its romantic idealization. They tend, in other words, to find the causes of change in certain trends among their constituents rather than in the inscrutable workings of history.

They admit, in brief, to the existence of a voter revolt. All of them would prefer (as would any Congressman) a happy relationship with their constituents which would give them the free hand that their ideological colleagues assert is their natural due. "A Congressman votes his convictions when he can, but votes the way his constituents want him to when he must," is a fair summary of the way they see their own problem. For the past several Congresses, more and more Southern Representatives have been forced—whether they admit it or not—to vote the way their constituents insist they should.

There is a surprisingly general agreement among all non-ideological Congressmen from the South as to the nature of the voter revolt that has caused so many of them to reverse themselves. Its principal component is protest, aimed less at foreign policy issues than at the rapid and painful changes through which the South and most Southerners have been passing in the years since the end of World War II. The comfortable political apathy that made the task of being a Southern Congressman so delightful has disappeared in many parts of the South. The voters are aroused, make insistent demands and ask embarrassing questions of their Congressman, and make explicit their determination that any failure on his part to do their bidding will evoke immediate and possibly drastic political consequences.

The protest these men recognize is not, of course, either informed as to facts or sophisticated as to alternatives; it is simplistic, emotional, slogan-ridden, and usually beside the point when focused on foreign policy. But none can be found who will deny its power, and none who dare consistently and overtly to defy it. The major effort of the sincere and open-minded Congressman would appear to be rather to contain the pressure of protest while at the same time avoiding being swept away by its effects.

Thus the big-city multilateralists managed to vote for foreign aid in the face of substantial protest against it at home, while the pragmatists concluded that on this issue at least they were forced to go along with the tide. The voting record on international issues of almost any Congressman from an urbanized and industrialized district with a relatively high per capita income is in fact no more than a disarmingly candid record of how he read the currents of protest and—less frequently and significantly—active support in his district at the time he cast each of his votes. Idealized evocations of conservatism, of patriotism, of fiscal responsibility, and of the virtues of rural life are all but meaningless to a Congressman facing a primary or a general election in which a complex of racial, regional, and economic prejudices are certain to figure largely. When protest becomes large enough to take seriously, he has only three choices open: he may resist it, he may identify himself with it, or he may submit to being destroyed by it. Understandably, none chooses the last alternative voluntarily.

If the change in Congressional attitudes reflects a widespread swing in voter outlook, and if the manifestation of

public feeling takes the form of greater political involvement, an important question next suggests itself: Who, to
put it bluntly, stirred the voters up? Why are so many cities
and towns so emphatic today on particular foreign policy
stands where only a decade and a half ago they were
perfectly willing to follow wherever their Congressman chose
to lead them? Answers from the Congressmen themselves
are almost embarrassingly explicit.

Many of them place the burden of blame for public
unrest on the operations of radical right pressure groups.
Almost all have had some experience with these gentry of
super-patriotic and militant doctrine, but none will admit
that he has been influenced by their work. There is no doubt
that the contemporary *brouhaha* of the far right wing has
found an appreciative and responsive audience in many
parts of the South. The simple and cliché-ridden appeal
to meretricious "patriotism," combined with the proffer of
scapegoats upon whom to vent all manner of pent-up
frustrations in the name of anti-Communism, admirably
suits the psychic needs of insecure people caught in the
tides of uncontrollable change. The call to direct action,
always a part of right-wing propaganda, has found many
takers in the South.

Closely connected with the work of the radical right
in this explanation is the alleged role of the Southern press.
Many Southern Congressmen are quite uneasy about the
role of the local newspapers that provide the bulk of the
political fare of their constituents. They claim that the press
gives oversimplified, heavily slanted, one-dimensional treat-
ment of foreign policy issues and that voters fed a steady
diet of this sort of material fall easy prey to the wiles of
agitators. Again, there is considerable evidence that the
heavy emotional content of some of the major news-gen-
erating domestic issues—racial integration, legislative reapportionment, corruption in government, and so on—helps
to create a climate of sensationalism for the presentation of

foreign questions as well. It would be too much to expect a Southern newspaper reader, with his emotions lashed by reports of inflammatory incidents and assiduously editorialized to the effect that his Southern way of life is under attack and facing extinction, to deal with foreign policy questions with cool detachment and judiciousness.

Also intertwined with the machinations of the extreme right wing, but a generally recognized difficulty in its own right as well, is the new outlook brought about by industrialization. Here too, only rarely will an individual Congressman admit that he has been influenced by particular industries or corporations, but many speak generally about this factor in districts other than their own. Probably the most frequently mentioned type of industrial pressure is alleged to emanate from the "textile interests," but many less specific accusations are also brought. Less attention is paid by Southern Congressmen to the potentially disruptive effect of labor unions, perhaps because only a relatively small number of districts have significant numbers of organized workers.

Many Congressmen will admit in private conversations that it was no accident that the great transformation in Southern attitudes set in in 1953. After twenty years of obediently following the leadership of two Democratic Presidents, almost by reflex the South tended toward generalized opposition to the first Republican President in two decades. A Congressman who defied a Democratic President on a foreign policy question would run something of a risk in thus breaking with an administration that might otherwise be willing to provide largesse in the form of federal grants of many sorts. Since the prospects of obtaining special favors from a Republican President were thought to be less rosy in any case, there was a much greater measure of safety in thus parting company with the general line of American foreign policy. It is also worth pointing out that 1953 was a year in which the Republicans (for only the second time in two decades) organized Congress and thus excluded the South from the positions of leadership in both Houses it had come to expect as no more than its due.

To argue that the South's new attitudes are a function of national party politics and thus not to be taken overly seriously (as several Congressmen have hinted) would, in logic, require also the claim that the multilateralist votes of Southerners in the pre-Eisenhower era can be explained as no more than routine allegiance to the Democratic party and its leadership. To equate a region's posture on national security and the world role of the United States with the party affiliation of the occupant of the White House is certainly political realism carried to its ultimate extreme.

Although this particular thesis may provide a persuasive explanation for the behavior of a small number of individual Congressmen, two contrary arguments tend to undermine its validity when applied to the South as a whole. First, the Republicans from Southern districts—as will be shown below—did not differ in any real sense from their Democratic brethren on foreign policy questions, and certainly Southern Republicans would seem to have little interest in discrediting the first president of their party for an entire generation. Second, throughout the last eight years of the decade under consideration, both Houses of Congress were under the domination of Democratic majorities, which meant in practice that Southerners occupied the leadership roles and committee chairmanships to which they fall heir when the Democratic party organizes Congress. In this case there was again little political capital to be won from outright opposition to even a Republican President.

The final refutation of the thesis, however, is provided by the figures on Southern support of the Kennedy administration's international ventures during the 87th Congress. There was, as the voting figures themselves show, something of an upsurge in support of certain types of multilateralist measures during the first session of the Congress, but the sharp decline that set in in 1962 (shown by the foreign aid and the United Nations bond purchase bills) revealed that even the persuasive Kennedy personality and the New Frontier's image of aggressive executive leadership were not making any real dent in the South's opposition. No more Democratic a President than John F. Kennedy could be imagined; if the South could not follow him, it is difficult to suggest another Democrat that would be satisfactory.

So the identification of Southern attitudes on foreign policy with the party holding power in the executive branch cannot be accepted as a valid explanation of the change except in a very few carefully chosen circumstances (in several districts in eastern North Carolina and east Texas, for example). Otherwise the data do not support the contention.

Neither rhetorically nor realistically will Southern Congressmen admit that the racial revolution in the South has had any direct or indirect influence on their votes on foreign policy—or, for that matter, on anything else. Its role in the generation of protest is obviously a major one, and its symbolism as forecasting the eventual disappearance of all that made the South unique is powerful. But the inflamed state of Southern attitudes on racial issues, as well as the slowly dawning new day of good sense and restraint, are both such explosive factors that on the surface, at least, Southern Congressmen prefer to pretend that the problem does not exist. Ideologists will on occasion link communism with school, bus, and lunch-counter integration, but even these more daring politicians are reluctant to touch off powerful forces the eventual effect of which no one can foresee.

THE SOUTHERN REPUBLICANS

No evaluation of the political impact of international issues on Southern Congressmen would be complete without some

detailed attention to that recently and increasingly significant phenomenon, the Southern Republican. Because by
1962 the Republican party had come to stay in many parts
of the South amid almost universal agreement that its future
was bright, two-party politics was destined to be an important factor in all political judgments in the formerly solid
South. The Republicans, although yet a tiny minority—only
in the election of 1962 did they garner as many as 10 per
cent of the South's seats—nevertheless have an impact beyond their numbers and constitute an interesting and possibly portentous fraction of the total Southern picture.

As of the close of the 87th Congress, ten seats in the
fourteen-state South were held by Republicans: Florida 1
(Tampa-St. Petersburg), Kentucky 8, North Carolina 10
(Charlotte), Oklahoma 1 (Tulsa), Tennessee 1, Tennessee 2
(Knoxville), Texas 5 (Dallas), Virginia 6 (Roanoke), Virginia 10 (Arlington-Alexandria), and West Virginia 1. In
addition, three others had been held by Republicans earlier
in the decade: Kentucky 3 (Louisville), West Virginia 4, and
Virginia 9.

Even a slight familiarity with the geography of the
South quickly reveals that these districts are of two types.
The first group consists of those located in mountain areas
of Virginia, West Virginia, Tennessee, and Kentucky with
a strong Republican tradition dating back to the Civil War;
the second and entirely different group is made up of rapidly
growing and, by and large, highly industrialized metropolitan areas that constitute a sample of the real "new South."
Tampa, Charlotte, Tulsa, Dallas, and the Virginia suburbs
of Washington, D. C., in no way comport with any traditional image of Southern folkways.

These ten districts, even though half are mountainous,
provide composite figures that contrast sharply with the
South as a whole. In sheer population they average 521,919
persons—more than 20 per cent above the regional average.
Two of the ten suffered population losses during the 1950's,

but even so the group's overall rate of population increase between 1950 and 1960 was no less than 28.1 per cent—a figure far beyond the Southern and national averages. The mean value added by manufacturing again far surpassed the South's average: their figure of $324,170,000 was above the national mean, even though only by approximately one million dollars.

The average age of the ten House Republicans in 1962 was 51.2 years, but here again the mean figure is deceptive. None of the ten was in this age bracket in reality; five ranged between 64 and 68 years and the other five between 29 and 44. Four of the five younger Congressmen represented rapidly growing districts and the fifth one heavily industrialized but declining in population. The five older Republicans represented two industrialized constituencies and three Appalachian Mountain Republican strongholds.

Only these three latter seats—Kentucky 8 and Tennessee 1 and 2—and Oklahoma 1 were in Republican hands prior to the election of 1952 that chose the 83rd Congress. Three more were elected that year and took office in 1953: North Carolina 10 and Virginia 6 and 10. Two more won their places in 1954 and entered the 84th Congress: Florida 1 and Texas 5. The recapture of West Virginia 1 took place in 1956.

Three additional seats won by the Republicans in 1952 were later lost again to the Democrats: Virginia 9 in 1954, Kentucky 3 in 1956, and West Virginia 4 in 1958. The votes these Republicans cast during their respective tenures are included in the totals given below.

The Southern Republicans still in the House in 1962 fell into the various attitude groups in no particular pattern except for one interesting point: with only ten members, the Republican delegation was able nevertheless to place at least one of its number in each of the six categories. One —Florida 1—qualified as a multilateralist, but not as one of the twenty-eight stalwarts. Three—North Carolina 10,

Tennessee 1, and West Virginia 1—fell into the pragmatic group. One—Oklahoma 1—was a waverer. Two—Kentucky 8 and Texas 5—were ideologists. Two—Virginia 10 and Tennessee 2—were classified as reversers (favoring foreign aid more strongly than the other multilateralist measures). Finally, one—Virginia 6—was a perfect example of a split position, dividing its votes almost equally on both foreign aid and the multilateralist bills.

How did the Republican bloc compare with the overall performance of the South? By and large the Republicans were inclined toward a somewhat greater opposition to multilateral foreign policy moves than was the Southern delegation as a whole. This is perhaps especially significant because between 1953 and 1960 they were under the leadership of a very popular president of their own party. Like the remainder of the South, the Republicans moved into overt opposition to foreign aid in 1957, although they never were unanimous and reached their 1-9 negative split only in 1962. After 1957, however, no more than four Republicans from the South ever voted in favor of an authorization bill for foreign aid.

For the ten years, the total vote of the Southern Republicans in the House on foreign aid was 48 "yeas" to 67 "nays," for an affirmative percentage of 41.7. This was perceptibly lower than the overall Southern figure of 49.5 per cent support. The only individual Congressman with a perfect affirmative record was the Representative of the tenth district of Virginia—who, interestingly enough, could show no better than an even division of his votes on the other fourteen multilateralist bills. Tennessee 1, Texas 5, and West Virginia 1 all produced perfect negative records on foreign aid, while North Carolina 10 (like the bulk of his Democratic colleagues from the state) voted "yea" in 1953 and never did so again.

On the multilateralist-measure yardstick, the Republicans again perceptibly trailed the Democrats. On balance they voted favorably on the entire package of bills for the ten years, but only by the relatively narrow margin of 67-62. Thus the Republican affirmative percentage of 51.9 was smaller than the South's overall 55.6. On only one occasion (vote number 3) did a majority of Southern Republicans support the multilateralist side of a question in opposition to the remainder of the Southerners, while on four issues (votes number 7, 8, 12, and 14) the Republicans chose the unilateralist side while the Southern group as a whole supported the opposite. On the other hand it should also be pointed out that on five of the fourteen votes (numbers 1, 5, 6, 11, and 13) the percentage of Republican support was above that of the Southern group in general.

It is clear that the influence of President Eisenhower and his vote-catching magic with Southerners had a measurable effect on the votes of the House Republicans between 1953 and 1960. This is amply demonstrated by the appreciably lower degree of support the ten Republicans gave the five Kennedy measures included in the group of fourteen (votes 10 through 14). Of 81 votes cast by them on the bills only 40 were affirmative, for a percentage of 48.7. The South as a whole, it will be recalled, supported the New Frontier's foreign policy proposals much more enthusiastically: 376-174, for a percentage of 68.4.

Five of the ten Republicans supported the Kennedy measures more than half the time—that is, at least three instances of support. None, however, could show perfect records, since no Southern Republican voted in favor of the United Nations bond purchase bill in 1962. Only two—Florida 1 and Virginia 6—supported all the remaining four, although Virginia 10 voted in favor of three and was not recorded on the Mutual Education and Cultural Exchange Act. The other Kennedy measure that drew a majority of "nays" from the Southern Republicans was the Peace Corps Act.

It would appear, therefore, that such weight as the Southern Republican bloc in the House was able to throw into the balance on foreign policy issues was primarily on the side of unilateralism. This general impression might suggest that any increase in Republican House strength would reinforce the regional trend toward this position. Yet only two of the ten Republicans could be classified as ideologists, and only one a waverer; although the samples are very small, it is worth pointing out that these percentages of 20 and 10 respectively are smaller than the corresponding figures for the South as a whole (24 and 15 respectively). There are grounds for arguing that the Republicans' approach to foreign policy contains a greater intrinsic flexibility than that of most Democrats, since 70 per cent of the group shows a record of some meaningful degree of support for either foreign aid or multilateralism in general.

Any increase in Republican strength from the South, furthermore, would on the basis of past performance be likely to occur in urbanized and industrialized constituencies as a result of the extension of real two-party politics. Only in exceptional cases, such as Texas 5 or Oklahoma 1, can a Republican from such a Southern constituency afford the luxury of rigid and ideological formulations of foreign policy issues. The fact that he will automatically face heavy opposition every two years will force him to assume the mantle of pragmatic politics with all its implications of flexible positions and a keen eye for the vote-catching worth of each issue. The same effect, of course, will be noted in the conduct of Democrats who hold their seats in the face of large-scale and dangerous Republican assaults.

The bulk of the Republican strength in the House during the decade consisted of a series of special cases. As the party matures in the South and gains experience in conducting campaigns and the sophistication that comes with holding a seat after it has been won, Republicans and Democrats alike will show much greater ranges of variation and maneuvering on international issues as well as on the more immediate problems of domestic policy.

VII
THE
DIMENSIONS
OF CHANGE

SOUTHERN Congressmen, in breaking away
to the considerable extent they have from the dominant
orthodoxy in foreign policy that is called "multilateralism"
in this study, have not all responded to the same motivations
nor gone in the same direction. There are today, as was
shown earlier, six different points of view that can be identified among Southerners in the House, each of which results
in a distinctive pattern of votes on international questions.
In large part these variations stem from certain differential
factors of political situation and outlook among the Congressmen themselves as each blends political reality with
the demands of statesmanship in such proportions as to him
seem both expedient and desirable. But to an even greater
extent, the key to the riddle of why the South's Representatives in Congress behave the way they do lies in the
districts from which these men draw their inspiration and
their orders. If there is a "problem" presented by the way
Southern Congressmen speak and vote on foreign affairs,
it is the South's problem and not the Congressmen's.

In this chapter, therefore, an attempt will be made to determine what kind of district is likely to have an ideological Congressman, a multilateralist Congressman, or any of the other four types. All Southern districts will be measured by certain socio-economic criteria, each of which throws light upon one facet of the society, and the combined force of which is to sketch at least the major outlines of the district's life. The aim is to isolate those characteristics of a district that not only correlate with its point of view on international affairs but that also will serve as useful predictive tools. If one or two of the criteria do in fact pinpoint various attitudinal probabilities, a valuable clue will have become available for subsequent use; if several do match the expressed international outlooks of Congressmen, something like a profile of a typical district of each type can be constructed. In either case the nature of the Southern phenomenon will be considerably clarified.

This enterprise will involve the application of four criteria to each of the 126 districts of the South: the rate of population growth during the 1950's, the percentage of urbanization in 1960, the value added by manufacturing in 1958, and the per capita income in 1959. Each of these has figured at some earlier point in connection with a discussion of particular attitude groups of Congressmen, but here they will be used across the board to discriminate the several groups from each other. In order, furthermore, to make the comparisons as complete and as accurate as possible, the sample to be used here is complete: that is, the two small groups not included in the discussions in the two preceding chapters (the dividers and the reversers) are included here, and the multilateralist category includes all forty-three members rather than just the core of twenty-eight "stalwarts" analyzed previously.

CRITERIA: 1. POPULATION GROWTH

The rate of population growth for the entire South between 1950 and 1960, it will be recalled, was 16.5 per cent. In certain discussions above, it was found useful to divide all Southern districts into three groups on the basis of this yardstick. The first consisted of those forty-four districts with a growth rate in excess of 16.5 per cent, the second of those fifty-one with a growth rate between zero and 16.4 per cent, and the third of those thirty-one that suffered a net decrease in population during the decade. Using these three categories, the districts representing the six identifiable points of view divided as follows:

TABLE 21

INTERNATIONAL OUTLOOK AND
POPULATION GROWTH, 1950-1960

GROUP	I Growth over 16.5%	II Growth 0-16.4%	III Net Loss
Ideologists (30)	6	16	8
Waverers (19)	9	9	1
Reversers (10)	4	3	3
Dividers (6)	1	3	2
Pragmatists (18)	8	7	3
Multilateralists (43)	16	13	14
TOTALS	44	51	31

In this discussion the two groups in the center of the range above, the reversers and the dividers, are not considered in detail, because both show themselves to be sharply divided and their overall number of districts is relatively small. In various of the tabulations that follow, however, their identification in terms of the criteria being used will be obvious.

In Table 21, the different bases for the distribution of each school of thought among the three classifications make meaningful comparisons difficult. The data become more relevant when transformed into percentages and compared with the percentage of the entire Southern group represented by each point of view. This information is summarized below:

Multilateralists hold: 34.1% of all Southern seats
36.3% of Type I districts
25.5% of Type II districts
45.1% of Type III districts

While:

Ideologists hold: 23.8% of all Southern seats
13.6% of Type I districts
31.4% of Type II districts
25.8% of Type III districts

Throughout the analyses in earlier chapters it has become clear that the eighteen pragmatic Congressmen are really multilateralists who feel obliged to vote against foreign aid, while the nineteen wavering Congressmen are ideologists at heart who are constrained by political considerations to make some gestures toward popular multilateralist measures. For the immediate purpose here, therefore, the pragmatic figures may be combined with the multilateralists and the waverers with the ideologists. On this basis the percentages change as follows:

Multilateralists/ 48.4% of all Southern seats
pragmatists hold: 54.5% of Type I districts
39.2% of Type II districts
54.8% of Type III districts

While:

Ideologists/waverers hold: 39.9% of all Southern seats
27.3% of Type I districts
49.0% of Type II districts
29.0% of Type III districts

What do these comparisons suggest? The most curious conclusion is that the generally pro-multilateralist districts neatly complement the generally unilateralist ones. The favorable groups together have more than their proportional share of both the high-growth and the declining districts and less than their appropriate number of the slow-growth type. Multilateralism is strongest in the declining districts, while pragmatism has its stronghold in high-growth areas. The combined negative groups, however, exceed their proportional share of the low-growth districts by almost exactly the same figure as they fall short of their fair share of the other two types. The extreme ideologists, of course, are fairly represented among the declining districts but win only half their share of the high-growth districts; this discrepancy is partially made up, however, by the skewed distribution of the wavering districts.

Thus the impressions to be drawn from the simple factor of population growth are suggestive rather than conclusive. There is a perceptible—albeit somewhat fuzzy—relationship between a low rate of population increase during the 1950's in a district and a negative attitude toward international questions expressed by its Congressman. A district, however, with either a high rate of increase or a record of net loss, is significantly more likely than not to be represented by a Congressman who voted in general support of the nation's multilateralist foreign policy. But the data cannot be used to draw any more precise conclusions; the distribution spelled out here is to be understood as no more than a generalized guideline to assist in the evaluation of the results reached in other ways.

CRITERIA: 2. URBANIZATION

Obviously connected with a generalized increase in population but much more immediate and explosive in its effect is the South's rapid urbanization. The mushroom growth of cities and metropolitan areas throughout the South is one extremely expressive demonstration of the extent to which the region is being finally incorporated into the major trends of American life. The 1950's, furthermore, were the second consecutive decade in which the movement of population into the city was the dominant element in Southern human mobility. What relationships can be discovered between the percentage of urbanization of a district and the international outlook of its Congressmen?

The fourteen states included in this study were more urbanized in 1960 than at any point in their history. The overall percentage for the region was 57, but on a district-by-district basis the spread ranged from over 95 per cent to less than 20. The median percentage, however, was 47.2, and the table that follows was constructed on this basis:

TABLE 22

INTERNATIONAL OUTLOOK AND PERCENTAGE OF URBANIZATION

GROUP:	I (Over 67%)	II (57- 66.9%)	III (37- 56.9%)	IV (27- 36.9%)	V (Under 27%)
Ideologists (30)	3	2	13	7	5
Waverers (19)	3	1	7	5	3
Reversers (10)	3	1	4	2	......
Dividers (6)	......	1	4	1	......
Pragmatists (18)	3	4	6	2	3
Multilateralists (43)	16	2	14	5	6
TOTALS	28	11	48	22	17

In terms of comparative percentages, the clusters form as follows:

Multilateralists hold: 34.1% of all Southern seats
57.1% of Type I districts
18.2% of Type II districts
29.2% of Type III districts
22.7% of Type IV districts
35.3% of Type V districts

While:

Ideologists hold: 23.8% of all Southern seats
10.7% of Type I districts
18.2% of Type II districts
27.1% of Type III districts
31.8% of Type IV districts
29.4% of Type V districts

The combined figures of the two positive groups compared with the two negative groups underscore the point:

Multilateralists/
pragmatists hold: 48.4% of all Southern seats
67.9% of Type I districts
54.5% of Type II districts
41.7% of Type III districts
31.8% of Type IV districts
52.9% of Type V districts

While:

Ideologists/waverers hold: 39.9% of all Southern seats
21.4% of Type I districts
27.2% of Type II districts
41.7% of Type III districts
54.5% of Type IV districts
47.1% of Type V districts

The percentages and the figures on urbanization tend to confirm and reinforce the impression conveyed by the simple growth data. The multilateralists, and the combined multilateralist-pragmatist group less so, show an affinity for districts of a high percentage of urbanization, the forty-three multilateralist districts including almost 60 per cent of all Southern districts that were more than 67 per cent urbanized. So great is the concentration of multilateralism within metropolitan areas that only in this classification (by only a very small margin) and in the lowest (Type V) category do multilateralist districts have a disproportionate share of the South's total. The pragmatic group, however, is more evenly distributed across the five categories with a slight preponderance on the side of high urbanization, and the combined figures for the two groups show concentrations in the two highest categories and in the lowest.

The ideologists, on the contrary, cluster at the lower end of the urbanization scale, with more than their fair share in each of the three lowest categories. Particularly noteworthy is the small number of ideological districts of Type I and the relatively large group that are of Type III. The wavering group is even more clearly oriented to the lower end of the scale and the combined ideologist-waverer figures only repeat the general panorama sketched out by the ideologists alone.

The generalized relationship may be shown by the following simplified table that divides each group into two categories depending on whether or not the district falls above the median level of urbanization for all Southern districts (Table 23).

Here again the relative differences are underscored. If the multilateralists and pragmatists are combined, thirty-six of these districts fall above the median and twenty-five below; the ideologist-waverer combination, however, shows only eighteen above and thirty-one below. The relationship

TABLE 23
PERCENTAGE OF URBANIZATION (Median: 47.2%)

GROUP	ABOVE MEDIAN	BELOW MEDIAN
Ideologists (30)	9	21
Waverers (19)	9	10
Reversers (10)	5	5
Dividers (6)	3	3
Pragmatists (18)	11	7
Multilateralists (43)	25	18

is perfectly neat, marred only by the perceptibly strong beachhead multilateralism still enjoys among heavily rural districts. Worth noting in passing also is the perfectly even division in the two small middle groups that represent the intermediate attitudes.

CRITERIA: 3. VALUE ADDED BY MANUFACTURING

The first two criteria applied to the several schools of Southern thought on international affairs were basically demographic in their inquiry. Separating population data from economic factors is a highly questionable procedure for social science analysis, since the sources of income available and the way economic rewards are distributed among individuals and groups obviously act upon and are in turn acted upon by the numbers and kinds of people available. The application of a critical economic yardstick to the Congressional districts of the South, however, again produces interesting and suggestive results that permit cross-checking with population figures on the one hand and with other types of indicators on the other.

The first of these economic criteria is the dollar value added by manufacturing per district. The average figure for the 126 Southern districts in 1959 was $201,000,000, but again the median figure was much lower at $139,000,000. Table 24 divides each group into five categories.

TABLE 24

VALUE ADDED BY MANUFACTURING (in millions of dollars)

GROUP	I (Over $350)	II ($200-$349)	III ($80-$199)	IV ($50-$79)	V (Below $50)
Ideologists (30)	3	6	15	3	3
Waverers (19)	1	4	6	4	4
Reversers (10)	2	3	2	2	1
Dividers (6)	1	2	2	1	......
Pragmatists (18)	4	3	10	1	......
Multilateralists (43)	8	5	19	6	5
TOTALS	19	23	54	17	13

Once again, transforming the figures from the table into percentages throws the differentials into high relief:

Multilateralists hold: 34.1% of all Southern seats
42.1% of Type I districts
21.7% of Type II districts
35.2% of Type III districts
35.3% of Type IV districts
38.4% of Type V districts

While:

Ideologists hold: 23.8% of all Southern seats
15.8% of Type I districts
26.1% of Type II districts
27.8% of Type III districts
17.6% of Type IV districts
23.1% of Type V districts

Consolidating the figures results in a minor change in the respective patterns:

Multilateralists/	48.4% of all Southern seats
pragmatists hold:	63.2% of Type I districts
	34.8% of Type II districts
	53.5% of Type III districts
	41.2% of Type IV districts
	38.4% of Type V districts

While:

Ideologists/waverers hold:	39.9% of all Southern seats
	21.1% of Type I districts
	43.5% of Type II districts
	38.9% of Type III districts
	41.2% of Type IV districts
	53.8% of Type V districts

Although much tends to be made in journalistic literature and semi-informed conversation about the impact of industrialization upon Southern attitudes, the evidence of these data lends only slight support to the notion that any connection can be made between manufacturing activity in the South and the international outlook of Southern Congressmen. It is true that there is a slight weighting of the multilateralists' percentages in the direction of a higher value added by manufacturing; this Type I is the only category in which the multilateralists are over-represented by any appreciable amount. This is balanced in some measure, however, by the very low percentage of Type II districts held by multilateralists and the fact that in the final three categories the multilateralists come very close to their proportional share of the seats. Something of the same sort of spread can be seen in the case of the ideologists: a heavy concentration around the median figure and a relatively even distribution through remaining categories except for a slight over-weight in the Type IV district.

Here the pragmatists merit some analysis in their own right, since their distribution on this scale is much different from the multilateralists with whom they otherwise have so much in common. These eighteen districts are almost entirely at the median or above; almost 40 per cent fall into Types I and II, compared with barely 30 per cent of the multilateralists. The waverers also contrast sharply with their fellow-traveling ideologists, if in a somewhat different way. The ideologists cluster in Type III; the waverers concentrate in Types IV and V. Over 40 per cent of the waverers are found in these latter categories, compared with 20 per cent of the ideologists, 25.5 per cent of the multilateralists, and only 5.6 per cent of the pragmatists.

The consolidated figures, therefore, are less meaningful than might be hoped. The affirmative group shows its clear affinity for Type I but also amasses more than its proportionate share of Type III. The negative pair is slightly above expectations in Type II and well above in Type V. But the bifurcated emphases of both groups throw considerable doubt on any but the most general conclusions that the higher the value added by manufacturing in a district, the more likely it is to have a Congressman with a generally favorable outlook toward multilateralist foreign policy, and *vice versa*.

If the districts are sorted out as being either above or below the median, however, an entirely different picture results (Table 25).

Thus a majority of the ideological districts falls above the median of value added by manufacturing, while a majority of the multilateralists falls below it. Each extreme position is somewhat conditioned by the performance of its nearest neighbor, however; the ideologists and waverers combined have twenty-four above and twenty-five below

TABLE 25

VALUE ADDED BY MANUFACTURING (Median: $139,000,000)

GROUP	ABOVE MEDIAN	BELOW MEDIAN
Ideologists (30)	16	14
Waverers (19)	8	11
Reversers (10)	5	5
Dividers (6)	5	1
Pragmatists (18)	11	7
Multilateralists (43)	19	24

the median, while the multilateralists and pragmatists combined have thirty above and thirty-one below. The only group that divides sharply on this question is—oddly enough —the dividers who break 5-1 above the median in spite of (or perhaps because of) their indecisive stand on the international issues.

It would appear that the principal effect of the criterion of value added by manufacturing is to separate the waverers from the ideologists and the pragmatists from the multilateralists rather than to establish polar positions for the two extremes. The pragmatists are heavily on the high side, the waverers heavily on the low side; the multilateralists and the ideologists are not so different from one another on this count as to be readily distinguishable. This is to say that a basically negatively-oriented district with a low value added by manufacturing is statistically likely to be a waverer, while a basically affirmatively-oriented district with a high value is more likely than not to be a pragmatic rather than a multilateralist constituency.

CRITERIA: 4. PER CAPITA INCOME

The final criterion to be applied in the measurement and classification of the districts represented by the different schools of thought is that of per capita income. If any single factor epitomizes the individual values implicit in the socio-economic revolution through which the South has been passing ever since the early years of World War II, it is the simple fact that personal cash incomes are rising everywhere throughout the region, if at an unequal rate. From an agricultural economy in which cash was a relative rarity in a culture in which the dominant groups lived on and from the land, the South is in the process of transforming itself into a money economy. The most consoling aspect of the contemporary upheaval in Southern folkways, at least for the bulk of the individuals personally affected by the change, is that as a result of their adjustments in habitation, employment, or way of life a much larger disposable income will become available. In measuring per capita income across the South, the analyst comes rather close to the heart of the matter.

Although per capita income in the South as a whole and in most of the individual states and districts is still well below the national average, the gap between the South and the rest of the nation is steadily narrowing while differentials within the South itself are growing greater. The lowest per capita income in the 126 districts in 1959 was $715, in the second district of Mississippi, while the highest was $2,557, in the tenth district of Virginia. The per capita income for the fourteen states of the South was $1,420 while the median per capita income per district was $1,277. The breakdown is shown in the table:

TABLE 26

PER CAPITA INCOME AND INTERNATIONAL OUTLOOK

GROUP	I (Over $1600)	II ($1377- $1599)	III ($1177- $1376)	IV ($1000- $1176)	V (Under $1000)
Ideologists (30)	2	4	7	8	9
Waverers (19)	3	2	5	7	2
Reversers (10)	3	2	2	......	3
Dividers (6)	1	2	1	2	......
Pragmatists (18)	3	5	6	3	1
Multilateralists (43)	12	11	9	7	4
TOTALS	24	26	30	27	19

Percentage figures show the relationships clearly:

Multilateralists hold: 34.1% of all Southern seats
50.0% of Type I districts
42.3% of Type II districts
30.0% of Type III districts
25.9% of Type IV districts
21.1% of Type V districts

While:

Ideologists hold: 23.8% of all Southern seats
8.3% of Type I districts
15.4% of Type II districts
23.3% of Type III districts
29.6% of Type IV districts
47.4% of Type V districts

The combined figures heighten the contrast:

Multilateralists/ pragmatists hold:	48.4% of all Southern seats
	62.5% of Type I districts
	61.5% of Type II districts
	50.0% of Type III districts
	37.0% of Type IV districts
	26.3% of Type V districts

While:

Ideologists/waverers hold:	39.9% of all Southern seats
	20.8% of Type I districts
	23.1% of Type II districts
	40.0% of Type III districts
	55.6% of Type IV districts
	57.9% of Type V districts

Here finally is a yardstick that seems to provide precise measurements. Each of the sets of percentages shown here corresponds exactly with the range of international attitudes of the Congressmen and their districts. The principle may be stated simply: the higher the per capita income in a district, the more likely the district is to have a multilateralist Congressman, while the lower the income, the greater the probability that the Congressman will espouse the ideological line or at least be a waverer. Indeed, one of the striking aspects of the results produced by the per capita income criterion is the extent to which it relates the waverers to the ideologists and the pragmatists to the multilateralists; each of the intermediate positions is much like its extreme associate, but with a somewhat blurred distribution. The waverers, for example, cluster in Types IV and V, while the pragmatist districts concentrate in Types I and II.

The relationship of each group to the median per capita income per district of $1,277 is shown in Table 27.

The closeness of the two negative groups to each other in the percentage of their number above the median is

TABLE 27

PER CAPITA INCOME (Median: $1,277)

GROUP	ABOVE MEDIAN	BELOW MEDIAN	% ABOVE MEDIAN
Ideologists (30)	9	21	30.0
Waverers (19)	6	13	31.6
Reversers (10)	6	4	60.0
Dividers (6)	4	2	66.6
Pragmatists (18)	11	7	61.1
Multilateralists (43)	26	17	60.5

remarkable; so also is the relationship of the two affirmative groups. The combined percentage above the median for the ideological-wavering aggregation is 30.6, while for the multilateralists-pragmatists it is 60.7. What these data suggest but do not make obvious is the fact that showed up clearly in Table 26: the ideological districts tend to have per capita incomes much further below the median than do the waverers, while the multilateralists have disproportionally many more very high per capita incomes than do the pragmatists.

The sheer statistical evidence seems to make apparent a positive correlation between the per capita income in a district and its international outlook that not only applies to extreme cases but also largely to intermediate positions as well. Note, for example, that in Table 27 only the two clearly negative positions have a majority of districts below the median, while the remaining four are close together and all more than 60 per cent above the median. Armed with no more information about a given district than its per capita income, an observer could, in other words, make a guess about that district's foreign policy grouping with significantly good odds in favor of putting the district in its correct place.

The multilateralists, with roughly one-third of the seats of the entire South, represent half the very high income districts and more than two-fifths of Type II. The ideologists, occupying nearly one-fourth of the seats, have less than one-tenth of the Type I districts and only 15 per cent of Type II. The multilateralists have markedly less than their proportionate share of Type IV and V districts, while the ideologists have slightly more than their share of Type IV and over twice their appropriate number of Type V districts. The percentages for the two extreme positions—which make up the largest groups of the six—are the clearest and the most conclusive, since both their smaller associated colleagues tend to cluster more toward the middle of the scale.

THE COMPOSITE CRITERION

Armed with the insight that per capita income in a district so closely coincides with the international point of view of its Congressman, and with his analytical vantage point buttressed by the less specific but nonetheless provocative insights into the impact of population growth, urbanization, and manufacturing activity, the analyst can next turn to the construction of a composite criterion. The data adduced in this chapter, in other words, can be so arranged as to develop a standardized district of each of the major types. These frames will provide the static base of analysis and the point of departure for subsequent consideration of dynamic factors.

The typical multilateralist district in the South between 1953 and 1962 had a per capita income in 1959 between $1,350 and $1,450, with the figure somewhat more likely to be on the high side (the median per capita income in these districts was $1,414). It was fairly heavily urbanized with its percentage between 50 and 55 per cent, but by and large not especially deeply committed to manufacturing. Its probable figure for value added would be between $125,-000,000 and $150,000,000 with a slightly greater likelihood of being closer to the smaller than to the larger figure, since the median for the group is $132,000,000. Its growth rate was between 5 and 15 per cent during the 1950-1960 decade.

On this basis, the multilateralist district that most closely approximated this norm was the sixth district of Kentucky. Its per capita income was $1,414—exactly the median figure; its percentage of urbanization was 50.8, and its growth rate during the 1950's was 8 per cent. It was slightly more industrialized than the model, since its figure for value added was $175,000,000, but this particular index is probably the least reliable of the four since so many other ways of producing fairly high per capita income may affect a district's rhythm. Other districts fairly close to the norm included Tennessee 3 (with, however, a very high value added by manufacturing) and Texas 3 (which was slightly below the postulated figures except in per capita income).

The typical pragmatic district differed somewhat from the multilateralist stereotype, but the essential similarity of the two is striking. The per capita income of the pragmatic ideal was somewhere between $1,300 and $1,350, while its percentage of urbanization of almost exactly 50 per cent was also somewhat below that of the multilateralist model. In value added by manufacturing, however, the pragmatic districts were significantly higher, with a figure in the neighborhood of $166,000,000; their rate of population growth as well was perceptibly above the regional average. The typical pragmatic district projects an image of a less sharply defined society gripped by the forces of transition from a stable—in some ways almost stagnant—agriculturally-based system into a new-industry urbanization.

Of the eighteen pragmatic districts none approximates this ideal as closely as the three cited as typifying the multilateralists. The closest in reality was Louisiana 6, with a per capita income of $1,313 and an urban percentage of

55.8. The value added by manufacture in this district, however, far surpassed the suggested norm; its total of $374,-000,000 in 1959 placed it in the upper 10 per cent of all Southern districts. Its rate of growth during the 1950's—thanks to "new industries" such as petroleum and chemicals—was also well in excess of the Southern average and within the suggested range of expectation.

The model of the wavering district is different from the first two in most respects and conveys an impression of a much different sort of society. The per capita income was much lower, between $1,150 and $1,200; the percentage of urbanization was between 45 and 49, at or slightly below the regional median. Value added by manufacturing was also perceptibly lower, being around $110,000,000, while its rate of population increase was very nearly at or slightly over the regional average of 16.5 per cent. Thus in two criteria—urbanization and population growth—the wavering districts approximated the Southern picture at large, while in the remaining two—per capita income and value added by manufacturing—they fell well below. The typical district of this type did not include a very large city or indeed any strong note of urban values. Manufacturing and other distinctively urban occupations were not as important as elsewhere. Change, however, was obviously on the way as the period drew to a close. The small cities in the wavering districts are growing rapidly and controlling rural social and political values are in the process of drastic revision. The new synthesis, however, had not been attained by 1962 and the wavering district showed itself clearly to be under considerable political tension.

The nearest example of the model to be found among the nineteen wavering districts is Louisiana 7. Its per capita income was $1,179, its urban percentage 47.4, and its rate of population increase 21.6 per cent. It surpassed the norm in value added by manufacturing by almost 50 per cent, but nevertheless conformed in reality largely to the generalized picture of a wavering district sketched above. Coming into the picture with a different set of statistics but projecting much the same image is Alabama 2, with a per capita income of $1,204 but with a higher urban percentage and lower figures on value added and on overall population growth.

Probably the most interesting and the most important of any of these models is that of the typical ideological district. Fortunately, the picture is clearer than for any other except perhaps its multilateralist counterpart. Its per capita income fell within the range between $1,090 and $1,150, probably on the lower end. Its percentage of urbanization was well below the regional average, between 38 and 42 per cent. The value added by manufacturing figure, however, was 30 per cent greater in the ideological district than in the wavering one; the figure of $130,000,000 compared rather neatly with the median of $132,000,000 for the multilateralists. The growth in population in the standard ideological district, however, was negligible during the 1950's, being scarcely more than 5 per cent.

How can one square the relatively great emphasis placed in the ideological district upon manufacturing with its low ratings on per capita income, urbanization, and growth rate? The most persuasive answer to this query draws a distinction between the kinds of industry common to the ideological district and those prevalent in the pragmatic and wavering types. The ideological district is given to "old industry," Southern style—textiles, wood products and food processing—that are low-wage, small-town, and relatively inelastic. This means that industrial production in an ideological district neither expanded dramatically during the 1950's nor attracted people into cities in any great numbers. The social impact of industry, therefore, was not conducive to great change in the ideological district, while the concentration of newer kinds of (and higher-paying) industrial establishments in growing and dynamic cities produced powerful tides of change.

No single ideological district meets all the specified criteria. Five, however, show a composite face that comes reasonably close to the model and each typified the general pattern. The relevant data on each of these are summarized below:

TABLE 28

RELEVANT DATA ON TYPICAL IDEOLOGICAL DISTRICTS

DISTRICT	PER CAPITA INCOME	% OF URBANIZA- TION	VALUE ADDED BY MANUFACTURING	GROWTH 1950-60
Arkansas 6	$1,087	42.7	$119,000,000	—3.3%
Georgia 9	$1,110	18.7	$144,000,000	10.5%
Mississippi 6	$1,154	48.9	$204,000,000	17.6%
South Carolina 1	$1,106	43.1	$108,000,000	21.8%
Virginia 5	$1,114	22.8	$310,000,000	2.9%

Each of these qualifies as typical on per capita income. The Arkansas and South Carolina districts come the closest to meeting the standard of urbanization, the Arkansas and Mississippi districts to the norm for value added by manufacturing, and the Arkansas and Virginia examples fit the growth pattern the most closely, with the Georgia district also close. Of all, Arkansas 6 probably most nearly meets the overall pattern, but none of the five need fear losing its classification as an exceptionally good example of an ideological district.

DISTRICTS SUSCEPTIBLE TO CHANGE

A second look at Table 26 that shows the distribution of the several types of districts according to per capita income reveals two clusters that seem to be definitely out of place: the fifteen multilateralist and pragmatic districts with a per capita income below $1,176, and the eleven ideological and wavering districts with per capita incomes above $1,377. Since the suggestiveness of per capita income figures in pointing to the international outlook of a district is so striking, and because no one who looks at the contemporary South can feel any confidence that the full course of change has been run, each of these two groups merits a closer analysis because of the incongruity of their overall identification with the single datum of per capita income. Do these districts match the other characteristics of their respective schools of thought, or are they in any sense exceptional? If the latter should prove true, it seems at least a hypothesis worth exploring that each cluster (or at least some of the districts included in each of the groups) should be considered as less than solid in the point of view expressed by their Congressmen and as potential candidates for early change.

The fifteen multilateralist districts with a per capita income so far below the median for their group were found in ten different states, with only Florida, Louisiana, South Carolina, and Texas failing to provide any examples. In the table that follows the districts are arranged in descending order of per capita income.

Particularly striking about this list is the relatively low level of urbanization characteristic of most and the truly remarkable incidence of population loss during the decade. For the group the median figures on the four criteria are: per capita income, $1,063; urbanization, 31.5 per cent; value added by manufacturing, $124,000,000; and growth rate, —6.5 per cent. These districts are truly a cross section of that part of the South that has been largely overlooked in the general prosperity of the region.

It seems a safe starting point to assume that the four pragmatic districts are prime candidates for early change since their Congressmen were long since moved to transfer their position on foreign aid from the affirmative to the negative side (none of these four districts was opposed to

TABLE 29

RELEVANT DATA, LOW-INCOME MULTILATERALIST
AND PRAGMATIC DISTRICTS

DISTRICT	PER CAPITA INCOME	% URBANIZED	VALUE ADDED BY MANUFACTURING	% POP. GROWTH
Georgia 6	$1175	53.8	$124,000,000	7.2
Georgia 1 (P)	1174	56.9	196,000,000	8.5
Alabama 5	1141	44.9	242,000,000	—1.5
Arkansas 3	1141	39.9	101,000,000	—7.5
Tennessee 6 (P)	1110	25.8	135,000,000	1.9
Alabama 4	1105	42.8	149,000,000	4.7
W. Virginia 5	1095	19.6	22,000,000	—16.5
Oklahoma 3	1063	34.8	19,000,000	—14.7
Tennessee 4	1017	27.4	126,000,000	—0.2
Virginia 9 (P)	1000	16.4	140,000,000	—6.5
Alabama 7	957	20.8	55,000,000	—13.5
Arkansas 2	910	17.1	26,000,000	—18.7
Kentucky 7	884	17.4	94,000,000	—13.6
N. Carolina 2 (P)	867	33.8	128,000,000	2.2
Mississippi 3	777	31.5	47,000,000	—10.2

(P - Pragmatic District)

foreign aid in 1953). Georgia 1 offers a set of figures, however, that is sufficiently high on all four criteria to suggest a somewhat greater staying power than might be estimated for the other three. Tennessee 6, although high on manufacturing and one of the five in the group that avoided a net loss in population, nevertheless shows such a low percentage of urbanization that its long-term stability in international outlook is open to serious question. Virginia 9 and North Carolina 2 would both seem to rely heavily on their relatively high level of manufacturing activity to keep them from a significant shift. None of the four, however, is immune to any of several dynamic political forces that might carry them all the way into the ideological camp. All, indeed, have shown some disposition in that direction already.

Of the eleven multilateralist districts on the list, all except Arkansas 2 were earlier classified among the "stalwarts" with only a stray negative vote or two marring the perfect affirmative record of each of them. In other words, in confronting this group of districts the analyst is dealing with Congressmen who have been unshakeable in their commitment to foreign aid and international co-operation. This would suggest that the struggle between the past (in the form of the paternalistic multilateralism of the Congressmen) and the future (represented by the changing socio-economic indices) that is so characteristic of the contemporary South comes to a special focus in these constituencies.

Three of the eleven show an overall profile not remarkably out of harmony with the more common multilateralist pattern except for the single important index of per capita income, and even so all three (Alabama 4, Alabama 5, and Georgia 6) are above the median for the group as a whole. Of the remaining districts in the upper half of the list, Arkansas 3 suffers from a low level of manufacturing activity and a sizeable loss of population, while West Virginia 5 offers mute but eloquent statistical evidence of a society suffering from widespread and wholesale stagnation and economic collapse. In the lower half, every district listed has at least two of the four indices startlingly out of harmony with regional or even multilateralist norms. In some way all but the first three are markedly atypical of the model of a multilateralist district.

How then can these constituencies remain committed to multilateralism in foreign policy (and, incidentally but interestingly, to a consistently high score on the ADA scale of liberalism)? Perhaps the most immediate answer is the remarkably low turnover among the Congressmen representing these fifteen districts. Only two of their number holding office at the close of the 87th Congress in 1962 had not answered the roll call opening of the 83rd in 1953; one of these two newcomers took office in 1955, and the other only in 1961. The latter, however, replaced an incumbent who had retired voluntarily after fourteen years of service.

Another relevant consideration is that of the fifteen, only four (Kentucky 7, Oklahoma 3, Virginia 9, and West Virginia 5) can be in any sense considered as two-party districts in which a Republican candidate regularly opposes the Democratic incumbent and polls a significant vote. This fact no doubt is related to the long service each of these Congressmen has enjoyed and contributes to the stability of their international outlooks. In districts like these, once a Congressman has established his personal organization and contacts and has become accepted by the politically articulate members of his constituency as part of the normal landscape, he comes to count on both long and relatively placid service and upon a singularly broad grant of discretion on all questions except those that directly affect the centers of interest and power in his district.

At the other end of the scale are found the eleven districts (six ideological, five wavering) with a negative attitude toward international co-operation but with socio-economic indices that comport with the bulk of the multilateralists. Five of the eleven are from Texas; the remainder includes one each from Arkansas, Florida, Georgia, Louisiana, Oklahoma, and South Carolina. All but one have per capita incomes in excess of $1,400. The relevant data on these atypical unilateralist districts are summarized in Table 30. As in the case of Table 29, the districts are arranged in descending order of per capita income.

The overall impression conveyed by this list is one of high per capita income, a high level of urbanization, a high manufacturing value, and remarkably rapid population growth. The median per capita income of the group, the

TABLE 30
RELEVANT DATA, HIGH-INCOME IDEOLOGICAL
AND WAVERING DISTRICTS

DISTRICT	PER CAPITA INCOME	% URBANIZED	VALUE ADDED BY MANUFACTURING	% POP. GROWTH
Texas 5	$2225	97.5	$810,000,000	54.8
Oklahoma 1 (W)	1958	77.9	324,000,000	18.7
Texas 22 (W)	1871	94.5	577,000,000	66.6
Texas 18	1862	64.7	198,000,000	25.6
Texas 16 (W)	1706	40.9	131,000,000	63.0
Florida 7	1663	61.7	128,000,000	75.3
Arkansas 5	1500	69.8	124,000,000	13.2
Louisiana 4 (W)	1471	34.1	147,000,000	17.6
Texas 21 (W)	1462	57.5	31,000,000	—2.3
Georgia 5	1413	91.0	567,000,000	33.2
South Carolina 4	1382	49.1	350,000,000	12.0

(W - Wavering District)

$1,663 of Florida 7, is nearly $250 above the overall Southern average and almost $400 above the median of the 126 Southern districts. Nine of the eleven are above the regional median in urbanization, three being above 90 per cent urban. Value added by manufacturing is generally quite high, five showing figures above $300,000,000 and seven of the eleven being above the Southern median figure. Only the relatively tiny figure for Texas 21 mars the general impression. Only Texas 21, furthermore, suffered a decline in population and only South Carolina 4 and Arkansas 5 lagged behind the Southern rate of population increase. Five had growth percentages of over 50.

Also notable in the list is the high incidence of districts from Texas. The status of the Lone Star State—whether "Southern" or "Western" in politics—has been a matter of considerable debate in recent years as figures from Texas have emerged on the national political scene with some apparent desire to disassociate themselves from any potentially embarrassing identification with the solid (and white-supremacy) South. Without attempting to settle this argument here, it may be safely pointed out that no more than half a dozen Texas districts are in any cultural or socio-economic way really Southern and that none of the larger Texas cities fit any Southern stereotype. But neither does Texas conform to any larger political pattern, since the state's one-party system remains relatively unshaken and Texans in Congress identify more frequently, more clearly, and obviously more comfortably with Southerners than with two-party delegations from the West.

This observation suggests that Texas ideologists draw their inspiration less from generalized Southern concerns (except possibly in east Texas) and more either from peculiarly Texas sources or else from the national thrust of the radical right. If and when any of the five Texas districts included here shows any signs of a relaxation in the militancy of its international outlook, it is probable that the reasons will prove to be rooted in Texas politics and Texas economic concerns. The five districts comprise Dallas, Houston, Amarillo, El Paso, and—the only non-metropolitan instance—San Angelo. Only the first two look eastward to "the South"; the remaining three are part of the "sagebrush West" and have little in common with Dixie.

The non-Texas districts make up a mixed bag. Oklahoma 1 is Tulsa, where oil interests and right-wing evangelism are dominant. Florida 7 includes west-coast and central Florida, with its center in Sarasota. Arkansas 5 includes Little Rock, the scene of the 1957 integration crisis. Louisiana 4 is the northwest corner of the state, centering in Shreveport. Georgia 5 is Atlanta. South Carolina 4 is "textile heaven," the Greenville-Spartanburg area in the Piedmont.

Florida 7 and Arkansas 5 lost their identities as a result of reapportionment after the census of 1960 and the subsequent redistricting of both states. The Congressman who had given Arkansas 5 its ideological orientation was squeezed out of the House as Arkansas lost two seats, although Little Rock itself is still represented by a Congressman with the same general point of view. The Congressman who represented Florida 7 remained a member of the House, but with a district smaller in population (although of the same general coloration) as Florida added four seats to its delegation. Of the remainder, Texas 16 suffered an upset in the election of 1962 and is now represented by a Republican with a record yet to make, while Georgia 5 (thanks to the final abolition of the county-unit system in the Democratic primary) finally retired its arch-ideologist Representative in favor of a younger Democratic replacement whose early impression suggests at the very least a tendency toward a pragmatic position.

This list of twenty-six districts that, on the evidence of the criteria used in this chapter, appear to be particularly susceptible to the forces of change in international outlook must be approached with great caution. It would be fatuous to predict that these—and only these—will change position during the next decade and that all others will remain where they were in 1962. The list merely includes those districts whose overall social and economic composition and dynamics sharply separate them from the bulk of the others that vote in the same fashion. Other districts may in fact change sooner or more extensively; entirely different factors may be at work. But the very symmetry of the groupings themselves makes these exceptional cases noteworthy, and a large portion of the twenty-six examined here will certainly be involved in whatever continued change takes place.

One additional datum might throw a modicum of further light. The affirmative districts of either type, it will be recalled, contained populations averaging 15 per cent Negro, while the two negative classifications averaged over one-fourth. Of the fifteen multilateralist and pragmatist districts on the low-income list, five show much greater concentrations of Negroes than the multilateralist norm: Alabama 4 (31.7 per cent), Georgia 1 (37.6), Georgia 6 (41.4), Mississippi 3 (65.6), and North Carolina 2 (50.5). If there is any correlative—let alone causative—relationship between the proportion of Negroes in the entire population of a district and the international outlook of its Congressman, these figures would certainly pinpoint these five districts as meriting close attention in the future. It is worth noting that two of them are included in the four pragmatic districts on the list; that is, they already are opposed to foreign aid.

By the same token, of the eleven high-income negative districts, only three equal or exceed the roughly 25 per cent Negro average for their group: Arkansas 5 (26.1 per cent), Georgia 5 (26.6), and Louisiana 4 (37.5). None of the five Texas districts ranks high; Dallas and Houston (Texas 5 and 22 respectively) show percentages of 14.7 and 14.9, while the three west Texas districts (16, 18, and 21) have 4.2, 2.6, and 2.9 respectively. Exempting the Texas districts from any generalizations about the South, it would thus appear that on this count alone the remaining districts on the list with low Negro percentages (Florida 7—16.1 per cent; Oklahoma 1—7.3; and South Carolina 4—21.3) might be less directly and intimately affected by whatever influence the Negro issue may have on foreign policy questions.

The analysis in this chapter, it should be repeated, has been static in the sense that the socio-economic setting for each type of district has been examined. The discussion in the preceding few pages, in isolating approximately one-fifth of the South's districts as out of harmony with the overall picture, obviously requires some evaluation of the dynamics of the Southern political scene as they affect the international behavior of Congressmen. This will be undertaken in the following chapter.

VIII
THE CHANGING SOUTH

THROUGHOUT the preceding chapters the theme of change has run almost without a break. The reversal in the international outlook of many Southern Congressmen is sharp and distinct, but the data in no way support the easy thesis that members of Congress from the fourteen Southern states vote differently today than they used to do simply because they have changed their individual and collective minds on the issues themselves. Congressmen, on the contrary, have themselves undergone fewer modifications in their personal positions than have the bulk of their people. They have changed their votes, in other words, simply because their constituents have changed their minds; the South is an entirely different phenomenon than it was only a decade ago, and the responses of its political spokesmen no more than reflect the new environment in which they must operate.

The political turmoil obvious throughout many parts of the South is a symptom of a much more fundamental and deep-seated malaise throughout the region. Bypassed by much of the past century of American history and permitted by fate to develop in its own way a society unique to the American norm, the South during the decade from 1953 through 1962 was brought suddenly face to face with the rest of the nation, the outside world, and the full impact of the twentieth century. Social and economic modernization, long delayed by a combination of inertia and deliberate design, has struck the once-placid landscape of the South a shattering blow. Major adjustments to an urbanized and industrialized era that other regions of the United States were given several generations to accept, have been forced on Southerners within the space of only a decade. The old society of the South is dissolving before the astonished eyes of the contemporary Southerner, and the new one that is taking shape with breakneck speed is neither familiar nor pleasing to him.

Being a Southerner today is a devastating experience. Criticized by outsiders and misled by his own leadership, his cherished values repudiated and his long-vaunted life pattern abruptly wrenched into alien forms, with even the fixed poles of his racial, political, and cultural systems drifting out of sight, he faces the world with a mixture of bewilderment, resentment, nostalgia, and hostility as his only defense, seasoned only irregularly by a dash of hope or anticipation. The South—particularly the "old" and tradition-ridden part—is not a happy place today.

With their senses newly sharpened and with an extensive bill of complaints against a world they never made, Southerners developed during the 1950's a touchiness and a querulousness unmatched in any earlier period in history except during the decade immediately preceding the Civil War. Since the Southern Congressman is a supremely political animal whose career in a one-party system depends upon his ability to sense and respond to constituent urges before hard and fast opposition develops, it is no more than natural that his votes throughout the decade were eloquent testimony to the way "his people" felt about a broad range of issues. Although the swing in the position of any individual Congressman cannot be used as a precise and accurate guide to the *magnitude* of the changes in his district, it is self-evident that the votes revealed quite accurately how he thought his district felt about the changes that had taken place. Objective factors can do no more than set the stage for political action; human responses to these external conditions constitute the real stuff of politics.

But if change is of the essence of the contemporary South, and if it is these very fundamental shifts in the conditions of Southern life today that provide the springboard for new and intensified forms of political action—the thesis of this chapter—it is essential that the nature of the change be examined. What exactly has been happening to the South? Many of the points to be made in this connection have been suggested earlier in different contexts, but here all the important threads will be pulled together to provide the outlines of a South in flux.

In general, it may be said that the South—at least half a century behind the rest of the nation—is rapidly metamorphosing from a rural and agricultural society with a stratified and astonishingly rigid social system to an urbanized, industrialized, pluralistic, and—at least as yet—flexible structure of interpersonal relations. The rural or small-town environment, the leisurely pace of affairs, the limited but self-satisfied point of view, and the snugly-rationalized system of race relations—all dominant in Southern life only a generation ago—are being eroded to the point of disappearance under the inexorable pressures of modernization.

But the values characteristic of a pastoral society are rooted in the peculiar conditions of Southern rural life and cannot be translated bodily to the congested circumstances and hectic pace of the city. Millions of middle and lower-middle class Southerners were perfectly well equipped psychically and personally to live full and satisfying lives in the rural South that is lost to them forever, but had no equipment to structure their behavior in their new urban environment. As a result, individual insecurities grew in number, in severity, and in frequency until they began to combine in mass hostilities that occasionally boiled over into simple panic. A mentality of crisis became a commonplace of Southern politics. The shift in the voting position of the region's Congressmen was thus no more than a natural consequence.

CITIES AND FARMS

Probably the most significant phenomenon on the Southern scene is the movement of the people across their own landscape. The fact that Southerners have finally become almost as mobile as other Americans is simultaneously a graphic demonstration of the final re-identification of the region with the rest of the country and a bleak reminder of how much the South has left its old ways behind. The proclivity of the Southerner to stay at or close to home was once proverbial, but in the 1950's, driven by a variety of powerful urges, at last he began to move.

The Southern migration was primarily in a single direction, from the farms to the cities. The increase in population of eleven of the fourteen states should not be taken as implying anything like an even distribution of people. On the contrary, of the total population increase of the fourteen states of about seven million people between 1950 and 1960, almost exactly four million (57.3 per cent of the total) of the increase was to be found in two states, Florida and Texas, while another 1.2 million occurred in Virginia and Louisiana. Thus the great surge of population in the South was primarily toward Florida and Texas, neither of them traditionally Southern, and secondarily toward two specially (and peripherally) located other states.

Regardless of the particular population increase (or decrease) any state may have experienced during the decade, in all the relentless rhythm of the rise of the city and the flight from the land played the dominant role. Of the 1,391 counties in the fourteen states, 804 (57.8 per cent) declined in population during the decade. More significantly (or perhaps, more ominously), only 227 counties (16.3 per cent) could boast a net increase through migration, while 360 owed what growth they enjoyed only to the excess of births over deaths and emigration combined.

In some states the flight of the farmer was astonishing in its pervasiveness. In Arkansas, for example, only 5 counties of 75 did not show a decline in population, in Mississippi only 22 of 62, in Oklahoma only 13 of 77, and in West Virginia only 14 of 55. Only Florida, Louisiana, North Carolina, and Virginia could show an increase in more than half of their counties, while South Carolina split exactly even, 23 of its 46 gaining. Only Florida had a majority of its counties with a net gain by migration; even Texas could only boast of 49 of its total of 254 counties that proved magnets to new residents.

It is interesting to note, however, that less than one-fifth of the South's county-seat towns—most of them small to middle-sized—suffered decreases in population. Although the hinterland on which they had long subsisted was being denuded of people, these towns continued to grow—although at a much slower rate than did the larger cities. Some garnered a new factory or two to provide jobs for displaced farmers and payrolls for the sustenance of their merchants, but generally the economic stability of these small urban centers was doubtful. There were few observers to be found who were optimistic about how long the Southern small town as a social system could continue to count on the fecundity of its residents to offset a flood of out-migration.

While the rural South was being decimated, the urban South was thriving. In 1950 the fourteen states were less than half urban in population; only 45.6 per cent of the people of the South lived in any kind of urban community. Thirty per cent of all Southerners lived in small cities (under 100,000) while 15.5 per cent lived in larger cities. There were only twenty-nine cities with more than 100,000 people in all the South, a fraction more than an average of two per state.

By 1960 one out of every ten living Southerners had moved from a rural environment to a city during the preceding ten years. The overall urban percentage had risen to 57.4; the total urban population had increased 45.9 per cent. The cities with more than 100,000 inhabitants had grown much more rapidly than the smaller ones; over half the urban population of the South in 1960 was to be found within the boundaries of its forty largest cities. One of every five Southerners, to put it another way, lived in a large city in 1960.

While the urban South was booming at a rate matched only by the hothouse growth of certain areas on the Pacific Coast, the farm population was dropping sensationally. Between 1954 and 1959, for example, the *number* of farms in cultivation decreased 27.5 per cent for the South as a whole. The states that suffered the most drastic declines were, in order, South Carolina, Mississippi, West Virginia, Georgia, Alabama, and Arkansas, all of them with percentages of decrease very close to 35 (the six states all fell within a span of less than 3 percentage points). The only states whose percentage of decline was less than the regional figure were Florida, Kentucky, Tennessee, Oklahoma, and Texas—none, be it noted, traditionally part of the classic rural pattern of the South except for some parts of Kentucky and Tennessee.

Closely linked with these figures in obvious ways was a marked decline in farm tenancy. In all fourteen states the percentage of all farms that were worked by tenants in 1959 was smaller than it had been only five years earlier, and in some states the drop was precipitous. In Mississippi, for example, nearly half of its farms were tenant-operated in 1954, but by 1959 less than one-third were sharecropped. In Georgia and Louisiana the decrease was from more than one-third to less than one-fourth of all farms. These data confirm the suspicion that the rural proletariat of the South —for so long the foundation-stone of traditional social structures—is being liquidated as agriculture becomes more fully a concentrated economic enterprise and less a myth-enriched way of life. The marginal farmer, be he sharecropper or small holder, held on in the South longer than anywhere else, but during the 1950's even he joined the stampede off the land.

Comparing the data on urban growth with those of agricultural decline, it seems obvious that for most Southern farmers the trip they took off the farm was a fairly short one. The major thrust was toward the city, but by and large the cities to which they moved were in the South. A somewhat larger proportion of ex-rural Negroes went to the North than did the uprooted whites, but in neither case was the flight from the land predominantly a flight from the South as well. Most settled in Southern cities, especially the larger ones. Here the tensions peculiar to the sudden confrontation of rural values with the rapid and jarring pace of life in a growing city were provided luxuriant grounds for growth.

INDUSTRY AND AGRICULTURE

With the great shift in residence patterns from farm to city in the South has come, of course, an equivalent redistribution of the Southern labor force as between industry and agriculture. The overall figures are stark in their simplicity and in the impact of the story they tell. Between 1950 and 1960, 46.7 per cent of the agricultural labor force of the South left farming for some other work, while over the same period the industrial labor force increased by 32.3 per cent. Thus nearly half the Southerners working on farms as owners, tenants, or wage laborers in 1950 had left ten years later, while for every three industrial employees in 1950 there were four in 1960.

It is interesting to compare these two trends of complementary change on a state-by-state basis. In Table 31, a general pattern shows up clearly, but so do also certain interesting exceptions:

TABLE 31

PERCENTAGES OF CHANGE, AGRICULTURAL
AND INDUSTRIAL LABOR FORCE, 1950-1960

STATE	AGRICULTURE, % DECLINE	MANUFACTURING, % INCREASE
Alabama	59.3	25.9
Arkansas	54.3	4.2
Florida	11.1	108.1
Georgia	54.8	22.9
Kentucky	46.0	31.3
Louisiana	51.6	42.7
Mississippi	52.7	44.8
North Carolina	43.1	24.7
Oklahoma	52.3	47.4
South Carolina	52.3	22.2
Tennessee	46.9	32.7
Texas	34.6	43.9
Virginia	40.6	27.2
West Virginia	60.2	5.9
SOUTH	46.7	32.3
UNITED STATES	38.6	20.2

Thus only Florida, with the smallest agricultural work force in 1950 of all Southern states except West Virginia, escaped the wholesale abandonment of agricultural employment that so forcefully characterized the entire region. Only Texas, in addition, had a percentage of decline of less than 40. At the same time, Arkansas and West Virginia alone did not manage to offset to some degree the loss of agricultural jobs by any substantial increase in their industrial work force. All other states did so to some extent—which no doubt helps to explain why Arkansas and West Virginia were the two Southern states that suffered substantial population losses during the decade.

It is also interesting to note that Virginia, the two Carolinas, and Georgia did not keep pace with the remainder of the South in increasing their industrial labor forces, although their rates of decline among farm workers were all in the neighborhood of the regional average. This relative sluggishness of the South Atlantic states will be encountered again in this chapter, and raises some interesting hypotheses about the proclivity of these states toward ideological unilateralism in foreign policy.

To put the matter another way, in 1950 the agricultural labor force in the South outnumbered the workers in manufacturing in every Southern state except Georgia, the two Carolinas, Virginia, and West Virginia. By 1960 only in Mississippi and Arkansas was this true, and the pace of change in both states made it likely that the slight preponderance of agricultural workers in their labor forces would soon disappear. In 1950 there were eight farm workers in the South for every seven industrial employees; in 1960 there were more than two industrial workers for every member of the region's decimated agricultural labor force.

Southern industrialization is a tremendously powerful force that is transforming the South at an incredible rate, but one significant statistic is highly suggestive. The South is the only major region of the United States in which workers producing non-durable goods outnumber those engaged in the production of durables. Only Alabama, Arkansas, Kentucky, and West Virginia—none with especially large labor forces and only Alabama with a major base in the coal-iron-and-steel complex—had more workers in 1960 in durable-goods industry than in the non-durables. Thus much of Southern industry is committed to "soft" goods and is, therefore, vulnerable to the cyclic instability intrinsic to low-wage and semi-skilled labor forces.

Running alongside the increase in industrial employment in any developing society is an almost automatic increase in the number and variety of establishments offering services. An urbanized system requires more services, and an industrially employed population with a high per capita income is better able to pay for them. Between 1954 and 1958, therefore, the number of service establishments in the South increased 31.1 per cent as compared with a national figure of 24.1 per cent. State by state, the figures paralleled the increase in industrial employment almost perfectly. Florida was far in the lead, and West Virginia and Arkansas brought up the rear. Interesting, because unexpected, were the records of Kentucky, Louisiana, and Tennessee, three states that followed Florida fairly closely, while Oklahoma and Virginia were relatively laggard.

Thus the industrial growth of the South—at least in terms of the increase in the numbers of workers in manufacturing—tended to concentrate during the 1950's in Florida and in the far Southwestern corner of the region in the states of Mississippi, Louisiana, Oklahoma, and Texas. The older "textile South" of the South Atlantic seaboard did not keep pace, and the border state group ranged from miniscule increases to virtually the level of the overall Southern average.

This is clear when the trends in the establishment of new factories are examined. During the period 1954 to 1959, there was a net increase in the number of industrial plants in the South of 5,301—9.5 per cent. This was a rate of expansion approximately two and one-half times the national figure. But again the differences among the several geographic sub-areas of the South and the extent to which certain states fell behind others are revealed by the details in Table 32.

This table shows the size and comparative vitality of the South's industrial boom. In all three categories of enterprise, the regional figures are well above the overall levels for the United States as a whole (in which, it must be kept in mind, the South's figures are included). Thus the South and the Pacific Coast were the only regions in which major

TABLE 32

MANUFACTURING ESTABLISHMENTS BY SIZE OF
WORK FORCE, 1954-1959

STATE	1-19 EMPLOYEES		
	1954	1959	% Increase
Alabama	2740	2732	—0.3
Arkansas	1859	1905	2.5
Florida	3762	4778	28.2
Georgia	3942	3952	0.3
Kentucky	1796	1923	7.1
Louisiana	2122	2190	3.2
Mississippi	1586	1671	5.4
North Carolina	4275	4660	9.0
Oklahoma	1607	1794	11.6
South Carolina	1885	1949	3.4
Tennessee	2691	2934	9.0
Texas	6277	7249	15.5
Virginia	3108	3033	—2.4
West Virginia	1509	1308	—8.5
SOUTH	39123	42150	7.7
UNITED STATES	196365	203142	3.5

industrial expansion went on during the 1950's; on a comparative basis, furthermore, the South virtually held its own.

Especially is this true in the third column, showing the numbers and rates of increase of large establishments with over 100 employees. Here the rate of expansion in the South was five times the national figure and only Louisiana and Kentucky were below the overall level and West Virginia close to it. Again the high growth rate of Florida stands out, but so also do the relatively surprising ones of Arkansas, Mississippi, and Oklahoma. The unspectacular performance of the South Atlantic states is once more notable; all four were well below Southern averages in the three categories

19-99 Employees			100 or more Employees		
1954	*1959*	*% Increase*	*1954*	*1959*	*% Increase*
746	756	1.3	407	439	7.9
397	466	17.4	172	200	16.2
839	1205	43.6	227	321	41.4
1131	1230	8.8	582	614	5.5
554	624	12.6	301	303	0.7
618	671	8.6	280	264	—5.7
473	505	6.8	193	238	23.3
1466	1645	12.2	904	984	8.8
388	412	6.2	136	160	17.6
471	548	16.3	364	391	7.4
829	933	12.5	538	583	8.4
1879	2253	19.9	734	836	13.9
852	899	5.5	438	482	10.0
325	319	—1.8	193	200	3.6
10768	12466	15.8	5439	6015	10.6
63884	68273	6.9	26567	27038	1.8

except for the single item of factories between 19 and 99 employees in South Carolina, in which a fractional advance over the regional average is shown.

But the sheer size of a state's manufacturing plant is by no means an infallible guide to the role industry plays in its life. The criterion of value added by manufacturing (used in the previous chapter as a comparative technique), when added to the data already adduced on work forces and numbers of establishments, can throw the matter of the South's industrialization into fuller perspective. Table 33 shows the rate of increase between 1954 and 1958:

TABLE 33
VALUE ADDED BY MANUFACTURING, 1954-1958 (in $1,000)

STATE	1954	1959	% INCREASE
Alabama	1,319,192	1,770,510	34.2
Arkansas	457,047	591,745	29.5
Florida	797,721	1,410,843	76.9
Georgia	1,592,411	2,102,332	32.0
Kentucky	1,236,760	1,781,969	44.1
Louisiana	1,181,649	1,429,580	20.9
Mississippi	467,625	642,175	37.3
North Carolina	2,210,463	3,083,448	39.5
Oklahoma	580,633	724,998	24.9
South Carolina	1,040,936	1,360,135	36.7
Tennessee	1,678,786	2,207,073	31.5
Texas	3,501,706	5,045,159	44.1
Virginia	1,629,041	2,122,652	30.3
West Virginia	988,274	1,214,775	22.9
SOUTH	18,681,744	25,487,394	36.4
UNITED STATES	117,212,837	141,380,886	20.6

Thus every one of the fourteen Southern states increased the value added by manufacturing in its factories at a more rapid rate than did the nation as a whole. Even the two obviously depressed Southern states—Arkansas and West Virginia—did better in this regard than did the nation, and of the fourteen only Louisiana was at all close to the national level. The six states that surpassed the overall Southern rate of 36.4 per cent increase included Florida and Texas (the true centers of the Southern boom), Kentucky, North Carolina, Mississippi, and South Carolina. In these terms the industrial power of the two Carolinas shows itself; industry in the mid-South may indeed be generally "old" and "soft-goods," but it yet retains considerable vitality.

It would seem that the South cannot escape its industrial future. All fourteen states are moving in the same direction, even though several are moving much more rapidly than the norm and one or two are lagging behind. The overall trend, however, has already gone too far ever to be stopped. For all that this development may bode for the South, the rural heritage of the region has been left behind forever and its future lies in the same kind of urban-industrial rhythm that is so characteristic of the rest of the United States.

THE NEGRO MIGRATION

By no means the least of the factors at work in the contemporary South, although of course not the absolutely controlling one, is the fact that the Negro is physically and psychically on the move in much the same way, in roughly the same directions, and in only moderately greater proportions than the white population. The surprising aspect of the statistics on migration among Southern Negroes is not the marked difference between them and equivalent data for the entire population or for the whites alone, but rather the close connections and near-identity of Negro patterns with those of the region as a whole.

For the South in general, between 1950 and 1960 the

Negro population increased 16.3 per cent—an insignificant 0.2 per cent less than the figure for all Southerners. That a generous element of out-migration of Negroes is concealed in this percentage is easily determined by the fact that nationally the percentage of increase in the Negro population was nearly 30 in contrast to an overall national percentage of only 18.5. Nonetheless, the increase of Negro population in the South virtually kept pace with the region, and the Negro's overall proportion of the Southern population decreased only 1.5 per cent during the decade, from 24.3 to 22.8.

State by state Negro figures approximated state totals with only a few significant differences. In only three states— Arkansas, Mississippi, and West Virginia—did an absolute decline in the number of Negroes in the population occur, and in each of these states, all of which suffered overall declines in population during the ten years, the rate of Negro depopulation was above that of the state as a whole. In six states forming a continuous band from Virginia south to Florida and sweeping westward to include Alabama, the rate of increase in the Negro population was more than 5 percentage points below that of the state as a whole, and only in Florida and Virginia was the increase more than minimal. In Louisiana and Texas, the Negro increase was well above the Southern average and approximated the relatively high rates of increase for the population as a whole. Finally, in Kentucky, Oklahoma, and Tennessee the Negro increase was well above the rate for the state as a whole, especially in Oklahoma where Negro population growth was two and one-half times the total increase for the state. Florida led the South in its rate of increase of Negroes, its 46.7 per cent increase more than doubling the 22.3 per cent of Texas and the 18.1 per cent of Louisiana, the next two states.

These state by state comparisons show one aspect of the Negro migration very clearly: the tendency of the

Negro population to leave the South Atlantic and Gulf states in much larger numbers than in any other parts of the South and to remain in (and to a significant extent, to immigrate into) the Southwest, Florida, and the border states. These general trends are in no respect markedly different from overall Southern performances, and reflect less any considered migration on a racial basis than a more generalized thrust in Southern society. It would seem to go without saying that in leaving Mississippi or South Carolina for Texas or Kentucky, Negroes are to an overwhelming extent simultaneously leaving rural life for the city and agriculture for industry. These are Southern, not Negro, trends.

This impression is corroborated by the data from the larger cities of the South. Of the forty cities with a population of over 100,000 in 1960, in exactly half the percentage of Negroes increased between 1950 and 1960, including—significantly—eight of the ten largest and four of the five largest. The two major cities in which the Negro percentage did not increase were Birmingham and Memphis; Houston, Dallas, New Orleans, San Antonio, Atlanta, Louisville, Fort Worth, and Oklahoma City—all with very high rates of growth—experienced even more rapid and extensive growth in their Negro population than in the city as a whole. It was probably no accident that of the eight cities mentioned, only Atlanta and New Orleans formed part of the traditional South; the remaining six were either Southwestern or border-state. Of the remaining thirty cities over 100,000, in only twelve was there a more pronounced increase among Negroes than in the overall population. Of these latter dozen, only three—Richmond, Jacksonville, and Greensboro—were in the South Atlantic-Gulf group of states. It is also interesting to note that Jacksonville and Richmond both suffered absolute decreases in population at the same time that their Negro populations were increasing.

In the larger metropolitan areas of which these cities formed the respective cores, in only fourteen instances did

the Negro percentage increase. Nine of the fourteen, furthermore, were in Texas and Oklahoma, one in Kentucky, one
in Florida, and only three—New Orleans, Greensboro, and
Little Rock—were in the traditional South. Three additional
smaller Southwestern metropolitan areas (Tulsa, Lubbock,
and Wichita Falls) showed the paradoxical condition of experiencing a greater increase in Negro population within the
metropolitan areas as a whole than in the central city alone.

It seems clear that urbanization is as powerful a force
among Southern Negroes as it is among Southern whites,
and that the pull of the larger cities is even more powerful
to Negroes than to whites. Naturally enough, in the South's
larger (and more rapidly growing) cities there are more job
opportunities, a broader range of housing and recreational
facilities, and—considering that most of the really large
cities are on the fringes rather than in the center of the
South—a greater measure of personal freedom from the
crueler inhibitions of segregation. Negroes, like whites, seek
economic opportunity and personal fulfillment when they
change their residences and exchange one way of life for
another; both these sets of goals are more convincingly at-
tained in the large urban centers of the South than in the
less dynamic smaller cities of the South Atlantic and Gulf
Coast regions.

Of course, the really powerful effect of the Negro migration to the cities of the South cannot be measured statistically. The decade of the 1950's was the era of the great
awakening as the Negro, supported by a series of court decisions and urged on by increasingly militant leadership, em-
barked on a campaign to win at last the promised rights so
long denied him. For any social group contemplating direct
action and extensive agitation in behalf of its members, large
concentrations of people are critically necessary, because
only in this way can the requisite momentum and dynamic
force be developed. Under the scattering intrinsic to rural
life the Negro was never able either to mobilize group senti-

ment or to mount a campaign of action; in the city, however, he can do both. The integration of the South's cities into the major currents of the American scene also helped Negro leadership by making it much easier and more effective to dramatize individual instances of injustice for the edification of national and world leadership.

The Negro's role in the South's larger cities is thus a far cry indeed from the place he occupied in the pastoral South. Nearing job and income equality with much of the white population and occupying jointly with the whites highly congested and dynamic urban landscapes, he is rapidly losing his traditional anonymity and is acquiring a direct and often disturbing personality. The larger numbers of Southern Negroes living in cities and actively participating in the newly refreshed patterns of Southern urban economic and political life would make up a much less meaningful phenomenon than they do if the Negroes themselves did not contribute the priceless ingredient of group self-consciousness and a determination to act on their own and each other's behalf.

THE POLITICS OF CHANGE

The several sets of data advanced in this chapter suggest something of the magnitude, the speed, and the direction of the massive change through which the South is passing. The transition from an agricultural to an industrial economic system is never simple for any society, and it has proved and is proving today to be an especially painful one for the South. The region is caught not only by an antiquated economic and social system but by anachronistic political patterns and the gnawing guilt left by its racial heritage. It is no wonder that the political behavior of the South since 1945 and especially since early in the 1950's has shown so many eccentricities.

In political terms, the most important single statistical

factor of the many examined throughout the preceding chapters is beyond doubt the region's mushrooming urbanization. The most important single characteristic of the cities of the contemporary South, furthermore, is that—except for climate—there is nothing distinctively Southern about them. The dominant rhythm of life in Atlanta, Mobile, or Memphis is rapidly becoming indistinguishable from that in Pittsburgh, Milwaukee, or Denver. The urbanized South can fulfill its potential only by finally ceasing to be Southern; the majority of Southerners will, in other words, become Americans first and Southerners second—assuming that to later generations the word "Southerner" will have anything like the unique connotation it has long had in the United States. The South of isolated farmsteads, rich plantations, and sleepy courthouse towns has finally given way to a new center of gravity.

This makes the city the focus of any analysis of contemporary Southern political norms, and raises the fundamental question: Who populates the urban centers of the South? How easy will the final transition be? Can the outsider assume that a large Southern city with ample industry and a major league baseball team is composed of substantially the same kind of people who live this way in other parts of the United States? Unfortunately, at least at the present time, he cannot; the Southern city yet has a way to go before it acquires full membership and participation in the standard American pattern.

In some measure, the South's urbanization owes a good deal to the in-migration of Northerners who have moved South to retire or to find a place in the region's economic boom. But only in Florida and a few widely scattered oases elsewhere do Northern immigrants bulk large enough in the population to give a non-Southern flavor to a particular city. The vast majority of the South's new city-dwellers are the same white and Negro rustics who have been uprooted (or who have succeeded in uprooting themselves) from the Southern countryside.

This means that the dominant element in the flight to the cities is the Southern rural poor white: the marginal farmer or small-town near-proletarian who for so long made up with the rural Negro the twin pillars on which the edifice of Southern culture was based. Unique in America and possessed of a special social technique and operational point of view, the poor white has in the twentieth century been a powerful figure in Southern politics. His role in the mechanism of protest will be examined in the next chapter; here, however, certain observations on the impact he has had on the city (and *vice versa*) are very much in point.

Whatever truth there may be in the old saw that "you can take the boy out of the country but you can't take the country out of the boy" is triply applicable to the Southern poor white. Perhaps the most insistently rural of any identifiable social group in America, the poor whites find the going difficult in the city. The rural Southerner who moves to an urban center remains a country boy still (and so, for that matter, do his sons), no matter how much his behavior may conform externally to his new life. He retains his values and his prejudices, his loves and his hates, his fears and his animosities. All his new environment (and it remains "new" even after twenty years) does for him is to heighten his inner tensions and to redouble the violence of his recurrent explosions. His rural myth, already inadequate to his changing back-country environment, turns out to be totally unsuited to the demands of his dramatically different situation in the city.

Why is this so? Why is the poor white incapable of an easy transition to urban existence? To begin with, in the city he becomes exposed to a much wider world than any he has ever known before. Much more information presses in on him: political, social, and economic controversy swirls about his ears. He sees newspapers (if not very good ones), he listens to the radio (with news bulletins every hour), he watches (national network) television. He becomes drawn into political dispute. He is herded into large groups for work and recreation. Everywhere he turns, whether he likes it or not, he is caught up in the press of human affairs. The peace, the leisureliness, and the solitude of the farm are all far away.

Even more devastating to his peace of mind, in the city he runs into the issue of race relations in terms and on a scale entirely foreign to his ideology and his experience. He meets the sophisticated and militant Negro for the first time and finds him an utterly different creature from the ostensibly servile types with whom he had enjoyed such an easy relationship "back home." Worse, there is no escape for him from the nagging moral conflict implicit in race problems, for he sees the Negro everywhere. School integration, bus transportation, lunch-counter sit-ins, pressure on housing, recreational facilities, and job opportunities all attack his sensibilities and his self-control at every point.

The personality and the philosophy the poor white brings with him from the back country are inadequate to cope with this abrasive environment. Wrenched from a stable and familiar setting and dropped into a way of life he had been taught to scorn as intrinsically inferior, his inner resources tend alarmingly often to fail. His innate instability breaks to the surface, and he accumulates resentments the way more successful men pile up money. Even the higher standard of living he usually enjoys does not succeed in soothing his outraged emotions. Everywhere in the urban South, poor-white in-migrants constitute a body of massed hurt feelings looking for an excuse to voice a protest and to attack what it feels are causes of its obvious malaise.

The urbanization of the South has been going on fairly steadily since the early years of the New Deal, but it picked up its contemporary velocity only as the result of World War II and the postwar boom. Except for local and sporadic outbreaks of pent-up hostility, there was no identifiable mass surge of protest between 1950 and 1954. The pressures were building up, however, and it was the school desegregation decision of the Supreme Court in 1954, breaking upon a startled and unprepared South (whose mass myth had taught for generations that white supremacy was the natural order of creation), that revealed the extent of the urban tension under the surface of the deceptive Southern calm.

It is no coincidence that the great race crises of the South since 1954 have taken place in major cities, swollen as most of them are by great floods of once-and-recently-rural poor whites. Little Rock, New Orleans, Montgomery, Birmingham, Nashville, Atlanta, Albany: the cities of the South have been and will continue to be the battlegrounds where the new racial synthesis will slowly win its final acceptance.

The city is the inevitable scene of the Southern climax because here is where the key ingredients are found: the activist Negro and the increasingly concentrated poor white. Here too are the several different types of Negro and white leadership, all prepared to capitalize on the historic crisis that finds race relations and the entire South gripped by the mysterious forces of great change. In the cities the struggle becomes public and open and loses its private and local character which was for so long the system's major defense. National and international attention today is riveted on the recurrent agony of the contemporary South, and the drama of racial readjustment is being played out before a global audience.

In the meantime, the struggle is having its effect on the rural and small-town environment the new city-dweller has left behind. It must not be forgotten that for many Southerners the move to "the city" involved only a transfer of household goods to the nearest county-seat town and the acceptance of a service or small-factory industrial job in a setting something less than fully metropolitan. With political power in the remaining one-party South still so firmly based in rural county machines, few Southern politicians are prepared to write off the small city and courthouse town as politically sterile. The farmers, although reduced in number, still exist and still can and do claim a sympathetic ear from their representatives at all levels of government from the county board to the United States Congress. And in this environment the saga of change is quite different.

The heady wine of higher incomes, national publicity, and mass organizations that intoxicates many big-city Southerners simply is not available in most smaller towns. Here the old folkways of Southern life are assiduously cultivated and any would-be boat-rockers are summarily disposed of in one way or another. Here race relations are, according to the dominant white, "just fine," at least as long as "outside agitators" do not "stir up our people." Only distant rumors of tension in Little Rock, New Orleans, or Nashville disturb the placid surface of small-town life.

The seeds of change, of course, are planted deep and are well-watered by the steady transformation of the economic and cultural centers of the South. But for most of the Southerners who have stayed behind, being left out or falling behind the general metamorphosis of the region is a cause for thanks rather than for alarm or regret. The relative paucity of payrolls may be worth a passing mention as "too bad," but even this sense of deprivation may well be cushioned by the reflection that the factory-that-never-came at least spared the town the anguish of adjusting to the new types of people an industrial establishment would have brought in, whether Northern-born managers, rural workers, or even more Negroes.

The outsider cannot help being impressed by, and experiencing a profound admiration for, the staunch spirit of these surviving custodians of the pure Southern ideal, while at the same time marveling at the extent to which they are missing virtually the entire point of what is happening in the South. Change through evolution—the abandonment of one life process as unsuitable to a changed environment in favor of adaptation to a new and effective one—is as close to an inescapable price for survival as anything can be. The Southern small town may blandly assume that no real readjustment in its racial, economic, social, or political processes is necessary, but the final day of reckoning will only be the more painful as a result. Certainly the pressures for a new rationale for Southern society are much less severe and less obvious in the non-metropolitan areas of the South today than in the crowded urban centers, but for the small-towner to assume that history will continue conveniently to pass him by is to expect far too much.

What is even more impressive is the extent to which these unaffected areas have begun actively to resist the tide of change. Ambitious and calculating politicians, sensing the uneasiness about the new trends among their rural constituents, have developed great skill at playing on these vague and relatively unfocused hostilities. They have gone far toward constructing massive reservoirs of opposition to change (symbolized most conveniently by the issue of race relations, but obviously extending into many other areas as well) in otherwise apathetic publics, and frequently succeed in converting these mass emotions into political instruments of real efficacy. Much Southern political tension, therefore, is rooted in paradox: those people most directly involved in the phenomena of change are frequently much less agitated by them (perhaps because they are busy adjusting to them) than are groups who watch the widespread modification of tradition without themselves participating in it, except vicariously.

A case can be made, therefore, that the most potentially politically explosive sections of the contemporary South are those that have been affected adversely—but not yet catastrophically—by the new trends in Southern life, but that have not yet succeeded in coming to either emotional or intellectual terms with them. Here are the strongholds of ideologically-oriented Congressmen, the centers of militant unilateralism. Here also are the wellsprings of last-ditch resistance to readjustment in race relations and the source of that half-instinctive urge to violence in times of political and social tension that has been noted so often. The boom areas of the South, on the other hand, have their own patterns of eccentricity, but the record indicates that growing metropolitan areas and dynamic smaller cities do not go so far or stay so long at the extreme as do the drowsy but now-stirring rural areas.

One final point should be made in this connection. The so-called "white citizens' councils," the action groups set up after 1954 to oppose school integration, were originally inspired, created, and led by traditional and respectable leadership in most Southern states—the type Northern liberals often call "racial moderates" in spite of their complete dedication to the mythology of white supremacy. These gentlemen professed undying loyalty to segregation and condemned the interference of Northern do-gooders in appropriately ringing language, but shrewdly covered their tracks by expressing also their commitment to something called "law and order."

This ambivalent position was immediately recognized as an advance admission of defeat, and fell generally on deaf ears. The poor whites would have nothing to do with equivocation; "law and order" is poor comfort to men who see their entire social system and personal values being undermined. Seized by disillusionment and frustration, the reluctant urbanites insisted on action. The inevitable happened; in state after state traditional gentry were stripped of the leadership they had enjoyed for twenty years and demagogues—waiting in the wings for their chance—took charge.

In some states like Alabama, old-line leadership was

elbowed aside almost completely in favor of militant activists. In others—Virginia and Arkansas, for example— traditional leaders who sensed the current of the times compromised with the "new men" of demagoguery and adopted enough of their vocabulary and tactics to retain a tenuous control over the official apparatus. The four years from 1954 to 1957 saw demagoguery and protest become the dominant themes in almost all the states of the South. A new crop of Southern leaders was voicing the complaints of the poor white.

Their favorite target was and is the "outsiders"—primarily journalists, but also scholars and politicians—who have committed the unpardonable sin of bringing the South and its problems to the attention of the nation and the world. Southerners feel that they are struggling against an open conspiracy and a totally hostile external environment and that they can never receive a fair hearing. Nothing inflames a poor white so much as to have some non-Southerner pass a highly critical judgment on the region and publish it in a national or international medium, with no opportunity available for rebuttal or contradiction.

Here the South has a point. Many—perhaps most—of the pictures of the South as a cesspool of prejudice, ignorance, and violence are generated by northern and foreign observers with strong ideological predispositions and no personal knowledge of the South or sympathy for the dilemmas Southerners face. There is a generous dash of supercilious condescension in many Northerners and Europeans as they blithely prescribe for Southern troubles. The demagogue is not alone in his anger at the mass-communications image of the South; he has considerable support among most well-intentioned Southerners as well on this particular point.

Southern opinion generally, in a word, feels that the pace the region is expected to set in the middle of the twentieth century is too fast for it. Whether or not the individual Southerner approves in the abstract of the direction in which the region is moving (and very many do indeed approve), or fights change in baffled rage as do the poor whites, he longs today for a breathing spell, a chance to relax. The South feels that it has already been pushed too far on too many fronts. Its message to the world, stripped to its essentials, may be freely translated as: "Leave us alone for a while!"

The new demagogues of the South, however, have been brought to a discouraging realization: the simple and negativistic white-supremacy crusade they head and on which they have ridden to power is slowly but certainly finding its inevitable end in a cul-de-sac. From Little Rock onward they have only a record of dismal, embarrassing, and undisguisable failure to show for all the flaming oratory and emotional fervor committed to the fight against desegregation. The nation's demand for fundamental change in the South's racial pattern is inescapable, and the demagogue cannot make good his promises.

But mass truculence has always been the demagogue's weapon. The mass movements still exist and he cannot afford to allow them to dissolve. If the issue of race cannot produce enough victories (or even enough sufficiently glorious defeats) to keep his operation prosperous, he must find new targets. Here the very frustration of his racial crusade in a strange way comes to his aid. If he cannot defeat the outside world within the South itself, he must do what he can to carry the battle to his enemies on their own ground. He must, in other words, strike directly at his external scapegoats.

So the old anti-Northern and anti-outside world bias of Southern provincialism has again been pressed into service to carry the burden of the demagogic appeal. The troubles of the South, the poor whites are told, arise directly from the machinations of malevolent individuals or groups, all operating or at least drawing their sustenance from outside the region. The list of the enemies of the South is long and tends to vary with the tactical needs of the moment, but it has recently always included Presidents Eisenhower and Kennedy, Chief Justice Warren, the NAACP, Prime Minister Nehru, the Communist party, the new nations of Africa, the Attorney-General of the United States (whoever he may be at the moment), the Secretary-General of the United Nations, and "weak" Southern politicians like Terry Sanford or the late Estes Kefauver.

The scapegoats perform a dual service. In the first place they are all safely beyond the reach of direct Southern political and governmental power, and thus the demagogue is not expected really to accomplish anything, only to conduct a campaign of harrassment. Second, they perform their ancient but valuable function of diverting the Southern voter's attention from what is going on in his state and local governments. As long as Ross Barnett, Orval Faubus, George Wallace, and James Eastland suffer martyrdom and heroic defeat in defense of "Southern traditions," what patriotic Southerner will question the efficiency or the integrity of his leaders or the direction in which they are taking him? Who worries about scandals in the highway department, the quality of public education, or the eccentricities in the purchase of insurance by the state government when the sanctity of the Southern home and the purity of Southern womanhood are at stake?

Patriotism may or may not in fact be the last refuge of the scoundrel, but it is unquestionably the line of last resistance for the Southern demagogue. No scapegoat has been more useful to him than Communism. Southern patriots of all shades of gentility argue vociferously that the desegregation decisions were initially masterminded in the Kremlin (with an assist from that "Swedish Socialist," Gunnar Myrdal), and that the abasement of white Southern culture ranks high on Moscow's list of priorities.

All this behavior is strictly in character. The contemporary formulation of poor-white protest in the South, however, is a much more significant phenomenon of contemporary American politics than the aberrant antics of earlier outbursts of demagoguery. National security and the maintenance of world peace are the major concerns of all Americans today, and any upset in the delicate balance of the national foreign policy consensus would have massive and unpredictable consequences. The contemporary demagogue is playing with desperately important issues today as he manipulates the shibboleths of unilateralist assertiveness for the enjoyment of his disciples.

IX
THE
UNILATERALIST
PROTEST

ALL CLASSES in the South—the most class-conscious and class-oriented section of the United States—have been materially affected by the tides of change that have swept the region in the past two decades. Every Southerner confronted by the new social and economic forces has made some adjustment, either cataclysmic or compensatory, in his own behavior patterns. The old upper classes, the several strata of long-time urban middle-class whites, and the entire pyramid of Negro society have all made some effort to come to reasonable terms with their new working environment. Only the poor white—for reasons suggested in the data presented in Chapter VIII—has found the transition so painful and so difficult to consummate as to create an infinity of problems and a succession of crises.

The most visible result of poor-white malaise in the postwar South has been the reappearance of a standard, if only intermittently recurring, regional political phenomenon: mass protest. Ever since 1900 the lowest socio-economic stratum of the white population—known colloquially in various localities as the "rednecks," the "woolhats," the "crackers," or the like—has been exploding in protest movements that usually have had their roots in difficulties of personal and group readjustment but have tended almost inevitably to find a final expression in political turmoil of varying degrees of severity. In this way, the historically "normal" political climate in most Southern states, marked by decorum and calm, has been repeatedly shattered by interludes of poor-white protest that brought political emotions to fever pitch. The impact of the poor white on Southern politics has always been negligible when he was inert and controlling when he decided to act.

The contemporary South is obviously in the grip of another of its long series of poor-white *crises des nerfs*. It is not only on issues of foreign relations that the Southern delegation in Congress has shown aberrant tendencies in the postwar period, but on an entire complex of problems of public policy. Southern unilateralism, the extent and the severity of which has been shown in many different ways in the pages of this book, can best be comprehended in terms of its place in the great protest movement rolling across the South today.

THE ROOTS OF SOUTHERN PROTEST

The roots of poor-white protest in the South go deep into the soil of the region as well as into its remote and recent past. There is no need here to retell the entire politcal history of the South since 1865; the story of protest as it is directly relevant to the contemporary era really begins in the latter years of the nineteenth century.

By roughly 1895, after the end of Reconstruction and the recapture of the South by local political forces, each state in the region had drifted into the absolute and oligarchic control of a small but acutely self-conscious leadership elite. The memories of the Civil War and Reconstruction were still very much alive and the South of that era was more than anything else a social monument to the Lost Cause. The oligarchs exercised their power with a fine mixture of aplomb and ruthlessness as they followed their inherent vocation for government. Each of these in-groups conformed to the peculiarities of its own state, but all were astonishingly alike in composition and point of view.

These "better people," from whose ranks responsible Southern political leaders came increasingly to be drawn after Appomattox, quite consistently had their origins in the socio-economic group that emerged from the cauldron of Reconstruction as the dominant voice of the "New South." This was an alliance of the remnants of the old pre-war Bourbons, the new entrepreneureal caste that sprang up after 1876, and urban banking and financial circles with Northern money of which to dispose. Their political strength grew from their monopoly of the only instrument of political power (and the only formal avenue of political advancement) in the South, the Democratic party. Their rule, although authoritarian, was nevertheless gentlemanly—often charming. They controlled their states in almost complete freedom from popular interference, thanks to their deliberate promulgation of a mass myth and the subtle inculcation of popular apathy.

The myth was indispensable to their rule. Its principal component was, of course, the "Southern way of life," with its roots in an idealized ante-bellum past and its major ingredients a rejection of the nationalizing trend of American life, a constant and deliberate glorification of the Lost Cause, and a blind faith in the sagacity, the courage, and the competence of the men who had led the South out of the nightmare of defeat and Reconstruction. There was always the impalpable (and never seriously articulated) but tantalizing half-promise that Southerners, if they remained true to their leaders and firm in the faith, might some day reverse the verdict of Appomattox and vindicate the principles (if not the system) for which the Confederacy had fought and bled. This found its way into folklore. "Save your Confederate money, boys; the South will rise again," Southerners joked and, joking, almost came to believe.

With Elysium thus safely in the past and Utopia somewhere in the indefinite future, there was nothing much for Southerners to do in the political present except to hold the line. Apathy that took its immediate toll in non-voting and its final exaction in almost total emotional uninvolvement in any but the most meretricious aspects of politics became the Southern norm. Southerners cared little for national or international affairs; the continued domination of the Federal government by the Republican party left the South nothing to concern itself with except regional and state politics. The operative dynamic of late nineteenth-century Southern politics all but guaranteed that, other things being equal, nothing could challenge the permanent supremacy of the all-but-official Establishment in each state.

What was true of Southerners generally applied especially to the rural poor white. He of all white citizens desperately needed the solace of the myth, both as an explanation and as a consolation for what was happening to him in politics. His state and local governments did little for him, and what little they did was dreadfully expensive; the low level of public services throughout the South in that era is almost unbelievable today. He drew his major satisfaction from his membership in the same race as his masters and in his identification with the community of the defeated, persuading himself (when he thought about it) that in these ways he shared—if only remotely and vicariously—in the perquisites of power. He lived out his political life as a helot, voting seldom and acting meaningfully almost never, contributing by his very passivity to the continued success of the oligarchy that ruled in his name.

As the 1890's wore on, however, some of the more

discerning poor whites began to be affected by the tides of protest that were beginning to flow from the Midwest. They looked about them with heightened perceptivity and discovered in surprise and anger something of the extent to which they had been and were being short-changed by their myth and their leaders. When this iconoclastic conviction passed the critical point of acceptance and enough poor whites began to talk to each other about the problems and to do something about them, poor-white protest was born. Something new thereupon appeared on the Southern political scene.

The Populist revolt in the South that followed the first real rupture of the myth of the "New South" was many things, most of them strange to the region. Not the least of its significant aspects, particularly in terms of its subsequent consequences, was the extent to which Populism became a bi-racial movement. The poor white, bent finally on achieving some redress for the social and economic injustices perpetrated on him by the oligarchy, took his allies where he found them. And the most convenient and available source of support was the Negro. For a time the Southern confrontation became nakedly one of exploited against exploiter, regardless of race. A disarmingly contemporary flavor still clings to the records of the controversies of that era.

The appeal of Populism, however, was short-lived. By the turn of the century the several Establishments were well on their way to the recapture and rationalization of their former hegemony. The traditional leadership elite, however, had learned a desperately important lesson during the hectic months of Populist agitation: they could never again afford to permit the controlling split in Southern politics to take place along economic and social lines. The poor whites must be prevented from making common cause with the Negro. The only way certainly to avoid any recurrence of this frightening realignment was to ensure that the crucial division in Southern society would henceforth be race. The "Southern way of life" to which all true Southerners would be expected to adhere was therefore decreed to be a white man's South. No more alliances of poor whites with poor blacks against rich whites would be tolerated; the pattern was evermore to be all whites, poor *and* rich, against all blacks.

As a result, despite the simple fact that slavery and the war were forty years gone and the equally glaring truth that the issues of the 1860's were monumentally irrelevant to existing Southern conditions, after 1900 race was elevated to the status of the supreme orienting factor in regional politics. The whole elaborate paraphernalia of segregation that was built up during this period, and the dismantling of which is causing such anguish today, had only one real purpose. Its explicit aim was to make racial identity the overriding fact in the life of the poor white; no matter how degraded his life or how miserable his lot, he was first and last a white man, a brother to all other whites and separated forever from all Negroes by an unbridgeable gulf. There was nothing really new in this idea. It had been developed generations earlier as part of pro-slavery doctrine. What made it novel at the turn of the century, however, was the stridency with which it became an accepted political faith and the speed with which it won almost total acceptance among those it was really designed to victimize, the poor whites themselves.

Race politics, in other words, was intended to deny the poor white any respectable avenue of political action in his own interests. On one side he faced an established political order that was either indifferent or inimical to his concerns and over which he could exercise no control; in a one-party system where only primary elections matter, he who controls the primary machinery rules the constituency. On the other side, however, he saw only the Negro and the combination of public odium and conditioned self-loathing that would be touched off if he admitted to the existence of any purposes or policies in common with the black community.

As the twentieth century multiplied the tensions of the poor white, his urge to protest struggled to find expression. Caught by the shrewd maneuver of his leaders, however, it seemed for a while as if his frustration was complete. Only religion or indiscriminate (and apolitical) violence seemed open to him as routes to catharsis. The high incidence of both fundamentalist revivals and Negro lynchings during this period indicates that both of these outlets found a good number of takers.

But, as it turned out, the oligarchs had not calculated correctly; the poor white was not after all completely boxed in by the iron doctrine of race. One way remained open for him to slip between the Scylla of the Establishment and the Charybdis of the Negro: to organize and act within the limits of his own large social class. Thus was born the poor-white protest movement necessarily led by that exotic regional growth, the Southern demagogue.

THE ROLE OF THE DEMAGOGUE

Poor-white protest in the South in this century has received its only effective leadership from demagogues whose special variations only heighten their essential similarity. The demagogue owes his position in politics entirely to the poor white; his approach to leadership, founded as it is so completely upon the special personality and psychic needs of his constituency, has not varied in any material degree during the half-century or more that he has been practicing his peculiar art. Most important in the demagogue's power is his unique role as the receptacle and the vehicle of the accumulated resentments of his followers. When the poor white goes on the warpath, he has two sets of enemies he wants to hurt: the middle and upper economic classes that oppress him, and the Negro that threatens him. The demagogue's strength lies in his proffer of a way to strike both adversaries at the same time.

The leaders of protest, therefore, normally mount a two-pronged offensive. Part of the time the demagogue rails against "the interests," attacking both economic oppression and social pretensions with complete abandon and playing to the personal and group insecurities intrinsic to any mass movement. He is likely to be something of a social and economic reformer of a showy if unsophisticated sort, with an eye more to the symbolism of a redress of the social and status balance than to any fundamental reordering of relationships. But protest has its racist side as well. The demagogue cannot of course outdo the traditional leaders in pure white-supremacy doctrine, for the "better classes" long ago forged a racial image that in totality and exclusivity is beyond embellishment by the most dedicated extremist. But the demagogue, freed of any necessity to behave like a gentleman before his own people, can and does outdo the traditional norm in the vehemence and the vulgarity with which he preaches his racial message.

Poor-white protest movements led by demagogues have been—at least until very recently—the only conceivable alternatives to oligarchic rule in all the Southern states. Thanks to the inexorable impact of demography, the poor white has been potentially the master of the political life of his region for many years. It required only the birth of mass awareness to make that potential an actuality. The rule of thumb that has governed Southern politics for more than a half-century may be simply stated: traditional leadership can control a state only so long as the poor whites remain relatively passive and unorganized. Once a protest movement attains its critical mass, demagogic victory is inevitable.

But why? From whence comes the urge to protest? What has there been in the political situation of the poor white that has touched off so many demagogic crusades that have spared no Southern state entirely and have kept several racked by almost continuous struggle? What has kept the demagogue alive in spite of the many premature obituaries pronounced over his apparently defunct corpse? To answer these critical questions the Southern political myth must be re-examined.

THE PROFANATION OF THE MYTH

The source of poor-white dissatisfaction, however much it may have varied in detail in place and time, has in essence been the same everywhere and always. For decades the lower socio-economic groups of the white population in the South have been suffering from the growing incompatibility of the social myth they profess with the reality of the South in change. To one who lives a dream, the invalidation of the very premises by which he guides his behavior is inescapably a shattering experience. When the discontinuity between ideal and reality has become great enough—usually in a time of crisis—the Southern poor white has gone on a rampage.

The norm of the idealized "Southern way of life" is rural or small-town in orientation, white Anglo-Saxon Protestant (WASP) in culture, individualistic in philosophy, and pragmatic and unintellectual in point of view: in no important way different in fundamentals, in other words, from the broader American viewpoint. What made the rural Southerner truly different was that the myth remained active in the South long after it had been sharply modified by urbanization and industrialization elsewhere. Until very recently, millions of Southerners saw nothing in their lives that contradicted their own beliefs. The North, the outside world, and even the urban South itself were for generations simply outside the ken of the bulk of the poor whites. Instead they lived in a society made in their own image, ignoring and being ignored by the main lines of American historic development. Even the grinding poverty that was their usual lot and the economic see-saw they rode as the result of the region's dependence on cash-crop agriculture were more or less calmly accepted as necessary costs of the best of all ways of life.

Even race relations seemed to be explicable in terms of the myth. In spite of the militancy of the racial dogma accepted as revealed truth, actual relationships between the races were for most poor whites relatively tension-free. Rural life meant that most came into personal contact with Negroes only seldom, and then only in carefully structured relationships as servants, employees, or service personnel. Here an easy *bonhomie* between the races lubricated the relationship and satisfied the poor white's never very exacting conscience.

The twentieth century, however, has been cruel to the myth. The rural South has lost the comfort of its cultural isolation as mass communications have made the region a national and world concern. The cotton economy has gone awry. The Negro—in defiance of what had long been accepted as a self-evident truth, that the Negro *liked* segregation—has become militant. And the rest of the nation has begun to insist on expecting the Southerner to act more like an American and less like a Southerner.

Even the comfortable rural life-pattern has been slipping away. The figures in Chapter VIII show how poor whites are being increasingly forced to adapt their personal lives to the requirements of a technological society, even to the point of leaving their ancestral bases on the soil to join the urban throngs. In the city they struggle with a completely alien way of living; the nervous tempo of urban life heightens their difficulties. Most upsetting is their jolting discovery of the huge and frightening world that always lay beyond their horizons but with which they could for so long remain uninvolved.

Southern protest, whatever its immediate referents in any particular place, grows ultimately from the almost inchoate resentments of the back-country farmer or small-towner (who may or may not have already moved to the city) in revolt against a changing society that denies him his old place but fails to provide a new and satisfying one. The poor white, facing and fearing a social system in which the old landmarks are being washed away one by one, turns in desperation to the demagogue who seductively promises both the punishment of those responsible for the tensions and the final re-establishment of the old values that are so jeopardized.

The demagogue has a standard set of scapegoats against which to focus poor-white animosity. The arch-enemy of the poor white has, of course, always been the urban Northeast, identified at various times with industry, finance, the Republican party, the Negro and the NAACP, the Roman Catholic Church, organized labor, or—increasingly in late years—Communism. Thus all deviations from the rural white Southern norm (including, significantly, the *urban* white Southern norm) can be, have been, and are today being pointed to as the source of the South's troubles. Against all of these the demagogue preaches a crusade to his constituents. If he is sufficiently convincing he receives a mandate to do battle.

This aspect of demagogic protest is really much more significant to Southern political life than is its simultaneous reformist bent. The local abuses against which demagogues strike are usually real and the reforms they urge occasionally meaningful, but the heart of all protest is the attack on the "enemies of the South." The poor white, inherently inert, will stir himself to political battle only when he becomes convinced that he is fighting for the preservation of his own identity in his own culture against those who for obviously sinister reasons would take it all away.

The great Southern demagogues of the past demonstrated this point with delicacy and clarity. United States Senators all, James Vardaman and Theodore Bilbo of Mississippi, Huey Long of Louisiana, Tom Heflin of Alabama, Tom Watson of Georgia, Cotton Ed Smith of South Carolina, and Robert Rice Reynolds of North Carolina were all adept at playing on the fears and hostilities of their heavily poor-white supporters. All did valiant battle—at least on the surface—with the poor white's enemies: all fought the urban Northeast and all its works, including especially the North's economic and political outposts in the South's larger cities.

As Senators, the demagogues were obliged to speak on foreign affairs. All ran completely true to type, being spokesmen for a short-sighted and belligerent nationalism identified in the popular mind with "isolationism." Each advocated the rejection of a dimly perceived outside world in favor of an obsessive fixation on "our own problems." Each painted a dark picture of the perils awaiting the nation on the international scene. Each foresaw entrapment, impoverishment, and mongrelization as the inevitable outcome of American entry into world affairs. Each professed himself to be striving to spare the long-suffering American (read "Southern") taxpayer the burden of subsidizing hordes of greedy, envious, slothful, and wily foreigners.

For none of these men, be it noted, was this strident unilateralism a matter of intellectual argument or personal belief. They preached "isolationism" because a Southern demagogue must sound like an isolationist; the constituency demands no less. A leader of protest must attack foreigners in the same way and for the same reasons as he must attack the Negro, the federal government, high taxes, and the city. Isolationism to the Southern demagogue is no more than a part of his kit of tools of political leadership. He keeps his power only as long as he can keep his protest movement alive, and foreign affairs—that never disappear, never lose interest, and never reach solution—are extremely useful in agitating the always-tender psyche of the poor white.

This was the fundamental rationale of the demagogic unilateralism of the South during the interwar period that co-existed uncomfortably with the more decorous "internationalism" of traditionalist leadership. The Southern isolationists of the 1920's and 1930's rode the crest of a wave of incensed provincialism. The Ku Klux Klan epitomized the up-country South indignantly denying the existence of a changing world and frantically seeking a set of fundamental truths on which to stand against it. Protestantism, white supremacy, and a chauvinistic nationalism filled the bill.

This was the doctrine each of the great pre-war demagogues served. Tom Watson—one of the originators of the technique—was indeed an "agrarian rebel," but ultimately he rebelled, in perfectly logical sequence, not only against industrialization and finance capitalism but also against the twentieth century and the entire world outside the rural South. Southern unilateralists, in spite of their assiduous manipulation of the crude symbols of "patriotism," were not nationalistic in any real sense; they were provincials on a rampage. Southern poor whites, their basic assumptions threatened by "alien" ideologies and their social and economic system tottering under crisis and change, reacted by turning their backs on hideous reality and seeking to escape into a purer and simpler world of fantasy.

Thus the politics of protest, necessarily unilateralist in foreign policy, conflicted constantly with the "internationalism" of the traditional Southern ruling class during the entire interwar period. The two philosophies agreed on only two points of foreign policy: low tariffs (a symbol for some but for others a stark necessity) and a strong national defense. Where protest was weak or disorganized enough to be kept suppressed, internationally-oriented leaders from the "better" strata of Southern society kept their states committed to their own views; where and when protest broke through, isolationist demagoguery took over. These swings of sentiment, however, were largely stilled by the New

Deal, World War II, and the postwar boom. Southern "internationalism" maintained control between 1945 and 1954 in spite of local and periodic outbursts.

The wave of protest that broke out after the Supreme Court decision on school desegregation in 1954, however, is the most impressive of all the poor-white thrusts to occur in this century. Today the poor white is not fighting merely economic injustice or even racial integration, but rather an enormous transformation of his entire society that will require decades to consummate and rationalize. The protestors in the South are consciously or unconsciously committed to a long period of political activism at a high level of volume and intensity. The voice of protest and all its attendant consequences will be heard in the South for many years more.

There is no doubt of the authenticity of the conversion of so many Southern Congressmen to a unilateralist point of view on foreign policy questions. In a one-party system, the capture of the party organization by the forces of protest confronts the beneficiaries of party politics with a simple and brutal choice: they must either become spokesmen of protest themselves or they must submit to being swept rudely into the discard. The belligerent nationalistic obtuseness that shows through the simple record of the roll calls in very small measure reflects the considered judgment of the Congressmen on the issues themselves, but is instead an eloquent evocation of the point of view on world affairs typical of the enraged poor white. The demagogue, having deliberately sowed the wind of provincialism, has recently been reaping the whirlwind of unilateralism.

THE FOREIGN POLICY OF PROTEST

Contemporary Southern demagogues and their followers go beyond their precursors in one important respect: they have a reasonably complete position on the foreign policy of the

United States. This proclivity to venture into global states-manship owes less to any increase in the general sophistica-tion of the leaders of protest than it does to their realistic appraisal of the political realities of contemporary America. Foreign affairs is a major concern of all Americans today; not even the most opinionated gallus-snapper in the most isolated canebrake seriously believes today that the world can be stopped so the South can get off. If Southerners excluded themselves from the national debate on interna-tional issues, they would shut themselves off from at least three-fourths of the real stuff of the political dialogue in the contemporary United States. So the South has a foreign policy literally in self-defense, and a Southern point of view finds expression on all manner of questions facing the United States in a troubled world.

Unlike his ancestors of the 1920's and 1930's, however, the general point of view of the postwar Southern dema-gogue on foreign policy has not been based on any illusion of secession and withdrawal by the United States. No one except the authentic lunatic fringe in the South today argues for any overt attempt to return to the mass ethos of the era of the rejection of the League of Nations. The foreign-policy rhetoric of protest instead emphasizes even greater American participation in world affairs and the rapid solu-tion of all important outstanding issues of American policy. In any crude quantitative sense, the Southern demagogue is as "internationalist" as the most sophisticated and cosmo-politan New Yorker.

The crucial watershed, therefore, between the foreign policy of Southern protest and the prevailing orthodoxy of the American national consensus should not be formulated so much in terms of "How much foreign policy?" as in those of "How is foreign policy conducted?" The distinction be-tween "multilateralist" and "unilateralist" detailed in Chap-ter I, and on which the analysis in this study has been based, fairly characterizes the difference. The Southern demagogue is a prime example of unilateralism in practice, and his whole theory of foreign policy is based upon this approach.

Unilateralism, it will be recalled, insists that the United States retain under all circumstances the maximum area of freedom of choice and action in foreign policy, while the multilateralist contends that the United States is no exception to the general principle of the interdependence of all states. The unilateralist sees the mission of the United States as requiring the projection of American will and power to arrange affairs in the world to the liking of the nation; the multilateralist defines the central purpose of American policy as one of adjusting as comfortably and safely as possible to an environment over which the United States can exercise no more than partial control.

Under the frustrating and tense conditions of the latter years of the cold war, unilateralism as defined above has made a strong comeback since its apparent death on the battlefields of World War II. The United States has had and is having serious difficulties with its allies, the costs of foreign policy and national defense have spiraled upward, and the international environment has evolved in strange, unpredicted, and complicated ways. Successive administrations in Washington have had little success in developing a consistent and effective foreign policy cast in terms simple and graphic enough to win mass acceptance. Thus disappointed and beset by complexities, buffeted by tensions that provide no compensating relief, and with its idealistic goals tarnished by contact with a corrupt world, the nation stands bemused at a historic crossroads.

Many men of good will in all parts of the country, despairing of their ability to cope with endless crises, have allowed themselves to slip into the trap laid by the simpler dogma of unilateralism. Although many of its detailed explanations and policy pronouncements are rejected, its illusory dynamics and gratifying self-image have promised solace and certainty. Let the rest of the world go hang, runs the argument; let the United States trust no one, retain its faith and its courage, keep its powder dry, and pursue only its own interests. This is the only possible route to national salvation.

This thesis, stripped of its intellectual content and presented with maximum emotional effect, is the general foreign policy message of Southern protest. The South today (along with much of the Southwest and scattered islands in the Middle and Far West) is the center of neo-unilateralism in the United States. The thirty ideological Southern Congressmen identified earlier are complete subscribers to the doctrine; the nineteen "waverers" fellow-travel with the militants with little sign of embarrassment or discomfort.

The three multilateralist aspects of current American policy that draw the sharpest fire from Southern demagoguery are the United Nations, foreign aid, and American policy toward the emerging nations, particularly the new states of Africa. Each of these three apparently insoluble and certainly interminable problems symbolizes the demands of a world the Southern protestor rejects as either beyond his comprehension or far removed from his interests. The United Nations, for example, is usually condemned as an unwarranted interference with American freedom of action; foreign aid is a waste of national resources that could be better spent at home or on military defense; the new nations, besides suffering from the basic shortcoming of being non-white in population, tend ominously toward the intolerable posture of neutralism, demand too much from the United States in a manner completely lacking in appropriate and necessary deference, and give far too little support to the United States in return.

Obviously there is a connection that links all three of these sore spots. The United Nations is conceived as dominated by a non-Western, non-white, anti-colonialist bloc that is at best blind to the issues of the cold war and at worst covertly pro-Communist. Most American foreign aid, furthermore, goes to those very states that repay American generosity with insults and a studied failure to "know their place." All in all, it seems to many Southerners as if the darkest predictions of Tom Heflin and Bob Reynolds are being fulfilled and that lesser breeds—outwitting idealistic but impractical American statesmen—have finally won access to the sources of American strength and are gorging themselves on the treasure accumulated by the efforts of earlier and sturdier generations of Americans.

If the Southern unilateralist is opposed to the United Nations, foreign aid, and the Afro-Asian bloc, what is he for? He is, first and foremost, in favor of the cold war, preferably fought to a finish. He has his own special reasons for being vocally anti-Communist as well as for enthusiastically embracing the nationally accepted set of hostilities; indeed, he modestly confesses himself to be the greatest Communist-hater of them all. To the demagogue, the cold war is to be fought at the maximum level of tension at all times; compromise is appeasement and relaxation cowardice. His announced goal is "victory," and he rings the changes on the sense of fulfillment and vindication that will ensue when the glorious triumph is finally in hand. In truth, however, a Soviet collapse and the final justification of American effort would suit his real purposes less than the indefinite prolongation of the struggle; with the reduction or elimination of the Communist threat would also disappear his major issue.

Southerners, however, tend to be more than a little dubious about the larger concepts Americans often use to define the heterogeneous grouping of states that make up the coalition the United States leads. Neither "the West" nor the "free world" is an especially popular term in the South, for far too many of the allies of the United States are found wanting in many Southern eyes. There is still a residue of the old Anglophilia, some admiration for German military efficiency, and—at least in some sections—a tolerant condescension toward Latin Americans. But France, Italy, and the smaller European states are all in some important way objectionable to the South. Non-European allies (with a few exceptions noted below) are simply untrustworthy and beneath serious attention, to be used on occasion for American purposes but to be kept safely under control at all times.

For it is important to bear in mind that to the Southerner, the cold war is conceived as a purely American operation. The United States pays the piper, and for it to call the tune is no more than simple justice. Intra-alliance disputes (except for an occasional squabble with Britain) are to be dealt with summarily and directly by the prompt exertion of American power and the early submission of the recalcitrant ally. All allies, as a matter of fact, are potential sources of trouble, prone to weakness or cowardice in the face of the Soviet threat. Any associate of the United States is to be judged almost entirely in terms of its commitment to American purposes and the military contribution it makes to American strength. Any failure in either dedication or performance materially reduces its value and to a corresponding degree the concern Americans should have for the erring state.

From the regional xenophobia are exempted, at least partially, a limited number of foreign countries. These preferred states—not all of them allies of the United States—form a rather disparate group, but each satisfies at least one important requirement. To be acceptable to the Southern unilateralist, a state must either make a substantial military contribution to the United States while accepting *de facto* American political domination (Turkey), be highly articulate and militant in its anti-Communism (Spain), flatter the United States overtly and uninterruptedly (South Korea, at least in the era of Syngman Rhee), or be on the same side as the South in racial or colonial policy (South Africa, Portugal). The strong pro-British bias in Southern thinking still exists but is much weakened; historically, this position has always been identified with traditional upper-class Southern society and has never had any great appeal for poor whites.

The demagogues are again consistent in backing their strong plea for unilateralism with a vigorous advocacy of a high level of military preparedness and defense spending by the United States. The South has always been a leader in this respect, supporting the armed forces with its sons as well as with its votes, the poor white no less than his higher-status brethren. Here real tradition and immediate regional interest neatly coincide, because (in spite of a heavy shift toward the West) a large share of the defense dollar has tended to be finally spent in the South, either for wages or for procurement.

The pro-military bias in unilateralist Southern thinking goes still further, and extends to the actual conduct of foreign relations. The South's reaction to international crisis has always been, and is more than ever today, geared toward direct—preferably military—action. Southerners have consistently shown a significantly greater "expectation of war" than has the remainder of the nation, and today seem more convinced that the final resolution of the dilemmas of the contemporary era will be found in military terms. In a crisis Southern spokesmen can be counted on to take the militant line, to make threats of military action by the United States, and to be free with the imagery of "meeting force with force."

What does all this mean? How does this distinct and powerful approach to foreign policy fit into the context of protest today? Why is unilateralism in the South linked with social change; why has the discovery of a new and larger world led to a demand that the South and the nation "take arms against a sea of troubles" in the forlorn hope of obliterating the demands of history? The crux of this entire study may be quickly suggested in the answer to these questions.

To the protesting South, foreign policy is more a means to a larger social end than it is an end in itself. The contemporary Southerner is at heart less interested in the discovery of solutions to international questions facing the nation than he is in the rediscovery of his own identity and of a viable place in a new society. He is therefore really only slightly involved in the specific issues that arise from the interplay of national policies on the world scene; on the contrary, he is obsessed with whatever personal, group, regional, and national value-gratifications are to be derived from the fact of American participation in international relations. He approaches foreign affairs, in a word, much more in terms of process than of substance.

This suggests that in his search for an improvement in his depleted store of self-respect and the rejuvenation of the myth of his mastery of the environment, he minimizes and conceptually often rejects the role of diplomatic finesse in foreign affairs. He finds satisfaction only in direct action. Very little personal vindication can be derived from a low-key compromise between the United States and any adversary, at least as compared with the psychic exhilaration that comes with the public humiliation of a capitulating enemy. The coercive implementation of foreign policy, the instinctual preference of most Southerners, thus generates a substantial domestic dividend that in some measure offsets its limited relevance to the realities of American policy. The ambiguities of contemporary Southern society, in other words, become easier for the poor white to endure if there are some satisfactions to be won vicariously through a strong international line taken by the United States.

All of this, admittedly, is in the grand tradition of American unilateralism and is by no means uniquely Southern. But Southerners are saying it today who never said it before, give much greater evidence of being willing to back their words with action, and lead the nation in their apparent commitment to the doctrine. Unilateralism is a key ingredient in Southern protest today, both in the extent to which the individual feels himself involved in the problem and in the evangelistic zeal with which believers reinforce their stand and aggressively seek new converts.

It is one thing for an "average citizen" to disagree with a resolution of the General Assembly of the United Nations, to be "against foreign aid," or to approve of *apartheid* in South Africa as a general principle. It is quite another matter, however, for him to attend a fiery mass meeting at which resolutions demanding the impeachment of the Chief Justice of the United States Supreme Court and condemning American purchase of United Nations bonds are whooped through as of equal relevance and importance.

If, in other words, the South is actually passing through an era of mass protest, mob violence in Mississippi and the Southern revolt against foreign aid are part of the same pattern. There is little especially right-wing about Southern unilateralism today, and nothing that is truly nationalistic. Shrewd demagogues may make their working alliances with established circles of economic power in their respective states (as several have done), but Southern protest—for all its long love affair with the symbolism of the Constitution— is not a conservative or reactionary movement. It is instead in the leveling tradition of Populism and Progressivism and except for the recurring appeal of the sloganizing call for tax reduction, none of the arguments of American big-business conservatism really receives a sympathetic hearing from the poor whites.

Nor, in reality, can any hard and fast conclusions be drawn from the rise of the Republican party and the birth of the two-party system in many Southern cities. Southern Republicans are not a party either of protest or of uni-lateralism. They draw only a few recruits from the poor whites, since their major appeal is to urban, upward-mobile, middle-class elements in both Negro and white populations. In particular situations, protest may be temporarily turned

to the benefit of local Republicans on non-presidential issues, but only if there is no sufficiently militant demagogue
within Democratic ranks. A multilateralist Democratic candidate for Congress in a dynamic and changing district, for
example, may be so unfortunate as to find both upper-
middle class Republicans and poor-white protestors arrayed
against him. When this situation arises, his electoral prospects are dim indeed.

What the foreign-policy arguments of Southern protest
amount to in the final analysis is little more than an
attempt to argue out of existence a world with which the
poor white feels he cannot cope, exactly as he hopes to argue
out of existence the new South in which he does not feel
at home. The states where the great foreign-policy shifts
have occurred are also the states where the impact of socio-
economic change has been the most difficult to absorb.
Crisis within a state has an almost automatic effect on the
international outlook of its Congressional spokesmen. The
changing relationships among the poor whites, their Southern environment, and the outside world form the keys to
the understanding of deviant Southern thinking on international affairs, whether in the poor-white suburbs of Baton
Rouge or Richmond or in the halls of Congress.

CONTEMPORARY SOUTHERN MULTILATERALISM

What of the multilateralist areas of the contemporary South?
How can one explain the fact that no less than forty-three
of the 126 Southern Congressmen showed themselves consistently committed to the traditional Southern position and
that nineteen others defected only on the issue of foreign
aid? Have social and economic change had no effect on the
political outlooks of these constituencies? Has protest passed
them by?

As a beginning point from which to develop answers to
these questions that so obviously bear upon the thesis of

this chapter, one postulate seems inescapable: there is no portion of the South that has completely escaped change and none in which some form of protest is not a factor in the political equation. But the point has already been made that it is not the mere birth and activity of a protest movement that is relevant to a change in the outlook of a Congressman or of an entire district, but rather a much more critical event: the capture of political control by the protestors and the subsequent registration of their opinions as policy. Looked at in this way, the questions in the previous paragraph come to one central concern: why has protest captured the districts it has but not succeeded in the remaining multilateralist (or at least non-unilateralist) areas?

The sixty-two districts that do not voice the foreign policy of protest in any important way can be broken down into two major classes. The first group consists of those in which the effects of change, although apparent and visible, have nonetheless been of a sufficiently limited nature to keep the resulting protest well below the critical point. This would suggest that smaller shifts away from agriculture and relatively minor increases in urbanization and industrialization—in other words, a less distinct move away from at least the externals of "normal" Southern life—tend to produce political climates less conducive to large-scale protest. The second type of non-protesting district would appear to be one with so advanced an urbanized and industrialized an economy and so dynamic a life pattern that further change can be taken in stride without unbearable tension. Here protest finds a plethora of outlets, thus making its concentration in political action less likely; here also the fabric of existence is much more varied, and individual frustrations can be worked off in a broad variety of areas of personal and social action without spilling over entirely into political affairs.

The two sorts of Congressional districts in which protest is less likely to seize control, in other words, are those in which change is either too small or too great to be productive of demagogic mass movements. It is the South-in-transition that is especially vulnerable to the unilateralist protest. Those parts of the South which have not yet entered the cycle of change and those parts in which change has gone so far as to create virtually an entirely new society all seem to have adequate, built-in resistance to the thrust of the demagogue.

But this generalization, supported though it may be by many quantitative data and corroborative correlations, should not be taken too literally. It is clear, for example, that by and large the smaller Southern city undergoing fairly rapid growth and industrial expansion is the most fertile hunting ground of the demagogue. Nevertheless there are some major Southern metropolitan areas which are and have been for several years hotbeds of protest. Many relatively stagnant areas are safely under the control of multilateralist Congressmen, but many others—statistically indistinguishable—are firmly unilateralist and counted as centers of unilateralist activism. If the roots of protest are ultimately psychic, all the rich variety of which human emotions are capable finds expression in the political life of the contemporary South and too rigid a formula is an invitation to analytical errors of awesome magnitude.

One of the intangible and literally immeasurable elements in this situation, for example, is the influence of individual Congressmen. At least a dozen districts could be cited in which multilateralist votes are cast by Representatives in defiance of large-scale actual or potential protest movements at home. Most of these Congressmen are very senior, quite influential, and compellingly prestigeful both in the House and at home. So long as they choose to retain their posts, they can afford to vote as they please, secure in the knowledge that their repudiation by the voters is an exceptionally remote possibility. But all of them are mortal. Some day they will retire and their constituencies, free from the impact of their personalities and their prestige, will be able to choose a successor more in keeping with their predispositions of the moment. The field will then be open for the protestors to take over the party machinery and the district.

Nor can one safely postulate how much change, how much urbanization, and how much of an increase in per capita income is enough to push a district safely over the line into big-city multilateralism and beyond the range of unilateralist protest. Here are too many variables to permit an abstract formulation: the gross number of unassimilated ruralites active in the population at any moment, the overall climate of political and social life, the relative frequency and severity of tension-producing crises, and so on. Each metropolitan center would appear to have its own unique critical point beyond which it is immune to the pernicious effects of protest. New Orleans, Atlanta, and Miami would appear to have passed this watershed stage; Birmingham, Richmond, and several Texas cities have not yet done so.

Those urban areas that are firmly beyond the reach of demagogic protest conduct a surprisingly mature discussion of international issues. The voices of the demagogue, the radical right, the religious fundamentalists, and other irrational appeals are heard, but—unlike in most other areas of the South—their arguments are met, answered, and on occasion refuted. Something approximating the tone of debate in other parts of the country takes place as alternative positions are formulated and pressed without leaving an almost clear field to the ministrations of the leaders of protest.

It should be kept in mind that the multilateralist areas are also those that evidence the greatest degree of "liberalism" in their Congressmen and that the unilateralist areas score the lowest on the same scale of liberalism. Here also the distinction should be drawn between those that merely tolerate a liberal Congressman because he has been in the House many years and "must know what he's doing," and those generating in some way local political support for and agitation in favor of particular measures that contribute to the liberal image. The logical conclusion here is borne out by the facts: each of the relatively unchanged multilateralist areas tends to allow its Congressman to vote the liberal line if he wishes, while the heavy metropolitan areas generally are more active in reinforcing whatever proclivity toward liberalism the Congressmen may themselves have.

The prognosis for multilateralism in the South, at least in roughly the next decade, must be on the available evidence a divided one. As the South continues its inevitable metamorphosis into an urbanized and industrialized part of the United States, that type of multilateralist position which is rooted in a dynamic metropolitan area with a political temper reminiscent of national patterns will become more common. Each such region, as it comes finally to terms with its social and economic destiny, will find fewer and fewer of its citizens interested in organized protest and less and less for these activists to protest about. Unilateralist ideology will thus cease to be an orthodoxy and will lapse into the same category as vegetarianism, prohibitionism, and anti-evolutionism as vaguely embarrassing eccentricities.

But, as the traditional South is passing away, so also must the traditional bases of multilateralism. The "country squire" theory of Congressional representation cannot outlive the constituencies that made it possible. There will be primarily rural districts in the South for an indefinite period, but by 1960 they had already ceased to be the Southern norm. The end of apathy and the birth of political awareness, neatly symbolized by the breakneck speed with which the two-party system is being extended in the South, will mean the final disappearance of the Congressman who can vote as he pleases. With him will go the last remnants of the kind of Southern "internationalism" which was largely responsible for the passage of the Lend-Lease Act in 1941 and the Marshall Plan in 1948.

A Southern Congressman a decade hence, in other words, will be multilateralist only to the extent to which he is supported by an active consensus at home. He will face unilateralist opposition indefinitely, although it will probably become progressively less ideological and therefore more susceptible to reasonable counter-argument. But he must reconcile himself to the same course of persuasion and the same cultivation of his sources of support as do his colleagues from other parts of the nation. Although his lot will be in this sense a more difficult one, at the same time it will permit him a broader range of choice and a more flexible agenda of discussion.

Thus, just as protest is clearly linked with the incidence of unilateralism on international questions, its longevity and lines of evolution contribute largely to the present and the future of multilateralist attitudes. The South is in transition, and any era of change is painful and upsetting. But no one should forget also that the South is changing *from* something *to* something else. The outlines of the South of the future are already apparent. It will be a South in which protest—although probably never disappearing—will be cast in terms and implemented in ways less exotically Southern and more in keeping with the political necessities of a mature nation. If this hopeful prediction is fulfilled, protest will cease to be an upsetting and disruptive force and will instead contribute to the vigor and vitality of the democratic process in the entire nation. The consequences for a healthy political community and an effective foreign policy for the United States cannot help but be favorable.

X
THE SIXTIES
AND AFTER

THE IMMEDIATELY preceding chapters have made one point with increasing emphasis: the South's Congressional delegation has been changing its position on international issues in response to the massive social, economic, and political changes that are shaking the region. Furthermore, the South has not yet completed its metamorphosis; the transitional era in which contemporary Southerners are destined to live has a great many years more to run. The data advanced in this study, therefore, are not purely historical and of an only retrospective significance, but instead point to a continuing and probably long-lasting cycle of change. The South's attitude toward world affairs, it would seem, will remain a matter of widespread concern for a long time.

There is considerable reason, therefore, for the attempt in this final chapter to develop some projections of future trends in Southern attitudes toward world affairs both in and out of Congress. Although it is true that the Southern shift, at least through 1962, had not succeeded in bringing about any real disruption of the national foreign policy consensus, who can be certain that this condition will endure indefinitely? Trends in other sections of the country would suggest that the role of the Southern bloc may well become critical to the passage of important legislation in future years. If the South continues to evolve toward a hard-line unilateralism, the task of national leadership will be that much more difficult, while a reversal of recent trends would provide a built-in cushion against the shock that would follow any new successes of the radical right in those non-Southern areas of the nation in which the movement is strong.

What evidence is available on which to base long-range predictions of the future course of Southern opinion on world affairs? Where will the South stand throughout the rest of the 1960's and in later decades? What factors will influence the course of Southern attitudes? Which of the contemporary points of view in the South is the wave of the future and which the voice of the past? The answers to these and similar questions will begin to sketch the dimensions of the new Southern consensus.

Change is the order of the day in the South. In political terms, the principal effect of relatively sudden and usually drastic overturns in the familiar rhythms of Southern life has been the rapid reappearance of political awareness among Southern citizens. The traditional norm of political life was long one of tolerant apathy toward matters of public policy and public office so long as the society remained familiar, relatively calm, and adequately rewarding to its members. The sudden uprooting of entire segments of the Southern way of life alerted millions of Southerners, the poor whites in the van, to the fact that something was afoot. Their political antennae, long atrophied from disuse, were rehabilitated with remarkable speed. The Southerner became in a special way a newly political animal.

The South today is looking for answers to its problems in a number of areas, of which the political is by no means the least important. A heightened political sensitivity, growing from and coupled with the general malaise incident to major social change, has produced and is still producing a generous harvest of unprecedented political fruit. Although many of these novel formulations—perhaps most—relate directly to the internal problems of the South and to "domestic affairs" generally, the figures cited throughout this study indicate that foreign affairs has come in for its share of attention as well.

Although it is safe to say that the South as a region has suffered change and undergone an increase in overall political awareness, not all Southerners nor all areas (or Congressional districts) in the South have endured the same kinds of shock or reacted with the same degree of increased sensitivity. The several points of view on foreign affairs discoverable among the South's House delegation may be used to separate all the 126 districts into rough categories using the criterion of change-plus-response as the device of classification.

In very general terms, three major groups existed in 1962 within the total number of Congressmen from the South. The most obvious was the unilateralists and their auxiliaries. The multilateralist-pragmatic contingent is larger than the unilateralists and waverers combined, but the quantitative difference between the two schools of thought becomes less significant when the multilateralists are, as they should be, divided in two. One sub-group of those Southern Congressmen who generally support the policies advocated by the executive branch draws its support from the relatively sophisticated constituencies in the larger urban (and urbane) centers, while the other—the anachronistic residual category from which almost all other points of view have been subtracted—reflects the feelings (or lack of feelings) of populations relatively untouched by the new trends and clinging to old patterns, points of view, and leadership.

In terms of the magnitude of change each group has undergone and the degree of escalation in its threshold of political awareness, these three major groups may be arranged in a rank order. The old-line multilateralists, who show the least response to change, form the first category; the unilateralists, caught in the middle of as yet undigested change, can be placed in the middle; the big-city multilateralists (without ascribing any superiority in insight or virtue to them) may be considered as the spokesmen for constituencies that have completed the essentials of the transition and which, therefore, reflect pretty much the same span of opinions as does much of the rest of the country.

In this way the predominantly rural and small-city districts that continue to send multilateralist Congressmen to Washington may be considered areas of incipient (but not yet realized) change. In many of these, as the statistics suggest, the principal effect of the new patterns of Southern life has been only somewhat to speed up the steady seepage away of population and to widen the gap between the income level of those who stay behind and their more aggressive brethren in the cities. Change so far, in other words, has been no more than peripheral. In certain other districts of this type, however, the transformation has already begun and the face of their societies is being sharply modified. Political awareness is on the rise and a perceptible thrust toward a modification in international outlook is operative. It cannot become controlling, however, because Congressmen from these districts tend to be veterans with all the awesome seniority and political impregnability that is the lot of the long-term Southern legislator. The Congressman himself, in other words, has not changed and does not feel that he needs to do so, freed as he is by the tenacious one-party principle from any direct reliance on short-term constituency consensus.

In either of the two cases, however, change is on the way. In the first type, the trends may be delayed in their effect but cannot be warded off indefinitely; in the second, even senior Southern Democrats are mortal and must some day be replaced by less solidly-situated and stubborn incumbents. If one adds such epicyclic factors as the continuing renaissance of the Republican party and the capricious way the expansion of industry sometimes occurs, the prospects of an eventual upset and about-face are increased. The old-line multilateral approach is a disappearing phenomenon because the social conditions that made this attitude workable in the first place are themselves being eroded.

In contrast, the militant unilateralist districts are, by and large, those in which the forces of change have bitten the most deeply and disruptively. Change to a district like this may take either of two forms. It may be negative, in that population and economic activity decrease absolutely, or at least increase far below regional norms; it may, on the other hand, be positive in the form of a sudden influx of population, industry and income. In either instance, for reasons examined in detail in Chapters VIII and IX, awareness comes to the bulk of the population suddenly and unpleasantly. This is the province of the poor white protestor and the happy hunting ground of the demagogue.

In this group one finds both the stagnating rural districts in which the most productive manpower drifts steadily away and the booming, newly prosperous, small-city constituencies with wholesale infusions of industrial payrolls and rising labor forces. Here also one finds, for somewhat different reasons, "old" Southern industry, trapped by high costs and inefficient techniques and beset by foreign competition. Here too one tends to encounter the new Southern managerial caste, technically well educated but caught within a sharply circumscribed socio-political outlook, working often in unadmitted alliance with local demagogues on the one hand and with the national network of the radical right movement on the other. All these disparate elements, each for its own reasons, have no reluctance to capitalize on the resentments of the poor whites.

Again without any implications that they are pre-eminent in wisdom or intellect, it would appear that the third group, the multilateralists from relatively urbanized and high-income districts, represent the South of the future. In these districts the tempo and the temper of political awareness is very much in keeping with national norms. The Congressmen these districts send to the House are in no way intrinsically superior to those of any other group—indeed, in personal characteristics they differ only in their marginally lower median age and somewhat broader range of experience. They are, however, directly responsible and responsive to a constituent consensus that is both broader and more pluralistic than that of either of the first two categories.

This family of districts seems to have won its way through to a mastery of the important ingredients of the Southern metamorphosis. Not that they have stabilized; actually, in most ways they are among the most dynamic parts of the South. But the shape of their future social and economic structure is already apparent, and later developments will almost certainly follow the lines already laid out. Their ultimate destiny is to be that of the rest of the nation.

Politically, this implies a new rationale. Two-party controversy is almost a reality already in most of them, and a Congressman from any of these districts must abandon any dreams of enjoying a blank-check mandate or serving as the voice of a single and tightly integrated consensus. Substantial change in the socio-economic sub-structure of

American politics has always brought about modifications in constituent opinion, and the shifting, coalition-based nature of voter support so characteristic of the representative function outside the South is becoming a commonplace thing to Southern Congressmen from these districts.

In international outlook this group is largely in tune with Northeastern, Western, and urban Midwestern attitudes. There is among their number a general acceptance of the principle of multilateralism on which American policy has been based since 1945, less for ideological or philanthropic reasons than in response to considerations of the most practical and immediate necessity. Such acquiescence in a general line, however, in no way implies a blanket endorsement of every maneuver but merely a basic predisposition toward sympathetic and usually favorable study of each new initiative. The multilateralist commitment of these Congressmen cannot be taken for granted in any single case, but must be won each time by the force of executive leadership exercised both upon the Congressman himself and upon public attitudes at large within the constituency.

So—to reiterate—the old-line multilateralists are in essence still successfully resisting change, the unilateralists are caught in the midst of change, and the new-type multilateralists have gone through the change and have figuratively come out on the far side. The first group either does not face enough organized protest to force a new approach or can successfully resist it, the second is serving as the voice of protest, and the third has kept protest to a sufficiently low level that it is no more than one factor in a complex equation rather than the dominant force.

Placing these three groups of districts along the change-awareness-response continuum raises a new possibility. Can one postulate a time sequence? Can it be argued that an old-line multilateralist district, once it has absorbed enough change and developed sufficient awareness, moves into a

unilateralist position, to remain there only until its transformation is completed and it evolves into new-type multilateralism as its permanent outlook?

Certainly some such formulation is accurate if applied
to the South as a whole. The sort of old-line multilateralism
characteristic of the South immediately after World War I
and immediately prior to World War II, the traditional
Southern outlook, is becoming passé today; its narrow political base and its motivations so obviously stemming from
the prejudices and interests of a particular social group are
inadequate for the needs of a South in change. It is also
evident that the major trend into unilateralism documented
in these pages is one reflection of the cataclysmic overturn
in Southern society. Certainly also, the South can reach a
new plateau of stability only after it has absorbed and
learned to live with the new rhythm history has forced
upon it. This time sequence is indeed the major argument of
this study.

But the South is far too complex a social, economic,
and political phenomenon to justify applying any such
mechanical diagnosis and prognosis to each district. Every
constituency will have to work out its own response to the
forces of change and develop its outlook on world affairs
in its own way. The several elements in the change will continue to have their effect in the future as they have in the
past in different combinations in different areas.

For example, Southern politics being what they are,
it is probable that a hard core of old-line multilateralists
will be found in the Southern House delegation for many
years regardless of what happens in their districts. Southerners have in the past showed a devotion to abstract principle and political ritual almost incomprehensible to outsiders, and there is no reason to believe that this preference
for the old ways will be speedily outgrown by all Southern
voters. One thinks in this connection of certain areas of
Alabama, Tennessee, Kentucky, Arkansas, east Texas, and

even Georgia in which multilateralist Congressmen will continue to be chosen by means of one-party rule and organization domination. Some of these men will undoubtedly cast some of their votes against particular programs—as many have done on foreign aid already—but by and large their response will continue to reflect tradition and propriety rather than any activist approach.

Another element of eccentricity is the unpredictable course of poor-white protest. Built upon an emotionalized rejection of social change, protest can be a powerful force, but it is also one of uncertain direction and duration. To the extent that a unilateralist posture in a Congressman is grounded upon short-term animosities in the lower social strata of his constituency, he must be always prepared to face the prospect of a sudden disintegration of the protest movement or at least its abandonment of foreign policy as an issue. The unilateralist, in Congress or not, who is persuaded of the rationality and morality of his position is personally prone to accept a comprehensive ideology of foreign affairs. If an ideological Congressman succeeds in incorporating such a formulation of international questions into the consensual base on which he operates, he has a much more solid and durable hold on his followers than if he merely rides the crest of a wave of hostility.

This is to say that a strong unilateralist Congressman needs something more than the sheer force of poor-white protest in order to make his position secure over the long term. He must have a network of doctrinal-oriented supporters in the party, the press, and the community of opinion generally. He must seek to lead and shape opinion rather than merely reflect it. He must aggressively satisfy both those whose protest grows from social and economic discontent and those for whom foreign policy raises larger issues of ideology.

Another ingredient in this complex problem, always difficult to specify or quantify, is the overall impact of race relations on the international outlook of a district. Although no clear relationship between foreign policy attitudes and Southern feelings about the changing status of the Negro can be pinpointed, that racial matters have a powerful effect on the Southern state of mind at any moment scarcely needs mentioning and obviously does not demand proof. The historical record suggests that a racial crisis in a state goes far to focus all forms of Southern protest on this single issue, and that at least some foreign-policy fallout may be expected from racial controversy.

Those states in which ideological unilateralism is the most widespread in foreign policy tend also to be those in which ideological absolutes shape racial attitudes; race crises have had a significant time connection with changes in foreign-policy outlook in Arkansas, Virginia, South Carolina, and Georgia.

It is probably safe to generalize that any particular region, district, metropolitan area, or even state in which a serious race crisis takes place may well, as a result, spill over into ideological unilaterialism or at least have its already-expressed opinion in this regard much strengthened. On the other hand, a constituency in which unilateralism has not yet become a powerful factor, or one in which it lacks a strong ideological base, may well be spared going all the way on foreign policy if it manages to avoid serious racial incidents.

These observations suggest the conclusion that an old-line district not yet responsive to change does not necessarily face a unilateralist phase before it finally adjusts to a modernized version of multilateralism. A constituency can accept the requirements of a new life pattern and with it a more broadly based view of world affairs without ever changing the overall tenor of the votes of its Congressman. Such a shift from old to new multilateralism, however, requires that several factors be present while change is taking place.

Most important probably is the pace at which events move. Change must be neither too rapid (which would tend to raise protest to an irresistible level) nor too slow (which would create other tensions appropriate to the appearance of a demagogue). The direction and content of change as well is also critical, for the statistical evidence of the importance of a high and rising per capita income to a multilateralist outlook is indisputable. There must also be, if the more extreme forms of unilateralist dogma are to be refuted, adequate alternatives to either the demagogue or the increasingly ineffectual traditionalist leadership in the form of political spokesmen who voice the newer issues in meaningful terms. If the correct set of conditions obtain (as they have in a number of districts that have already made the change), the constituency may avoid unilateralism entirely.

Nor can it be argued that the direction of a district presently unilateralist is inevitably toward some form of more sophisticated multilateralism. Many unilateralist constituencies are continuing to change, but in directions that reinforce controlling tendencies rather than offset them. Population loss, increasing reliance on low-income industry and declining agriculture, and a greater and greater disparity in per capita income compared with regional and national averages are trends that do not argue for any early awakening of greater international sophistication. It would seem rather that such unilateralist districts will find in their steadily worsening situations confirmation of their darkest suspicions about the new order and a stronger tendency to resist rather than to accommodate to its demands. Eccentricity and (in a statistical sense) abnormality are by no means uncommon in Southern politics even in routine circumstances; under the impetus of increasing tensions, it seems at least possible that they will continue to be so.

For a unilateralist district to reverse itself into broad-gauge multilateralism will in most cases require more than a conscious effort of will on the part of its leadership. The social and economic trends that made unilateralism possible in the first place will have to be reversed and a new basis for consensus developed. Neither of these is an easy or simple task; both will require long effort and considerable time to consummate. From this generalization, of course, should be excepted those few unilateralist constituencies in which the bases for multilateralism are already present and in which the transformation can be effected by means primarily political. In the bulk of the cases, however, no such quick and easy formulation is possible.

Unilateralism, therefore, will continue to constitute a part of the Southern approach to foreign policy for many years. It will be a factor in the consensus in almost every district, and will be dominant in a sizeable number. The influence of ideology—always a solace in time of trouble—will show no signs of disappearance. One may assume, therefore, that the unilateralist position will continue indefinitely to attract supporters and advocates.

Finally, there seems little ground to assume that the new-type multilateralists will do very much back-sliding. Not all of them, of course, have thoroughly digested the implications of their new place in the American scene, and counter-pressures are constant. Political controversy, already high, will probably grow in intensity and ubiquity, and the possibility exists that the interactions of electoral and party struggle will result in the appearance in the House from time to time of unilateralist Congressmen from normally multilateralist districts. This is to be expected in any constituency in which there is a pattern of active political life and in which clearly opposed points of view are pitted against each other in rough equality. But, by and large, the multilateralists who have survived the metamorphosis will remain in control.

Their number, furthermore, seems destined to grow. A

few major metropolitan areas in the South, in defiance of the clear regional trend, are firmly unilateralist, but most have placed themselves clearly in the multilateralist camp. As other urban centers increase in population, economic activity, and sophistication to the point where they can be logically included with the ten or dozen really modern centers in the contemporary South, they will in turn probably make their final identification with the multilateralist rationale of foreign affairs. The South is a far cry from megalopolis, but the more it approximates the life-rhythms of the urban Northeast the more its international outlook will be the same as its model.

For the remainder of the 1960's and thereafter, Southern thought and action in international affairs will continue and in some ways intensify the trends made visible during the 1950's. The pattern of unilateralism so obvious after 1957 will certainly remain operative and will probably grow. But it would be both premature and unjustified to predict that rigid unilateralism is the true wave of the future in Southern attitudes or that its advocates will ever completely dominate Southern thought. Unilateralism is a factor of great importance and self-evident force, but it is by no means the entire Southern story.

Multilateralism as well will be a major factor in the Southern equation. It is impossible to foretell its exact course; no one can be certain that the inevitable increase in the new-type multilateralism will be so rapid as to offset the defection of old-line multilateralist districts to resurgent unilateralism. If a prediction must be made, it seems likely that the unilateralist inroads into the mutilateralist group will bulk—at least for several more Congresses—larger than the slipping away of unilateralist Congressmen to the multilateralist camp.

This is, however, a relatively short-run view tied to that frame so beloved of all analysts, the "foreseeable future." In the long run the South cannot escape its ultimate fate of complete integration with the main stream of American life. In so finally rejoining the United States, this unique region will fall heir to the common American lot of political outlooks and social dynamics. This clearly implies that the South's international point of view will some day come to rest pretty much within the bounds of the controlling national consensus of the time. Since 1945, the national norm has been one of pragmatic multilateralism, while the South has evolved in a contrary direction. No one can now foresee the time or the historic circumstances under which the South's path of development will again intersect that of the nation as a whole.

In its final rendezvous with America, the South will display and voice a complete range of international opinions. None of the attitudes it will incorporate, however, will any longer be especially Southern. Big-city multilateralism in the South today grows to only a very minor extent from unique Southern conditions, but partakes of the broader (if not necessarily deeper) ebb and flow of opinion within the nation. Southern unilateralism, on the other hand, is still part and parcel of the peculiar dynamics of contemporary Southern life, while old-line multilateralism is increasingly an echo from the past speaking for a region and a society that is dying out. The newly Americanized South will share all the strengths and all the weaknesses, all the breadth of vision and all the petty shortsightedness, that mark the national process of establishing consensus on any issue.

All this is far in the future. Of much more immediate importance is the role the Southern delegation in Congress will play in coping with foreign policy legislation in the next decades. Here projection is not as far-fetched since both trends in Southern behavior and the instructive example of the Midwest serve as guides to analysis.

To pick up the second point first: the Midwest and its history of "isolationism" provides a number of surprisingly apt parallels with the contemporary South. The second and third decades of this century saw social and economic changes in this region that are clearly analogous to the current dilemmas of the South. Midwesterners between 1910 and 1930 left the land in droves while industry drew them to the cities. A rural value system clashed with urban society, and a wave of protest shook the prairies. Lacking the nettle of race and the special social ingredient of the poor white, Midwestern protest never assumed the particular forms associated with the Southern brand. But protest was present in large amounts, and its effect on politics was clear and explosive.

A strong case can be made that the rejection of the outside world so characteristic of Midwestern politics during and after this period was directly linked to the major transformation in society. Like the Southerners a generation later, Midwesterners tended to blame "outsiders" for their troubles and attempted to escape external influences by turning their backs on them. They rejected foreign peoples and concerns in much the same way and for the same reasons as they did Eastern urban society—just as Southerners do today. Even the Ku Klux Klan, that eloquent testimony to a society in turmoil, had its day in the Midwest.

But the heartland of America, torn by stress and given to militant unilateralist rhetoric up to the eve of World War II, finally settled down after the war and joined— with only moderately stronger reservations than the East or the West—the national consensus. Today, although the unilateralist frame of mind has by no means died out, the Midwest's approach to international relations tends to be much more flexible than ever before in this century and to show much less susceptibility to ideological absolutes.

The same time frame, if applied to the South, suggests that at least another decade and possibly two will be necessary before the South finally arrives at the kind of stability in international outlook the Midwest enjoys today. If 1953 or 1954 is taken as marking the beginning of the shift, it will be well into the 1970's or perhaps later before even the speeded-up Southern process is completed. The irrelevancy of race relations and the clearly layered structure of Southern society will both make the Southern transformation slower and more painful.

The South's effect on Congressional action in foreign policy matters will therefore continue on balance to be a disruptive one, at least for the next several national administrations. Unilateralism, tending steadily toward ideological militancy, will speak for a major sector of Southern opinion and will for much of the time succeed in throwing Southern multilateralism on the defensive. If the solidity of the consensus in areas outside the South should ever be broken, this aberrant Southern trend may well become a major control over events instead of the digression it has remained up to the present time.

Some observers of the processes of American politics have very recently become concerned about this latter possibility. The tensions of the cold war era, they fear, have begun to erode the reservoir of consensus upon which successive administrations have called since 1945. Extreme solutions, wholesale reversals of direction and emphasis, and the abandonment of large parts of existing programs are being urged before increasingly large and sympathetic audiences. The problem of winning enough support in Congress and in the general public for particular multilateralist measures may become much more difficult.

If these pessimistic judgments are accurate, it would be indeed a cold comfort to appreciate that the South's contribution to this state of eccentricity would be almost by definition a temporary phenomenon. The tragedy of making foreign policy in a democracy is that there is so little margin for error; any major miscalculation by the public may well prove fatal to the best-laid plans of the most dedicated and able diplomats. A temporary failure may be costly on the scales of history as a long-standing dedication to wrong-headedness.

So the South's position is indeed crucial. With Congress so central to all major foreign policy programming, and with the Southern delegation as willing as it has proved to be to go against the tide of national opinion and the recommendations of experts, the state of Southern Congressional opinion is, or at any rate ought to be, a matter of national concern. Everyone with an interest in world affairs will have to look South anxiously for many years.

APPENDIX I

BASIC DATA, 126 CONGRESSIONAL DISTRICTS

District		Population 1960	% Population Increase 1950–1960	% Urbanized 1960	Value Added by Manufacturing 1959	Per Capita Income 1959
Alabama	1	441,490	19.0	66.2	$234,405,000	$1282
	2	386,075	4.2	55.7	96,384,000	1204
	3	310,947	2.4	45.3	77,204,000	1000
	4	315,817	4.7	42.8	149,673,000	1105
	5	305,941	- 1.5	44.9	242,000,000	1141
	6	251,765	0.4	38.9	113,873,000	985
	7	236,216	-13.5	20.8	55,591,000	957
	8	383,625	19.3	49.2	210,838,000	1332
	9	634,864	13.6	84.6	587,027,000	1647
Arkansas	1	360,183	-11.6	30.7	61,810,000	922
	2	182,314	-18.7	17.7	26,289,000	910
	3	299,727	- 7.5	39.9	101,559,000	1141
	4	301,286	-10.6	40.9	146,887,000	1108
	5	320,757	13.2	69.8	123,547,000	1500
	6	322,005	- 3.3	42.7	119,301,000	1087
Florida	1	820,443	88.0	82.1	236,091,000	1741
	2	474,946	49.2	83.1	178,837,000	1710
	3	563,646	39.2	49.7	250,700,000	1352
	4	982,968	87.2	94.4	253,729,000	2000
	5	739,006	98.9	59.4	183,119,000	1705
	6	743,966	161.6	80.9	84,452,000	1414
	7	386,593	75.3	61.7	127,776,000	1663
	8	239,992	14.0	37.4	82,705,000	1188
Georgia	1	379,933	8.5	56.9	196,359,000	1174
	2	301,123	5.4	47.3	67,657,000	1016
	3	422,198	10.2	53.9	139,999,000	1208
	4	323,489	8.5	39.1	184,722,000	1243
	5	823,680	33.2	91.0	567,316,000	1413
	6	330,235	7.2	53.8	124,550,000	1175
	7	450,740	22.6	39.4	384,942,000	1411
	8	291,185	9.1	47.1	153,000,000	989
	9	272,154	10.5	18.7	144,398,000	1110
	10	348,379	8.8	50.3	135,653,000	1191
Kentucky	1	317,436	3.0	31.1	136,941,000	1247
	2	321,303	1.8	39.1	125,193,000	1214
	3	610,947	26.1	88.5	1,061,094,000	1879
	4	303,431	10.3	17.4	65,247,000	1200
	5	329,116	12.0	58.9	94,782,000	1595
	6	411,459	8.0	50.8	175,700,000	1414
	7	420,816	-13.6	17.4	94,092,000	884
	8	323,648	-19.0	18.4	24,232,000	739

District		Population 1960	% Population Increase 1950–1960	% Urbanized 1960	Value Added by Manufacturing 1959	Per Capita Income 1959
Louisiana	1	449,491	28.3	94.3	$123,293,000	$1390
	2	499,561	27.2	89.3	123,292,000	1954
	3	387,207	29.2	49.3	71,305,000	1258
	4	391,541	17.6	34.1	146,970,000	1471
	5	345,013	6.5	40.3	112,004,000	1035
	6	536,029	28.3	55.8	374,000,000	1313
	7	384,330	21.6	47.4	158,979,000	1179
	8	263,850	5.6	36.7	35,198,000	1027
Mississippi	1	364,963	− 4.8	35.4	118,340,000	899
	2	237,887	− 9.5	18.6	34,000,000	715
	3	370,554	−10.2	31.5	47,514,000	777
	4	460,100	7.9	45.3	161,651,000	1198
	5	295,072	− 5.2	25.9	·71,258,000	854
	6	449,565	17.6	48.9	204,825,000	1154
North Carolina	1	253,511	2.3	30.5	51,029,000	880
	2	313,728	2.2	33.8	128,380,000	867
	3	382,124	23.9	21.7	48,137,000	989
	4	442,059	10.0	38.9	196,826,000	1228
	5	408,992	15.2	44.4	624,226,000	1408
	6	487,159	22.3	80.4	651,525,000	1687
	7	455,630	15.6	33.6	103,704,000	1032
	8	396,369	7.3	25.4	203,955,000	1135
	9	364,561	7.6	38.6	291,962,000	1278
	10	452,732	25.6	58.5	348,955,000	1646
	11	307,575	4.0	39.5	267,911,000	1222
	12	291,715	2.5	31.0	176,564,000	1313
Oklahoma	1	521,542	18.7	77.9	324,054,000	1958
	2	368,976	− 6.6	44.2	115,000,000	1447
	3	227,692	−14.7	34.8	19,130,000	1063
	4	252,208	−14.4	53.6	63,969,000	1348
	5	552,863	26.6	96.0	148,202,000	1888
	6	405,003	1.1	46.9	53,292,000	1472
South Carolina	1	421,478	21.8	43.1	108,489,000	1106
	2	531,555	27.8	47.4	267,139,000	1210
	3	318,809	3.6	36.7	242,375,000	1176
	4	444,230	12.0	49.1	350,218,000	1382
	5	272,220	2.1	35.2	265,000,000	1065
	6	394,302	2.7	27.8	131,192,000	839
Tennessee	1	460,583	6.1	32.1	332,000,000	1181
	2	497,121	6.2	51.4	407,500,000	1396
	3	412,664	8.4	56.1	417,281,000	1398
	4	389,563	− 0.2	27.4	126,707,000	1017
	5	399,743	24.2	87.7	283,073,000	1771
	6	324,357	1.9	25.8	135,988,000	1110
	7	232,652	− 6.2	27.1	56,062,000	941
	8	223,387	− 9.9	27.4	50,820,000	926
	9	627,019	30.0	87.8	393,652,000	1588

District		Population 1960	% Population Increase 1950-1960	% Urbanized 1960	Value Added by Manufacturing 1959	Per Capita Income 1959
Texas	1	245,942	-11.2	45.8	$132,000,000	$1216
	2	420,402	23.1	72.5	404,276,000	1791
	3	293,942	- 0.2	31.8	78,065,000	1436
	4	216,371	- 5.0	52.9	77,754,000	1363
	5	951,527	54.8	97.5	810,317,000	2225
	6	248,149	- 7.2	41.4	47,253,000	955
	7	265,629	- 6.6	31.3	83,934,000	904
	8	568,193	41.5	94.5	576,984,000	2223
	9	498,775	22.8	56.9	570,000,000	1438
	10	353,454	12.4	69.3	49,862,000	1437
	11	322,484	14.2	64.8	145,000,000	1420
	12	538,495	49.1	94.6	514,385,000	2082
	13	326,781	4.5	67.3	62,303,000	1591
	14	539,262	17.9	68.7	187,000,000	1289
	15	515,716	13.2	70.5	48,000,000	909
	16	573,438	63.0	40.9	131,420,000	1706
	17	287,889	6.2	56.7	79,000,000	1303
	18	363,596	25.6	64.7	197,683,000	1862
	19	424,774	30.3	62.4	85,616,000	1803
	20	687,151	37.3	93.4	155,891,000	1530
	21	262,742	- 2.3	57.5	31,123,000	1462
	22	674,965	66.6	94.5	576,984,000	1871
Virginia	1	422,624	37.6	63.2	132,626,000	1588
	2	494,292	22.4	95.0	131,347,000	1626
	3	418,081	25.1	82.8	452,606,000	2526
	4	352,157	4.0	27.4	247,000,000	1071
	5	325,989	2.9	22.8	310,000,000	1114
	6	378,864	12.1	56.9	275,000,000	1512
	7	312,890	8.0	29.5	249,778,000	1339
	8	357,461	20.4	18.8	142,027,000	1161
	9	364,973	- 6.5	16.4	140,086,000	1000
	10	539,618	77.9	88.8	33,549,000	2557
West Virginia	1	273,107	- 2.4	61.6	410,000,000	1717
	2	276,874	- 8.4	22.7	67,347,000	1275
	3	268,334	-14.9	22.8	93,500,000	1181
	4	345,208	4.3	48.3	301,000,000	1477
	5	275,813	-16.5	19.6	22,475,000	1095
	6	421,085	- 5.7	47.1	322,885,000	1520

APPENDIX II

ROLL CALL VOTES ON FOREIGN AID AUTHORIZATIONS,
126 SOUTHERN CONGRESSMEN, 1953-1962

District		1953	1954	1955	1956	1957	1958	1959	1960	1961	1962	Total (Y-N-NV)
Alabama	1	Y	Y		Y		Y		Y	Y	Y	07-00-03
	2	Y			N	N	N	N		N	N	01-06-03
	3	N	N	N	N	N	N	N	N	N	N	00-10-00
	4	Y	Y	Y	Y	Y	Y	Y		Y		08-00-02
	5	Y	Y	Y	Y	Y	Y	Y		Y		08-00-02
	6	Y	N	Y	Y	Y	Y	Y	Y	Y	Y	09-01-00
	7	Y	Y	Y	Y	Y	Y	Y	Y	Y	Y	10-00-00
	8	Y	Y	Y	Y	Y	Y	Y	Y	Y	Y	10-00-00
	9	Y	N	Y	Y	Y	Y	Y	Y	Y	Y	09-01-00
Arkansas	1	Y	Y	Y	Y	Y	Y	N	N	Y	N	07-03-00
	2	Y	N	N	N	N	Y	Y	Y	Y	Y	06-04-00
	3	Y	Y	Y	Y	Y	Y	Y	Y	Y	Y	10-00-00
	4	Y	Y	N	Y	N	Y	N	N	N	N	04-06-00
	5	Y	Y	Y	Y	Y		N	N	N		05-03-02
	6	N	N	N		N	Y	N	N	N	N	01-08-01
Florida	1	Y	Y	Y	Y	Y	Y	Y	Y	Y	N	09-01-00
	2	Y	N	Y	Y	N	Y	Y	Y	Y	Y	08-02-00
	3	Y	N	N	N	N	N	N	N	N	N	01-09-00
	4		Y	Y	Y	Y	Y	Y	Y	Y	Y	09-00-01
	5		N	N	N		Y		Y	Y	Y	04-03-03
	6	Y	N	N	N	N	N	N	N	N	N	01-09-00
	7	Y	N	N	N	N	N	N	N	N	N	01-09-00
	8	Y	Y	Y	Y	Y	Y	Y	Y	Y	Y	10-00-00
Georgia	1	Y	Y	Y	Y		N	N	N	N	N	04-05-01
	2	Y	Y	Y	Y	N	N	N	N	N	N	04-06-00
	3	Y	Y	Y	Y	N	N	N	N	N	N	04-06-00
	4	Y		Y	N	N	N	N	N	N	N	02-07-01
	5	Y	Y	Y	Y		N	N	N	N	N	04-05-01
	6	Y	Y	Y	Y	Y	Y	Y	Y	Y	Y·	10-00-00
	7	Y	Y	Y	Y	Y	N	N		N	N	05-04-01
	8	N		N	N	N	N		N	N		00-07-03
	9	N	N	N	N	N	N	N	N	N	N	00-10-00
	10	Y	Y	Y	Y	N	N	N	N	N	N	04-06-00
Kentucky	1	Y	Y	Y	Y	Y		Y	Y	Y	Y	09-00-01
	2		Y	Y	Y	Y	Y	Y	Y	Y	Y	09-00-01
	3	Y	Y	Y	Y	Y	Y	Y	Y	Y	Y	10-00-00
	4	Y	Y	Y	Y	Y	Y	N	Y	Y	Y	09-01-00
	5	Y	Y	Y	Y	Y	Y	Y	Y	Y	Y	10-00-00
	6	Y	Y	Y	Y	Y	Y	Y	Y	Y	Y	10-00-00
	7	Y	Y		Y	Y	Y	Y	Y	Y	Y	09-00-01
	8	N	Y	N	N	N	N	N	N	N	N	01-09-00

295

District		1953	1954	1955	1956	1957	1958	1959	1960	1961	1962	Total (Y-N-NV)
Louisiana	1	Y	Y	Y	Y	Y				Y	Y	07-00-03
	2	Y	Y	Y	Y		Y	Y	Y	Y	Y	09-00-01
	3	N	N	N	N	N				N	N	00-07-03
	4	N	N	N	N	N	N	N	N	N	N	00-10-00
	5	N	N	N	N	N	N	N	N	N	N	00-10-00
	6				Y		N	N	N	Y	Y	03-03-04
	7	N	N	N		N		N		N		00-06-04
	8	N		N	N	N		N	N	N		00-07-03
Mississippi	1	N	N	N	N	N	N	N	N	N	N	00-10-00
	2	N		N	N	N	N	N	N	N	N	00-09-01
	3	Y	Y	Y	Y	Y	Y	Y	Y	Y	Y	10-00-00
	4	N	N	N	N	N	N	N	N	N	N	00-10-00
	5	N	N	N	N	N	N	N	N	N	N	00-10-00
	6	N	N	N	N	N	N	N	N	N	N	00-10-00
North Carolina	1	Y	N	N	N			N		N	N	01-06-03
	2	Y	N	N	N	N	Y	N	N	Y	N	03-07-00
	3	N			N	N				Y	N	01-04-05
	4	Y	N	N	Y	N	Y	Y		Y	Y	06-03-01
	5	Y			Y	N		N	N	Y	N	03-04-03
	6	Y	N	N	Y	Y	Y		Y	Y	N	06-03-01
	7	N	N	N	N	N		N	N	N	N	00-09-01
	8	Y	N	Y	Y	N	N	N	N	N	N	03-07-00
	9	Y	N	N	N	N	N	N	N	N	N	01-09-00
	10	Y	N	N	N	N	N	N	N	N	N	01-09-00
	11	Y	N	N	N	N	N	N	N	N	N	01-09-00
	12	Y	N		N	N		N		Y	N	02-05-03
Oklahoma	1	N	N	N	N	N	N		N	Y	N	01-08-01
	2	Y	Y	Y	Y	N	Y	Y	Y	Y	Y	09-01-00
	3	Y		Y	Y	N	Y	Y	Y	Y	Y	08-01-01
	4	Y	Y	Y	Y	N	N	N	N	Y	N	05-05-00
	5	Y	Y	Y	Y	N	Y	Y	Y	Y	N	08-02-00
	6	Y	Y	Y		N		N	N	Y	N	04-04-02
South Carolina	1		Y		Y	N	N	N	N	N	N	02-06-02
	2	Y		Y	Y	N		N	N	N		03-04-03
	3	N	N	N	N	N	N		N	N	N	00-09-01
	4	Y	N	N	N	N	N	N	N	N	N	01-09-00
	5	Y	Y	Y	Y	N	N	N	N	N	N	04-06-00
	6	Y	N	Y	N	N	N	N	N	N	N	02-08-00
Tennessee	1	N	N		N	N	N	N	N	N	N	00-09-01
	2	Y	Y	Y	Y	Y	Y	Y	Y	N	N	08-02-00
	3	Y	Y	Y	Y	Y	Y	Y	Y	Y		09-00-01
	4	Y	Y	Y	Y	Y	Y	Y		Y	Y	09-00-01
	5	Y	Y	Y	Y	Y	N	Y	Y	Y	Y	09-01-00
	6			N	N	N	N	N	N	Y	Y	02-06-02
	7	Y		Y	Y	N	N	N	N	N	N	03-06-01
	8	Y	Y	Y	Y	Y	N	N	N	Y	Y	07-03-00
	9		Y	Y	Y	Y	Y	Y				06-00-04

District		1953	1954	1955	1956	1957	1958	1959	1960	1961	1962	Total (Y-N-NV)
Texas	1	Y	Y	Y	N	N	Y	Y	N	Y	Y	07-03-00
	2	Y	Y	Y	Y	Y	Y	Y	Y	Y	Y	10-00-00
	3	N	N	N	N	Y	Y	Y	Y	Y	Y	06-04-00
	4	Y	Y								Y	03-00-07
	5	Y		N	N	N	N	N		N	N	01-07-02
	6		Y	Y	N	N		N		N	N	02-05-03
	7	N	N	N		N	N	N		N	N	00-08-02
	8	N	N	N	N	N	N	N	N	Y	N	01-09-00
	9	Y	Y	Y	Y	N	N	N	N	Y	Y	06-04-00
	10	Y	Y	Y			Y	Y	Y	Y	Y	08-00-02
	11	Y	Y	Y	N	N	N	N	N	N	N	03-07-00
	12	Y		Y	Y	Y	Y	Y	Y	Y	Y	09-00-01
	13	N	Y	Y	Y	N	Y	Y	Y	Y	Y	08-02-00
	14	Y		N		N	N	N		N	N	01-06-03
	15	N	N	N	N	N	N	N	N	N	N	00-10-00
	16			N	N	N	N	N	N	N	N	00-08-02
	17	Y	Y	Y	N	N	N	N		N	N	03-06-01
	18	N	N	N	N	N		N		N	N	00-08-02
	19	Y	Y	Y	Y	N	Y	Y	Y	Y	Y	09-01-00
	20		Y	Y	Y	Y	Y	Y	Y	Y	Y	09-00-01
	21	N	N	N	N	N	N	N		N	N	00-09-01
	22		N	N	N	N		N	N	N	N	00-08-02
Virginia	1	N	N	N	N	N	N	Y	Y	Y	Y	04-06-00
	2	Y	Y	Y	Y	Y	Y	Y	Y	Y	Y	10-00-00
	3	Y	Y	Y	Y	Y	Y	Y	Y	Y	Y	10-00-00
	4	Y	N	N	N	N	N	N	N	N	N	01-09-00
	5	Y	N	N	N	N	N	N	N	N	N	01-09-00
	6	Y	Y	Y	Y	Y	N	N	N	N	N	05-05-00
	7	Y	N	N	N	N		N	N		N	01-07-02
	8	Y	N	N	N	N	N	N	N	N	N	01-09-00
	9	Y	Y	N	N	N	N	N	N	N	N	02-08-00
	10	Y	Y	Y	Y	Y	Y	Y	Y	Y	Y	10-00-00
West Virginia	1	Y	Y	Y	Y	N	N	N	N	N	N	04-06-00
	2		Y	Y	Y	Y	Y	Y	Y	Y	Y	09-00-01
	3	Y	N	N	N		N	N	N	Y	Y	03-06-01
	4	N	N	Y	Y	N	N	Y	N	Y	Y	05-05-00
	5		Y	Y	Y	Y	N	Y	Y	Y	Y	08-01-01
	6	Y	Y	Y	Y	Y	N	Y	Y		Y	08-01-01

APPENDIX III

ROLL CALL VOTES ON FOURTEEN SELECTED INTERNATIONAL
ISSUES, 126 SOUTHERN CONGRESSMEN, 1953-1962

1 – Wheat for Pakistan (1953)
2 – Refugee Act of 1953
3 – Motion to recommit Emergency Famine Relief Act (1953)
4 – Amendment to reduce United States contribution to international organizations (1957)
5 – Revision of immigration laws to relieve certain hardship cases (1957)
6 – Increase in United States subscription to International Monetary Fund and World Bank (1959)
7 – United States participation in Inter-American Development Bank (1959)
8 – The International Health and Medical Research Act (1960)
9 – United States participation in the International Development Association (1960)
10 – The Alliance for Progress (1961)
11 – The Mutual Education and Cultural Exchange Act (1961)
12 – The Peace Corps Act (1961)
13 – Creation of the United States Arms Control Agency (1961)
14 – United States purchase of United Nations bonds (1962)

NOTE: In the "Total" column, a "yea" vote in votes 3 and 4 is counted as a "nay,"
and vice versa.

Vote Number:	1	2	3	4	5	6	7	8	9	10	11	12	13	14	Total (Y-N-NV)
Alabama 1	Y	N	Y	Y	Y				N	Y	Y	Y	Y	N	06-05-03
2	Y	N	Y	Y	N	N	Y	Y	N	N	N	Y	Y	N	05-09-00
3	Y	N	Y	Y	N	N	Y	Y	N	Y	Y	N	Y	N	05-09-00
4	Y	N	N	N	Y	Y	Y	Y	N		Y	Y	Y	Y	11-02-01
5	Y	N	N			Y	Y	Y	Y	Y	Y	Y			09-01-04
6	N	N	Y	Y	N	Y	Y	Y	N	N	Y	Y	Y	N	06-08-00
7	Y	N	N	N	Y		Y	Y	N	Y	Y	Y	Y	Y	11-02-01
8	Y	N	N	N	Y	Y	Y	Y	N	Y	Y	Y	Y	Y	12-02-00
9	Y	N	Y	Y	Y	Y	Y	Y	N	Y	Y	Y	Y	N	09-05-00
Arkansas 1	Y	N	N	Y	N	Y	N	Y	Y	N	Y	N	N	N	06-08-00
2	Y	N	Y	N	N	Y	Y	Y	Y	Y	Y	Y	Y	Y	11-03-00
3	Y	N	N	N	Y	Y	Y	Y	Y	Y	Y	Y	Y	Y	13-01-00
4	N	N	Y	N	N	Y	Y	Y	N	N	Y	Y	Y	N	07-07-00
5	Y	N	N	N		N				N	N	N	N	N	03-07-04
6	N	N	Y	N	N	Y	Y	N		N	Y	N			04-07-03
Florida 1	Y	N	N	Y	Y	Y	Y	Y	Y	Y	Y	Y	Y	N	11-03-00
2	Y	N	N	Y	N	N	Y	Y	Y	Y	Y	Y	Y	Y	10-04-00
3	Y	N	N	N		N	Y	Y	Y	Y	Y	Y		N	09-03-02
4	Y	N	N	N		Y	Y	Y	Y	Y	Y	Y	Y	Y	12-01-01
5	N	N	Y	Y	N		Y	N	Y		N	Y	Y	N	04-08-02
6	N	N	Y	Y	N	N	Y	Y	N	Y	Y	Y	Y	N	07-07-00
7	N	N	N	Y	N	N	Y	N	N	N	N	N	N	N	02-12-00
8	Y	N	Y	Y	N	N	Y	Y	Y	Y	Y	N	Y	Y	08-06-00
Georgia 1	Y	N	Y	N		Y	Y	Y	N	N	Y	Y	Y	N	08-05-01
2	Y	N	Y	N			N			N	N		Y	Y	04-05-05
3	N	N	Y		Y	N	N	N	N	N	Y		Y	N	03-09-02
4	Y	N	Y	Y	N		N	N	N	N	N	N	Y	Y	03-10-01
5	N	N	Y				N	N	N	N		N	N	N	00-10-04

Vote Number:		1	2	3	4	5	6	7	8	9	10	11	12	13	14	Total (Y-N-NV)
Georgia	6		N	N				Y	Y		Y				Y	05-01-08
(continued)	7	Y	N	Y	N	Y		N	Y	Y	Y	Y	Y	Y	Y	10-03-01
	8	N	N	Y			N			N	Y	N		Y		02-06-06
	9	N	N	Y	Y	N				N	N		Y	Y		02-07-05
	10	Y	N	N	N	N	Y	Y	Y	N	Y	Y	Y	Y	Y	11-03-00
Kentucky	1	Y	N	N			N	Y	Y	Y	Y	Y	Y	Y	Y	11-02-01
	2				N	Y	Y	Y	Y	Y	Y	Y	Y	Y	Y	11-00-03
	3	Y	Y	N	N			Y	Y	Y	Y	Y	Y	Y	Y	13-00-01
	4	Y	N	N	Y	Y				Y	N	Y	Y	Y	Y	09-03-02
	5	Y	Y	N	N	Y	Y	Y		Y	Y	Y	Y		Y	12-00-02
	6	Y			N	Y	Y			N	Y	Y	Y	Y	Y	09-01-04
	7	Y	Y	N	N		Y	Y	Y	N	Y	Y	Y	Y	Y	12-01-01
	8		N	N	Y	Y	N	N	N	N	N				N	02-08-04
Louisiana	1	Y			Y	Y		Y		Y	Y				N	05-02-07
	2	Y	N	N	N	Y	Y		Y	Y	Y	Y			Y	10-01-03
	3	N	N	Y		Y		Y			Y		Y		Y	05-03-06
	4	N	N	N	Y		Y		Y	N	Y				N	04-05-05
	5	N	N	Y	Y	Y	Y	N	Y	N	Y	N	N	N	N	04-10-00
	6		N	N						Y	Y	Y	Y	Y	Y	07-01-06
	7	N	N	Y		N	Y				Y		Y		Y	04-04-06
	8	N	N	Y	Y	Y	Y	Y			N		Y	Y	Y	06-05-03
Mississippi	1	N	N	N	Y	N	N	N	N	N	N	N	N	Y	N	02-12-00
	2	Y	N	N	Y	N	Y		N	N	N	N	N		N	03-09-02
	3	Y	N	N	N	Y	N	Y	Y	Y	Y	Y	Y	Y	Y	12-02-00
	4	N	N	N	Y	N	N	N	N	N	N	N	N	N	N	01-13-00
	5	N	N	N	Y	N	N	N	N	N	N	N	N	N	N	01-13-00
	6	N	N	N		N	N	N	Y	N	N	N	N		N	02-10-02
North	1	N	N	Y	Y			Y		N	Y	Y	Y	Y	Y	06-05-03
Carolina	2	N	N	Y	Y	Y	Y		N	Y	Y	Y	Y	Y	Y	08-05-01
	3	N	N	Y	Y					N	Y	N	Y	Y	Y	04-06-04
	4	Y	N	Y	N	Y	Y	Y	Y	N	Y	Y			Y	09-03-02
	5			Y	N	N	N		N	N	N	Y	Y	Y	Y	03-07-04
	6	N	N	N	Y	Y	Y	Y		N	Y	Y	Y	Y	Y	09-04-01
	7	N	N	Y	Y	Y	N	N		N	Y	N	Y	Y	N	04-09-01
	8	Y	N	Y		N	N	N	N	N	N	N	Y	Y	Y	04-09-01
	9	N	N	Y	Y	N	N	N	N	N	Y	N	Y		Y	03-10-01
	10	Y	Y	N	Y	Y	Y	Y	Y	N	Y	N	N	Y	N	09-05-00
	11	N	N	Y	Y	N	N	N	N	N	Y	N	Y	Y		03-10-01
	12	N	N	Y	Y	N	N	N		N	Y	N	Y	Y	Y	04-09-01
Oklahoma	1	Y	N	N	Y	Y	Y	N	N	Y	N	N	N	Y	N	06-08-00
	2	Y	N	N	N	Y	Y	Y	Y		Y	Y	Y	Y	Y	12-01-01
	3	Y	N	N	N	Y	Y		Y	Y	Y	Y	Y	Y	Y	12-01-01
	4	Y	N	Y				Y		Y	Y		Y		Y	06-02-06
	5	Y	N	N	N	Y	Y		Y	Y	Y	Y	Y	Y	N	11-02-01
	6	Y	N	N	N	Y	Y	Y			Y	Y	Y	Y	Y	11-01-02
South	1	N	N	N	Y	N			Y	N	N	N		N		02-08-04
Carolina	2	Y	N	N	N	N	Y	Y	Y	N		N	Y	N	N	07-06-01
	3	N	N	Y	Y	N	N	N	N	N	N	N	N	N	N	00-14-00

Vote Number:	1	2	3	4	5	6	7	8	9	10	11	12	13	14	Total (Y-N-NV)
South Carolina (continued) 4	Y	N	Y	Y	Y	N	N	N	N	N	N	N	N	N	02-12-00
5	Y	N	N	Y	N	N	N	Y	N	N	Y	Y	Y	N	06-08-00
6	Y	N	Y	Y			N	Y	N	N	N	N		N	02-09-03
Tennessee 1	Y	Y	N		N	Y	Y		Y		Y	N	Y		08-02-04
2	Y	N	N	Y	Y	Y	N	N	Y	N		N	Y	N	06-07-01
3	Y	N	Y	Y	Y	Y	Y			Y	Y				06-03-05
4	Y	N	N	N	Y		N	Y	Y	Y		Y	Y	Y	10-02-02
5	Y	N	Y					Y	N	Y	N	Y		Y	05-04-05
6	N	N	Y	N	Y		N	Y	N		Y	Y		Y	06-05-03
7	N	N	Y	Y	N	N	Y	N	N	Y	N	N	Y	N	03-11-00
8	Y	N	Y	N	N	Y	Y	Y	N	Y	N		Y	Y	08-05-01
9	Y	N	Y	N	Y			Y	Y	Y		Y	Y	Y	09-02-03
Texas 1	Y	N	Y	Y	Y	Y	Y	Y	N	Y	Y	Y	Y	Y	10-04-00
2	N	N	N	N	Y	Y	Y	Y	N	Y	Y	Y	Y	Y	11-03-00
3	N	N	Y	N	Y	Y		Y	Y	Y	Y	Y	Y	Y	10-03-01
4	Y	Y	Y											N	02-02-10
5	N	N	Y	Y		N	N	N	N	N			N	N	00-11-03
6	Y	N	Y	Y		Y	N	Y	N		N	N	N	N	03-09-02
7	N	N	Y	Y	N	Y	N	N	N	N	N	N		N	01-12-01
8	N	Y	Y	Y	Y	Y	Y	Y	Y	Y	Y	Y		Y	10-03-01
9	Y	Y	N	N	Y	Y	Y	Y	Y	Y	Y		Y	Y	13-00-01
10		N	N	N	Y	Y	Y	Y	Y	Y	Y	Y	Y	Y	12-01-01
11	Y	N	Y	N	Y	Y	Y	Y	N	Y	Y	N	Y	N	09-05-00
12		N	Y	N	Y	Y	Y		Y	Y	Y	Y	Y	Y	10-02-02
13		N	Y	N	N	Y	Y	Y	Y	Y	Y		Y	Y	09-03-02
14	N						Y	Y	Y	Y	Y	Y	Y	Y	08-01-05
15	N	N	N	Y	Y	Y	Y	N	Y	N	N	N	Y	N	06-08-00
16		N	Y	Y	N	Y	Y	Y	Y	Y	Y	Y	N	N	07-06-01
17	N	N	N	Y	N	Y	N	Y	N	N	N	N	N	N	03-11-00
18	N	N	Y	Y	N	N	Y	Y	N	N	N	N		Y	03-09-02
19	Y	N	N	Y	N	Y	Y	Y	Y	Y	Y	Y	Y	Y	11-03-00
20	Y		Y	N	Y	Y	Y	Y	Y	Y	Y	Y	Y	Y	12-01-01
21	N	N			N	Y	Y	Y	Y	N			N	Y	N	06-05-03
22						Y	N	Y	N	Y	Y	Y	N	N	N	04-05-05
Virginia 1	Y	N	Y			N	Y	N		N	Y	Y	Y	Y	07-05-02
2	N	N	N	Y	Y	Y	N	Y	N	Y	Y	Y	Y	Y	09-05-00
3	N	N	N	Y	N	Y	N	Y	Y	Y	Y	Y	Y	N	08-06-00
4	N	N	N	Y		N	N	N	N	N	Y	N	N	N	03-10-01
5	N	N	N	Y	N	N	N	N	N	Y	N	N	Y	N	03-11-00
6	N	N	N	Y	Y	Y	N	N	N	Y	Y	Y	Y	N	07-07-00
7	N	N	N	Y	N	Y	N	Y	N	Y	Y			N	05-07-02
8	Y	N	N	Y	N	N	N	N	Y	Y	N	N	Y	N	05-09-00
9	N	N	N	Y	Y	Y	N	Y	N	Y	Y	Y	Y	Y	09-05-00
10	N	N	N	Y	Y		Y	N	N	Y		Y	Y	N	06-06-02
West Virginia 1	Y	Y	N	Y	Y	Y	N	Y	N	N	Y	N	Y	N	09-05-00
2	Y	Y	N	N	Y	Y	Y	N	N	Y	Y	Y	Y	Y	12-02-00
3	Y	Y	Y	Y	Y			N	N	Y	Y	Y	Y	Y	08-04-02
4	Y	N	N	Y	Y	Y		N		Y	Y	Y	Y	Y	09-03-02
5	Y	N	N	N	Y	Y	Y	N	N	Y	Y	Y	Y	Y	11-03-00
6	Y	N	Y	Y	Y	Y	N	N	N	Y			Y	Y	07-06-01

APPENDIX IV

MAPS OF SOUTHERN
CONGRESSIONAL DISTRICTS

ALABAMA (9 districts)

ARKANSAS (6 districts)

SCALE IN MILES

FLORIDA (8 districts)

GEORGIA (10 districts)

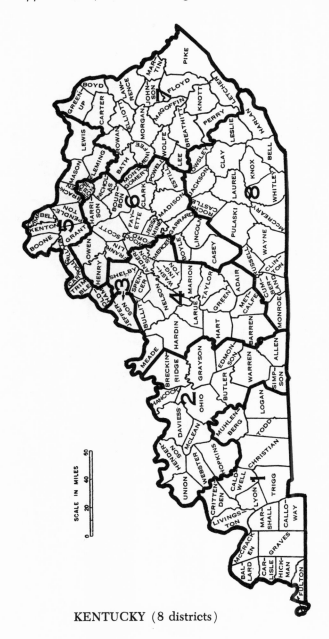

KENTUCKY (8 districts)

LOUISIANA (8 districts)

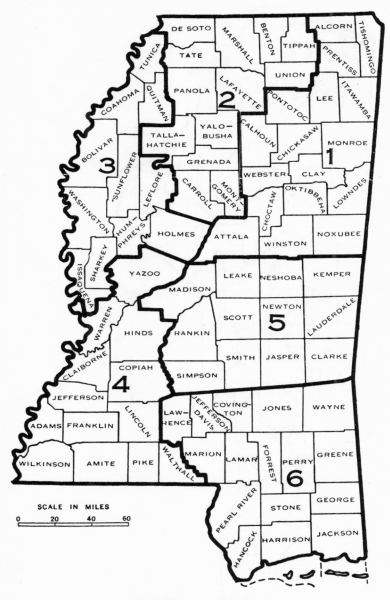

MISSISSIPPI (6 districts)

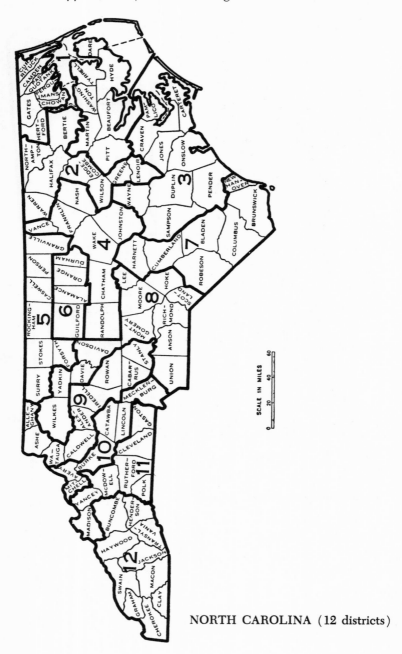

NORTH CAROLINA (12 districts)

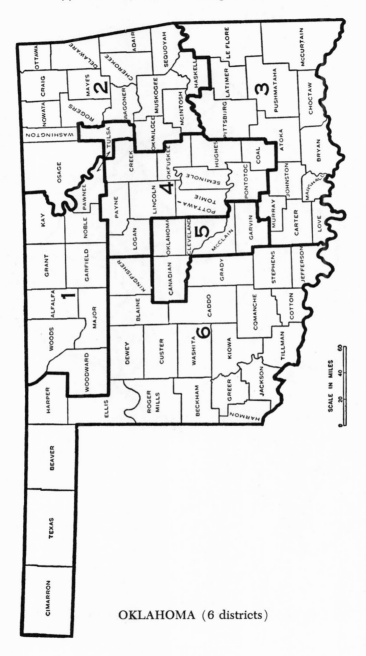

OKLAHOMA (6 districts)

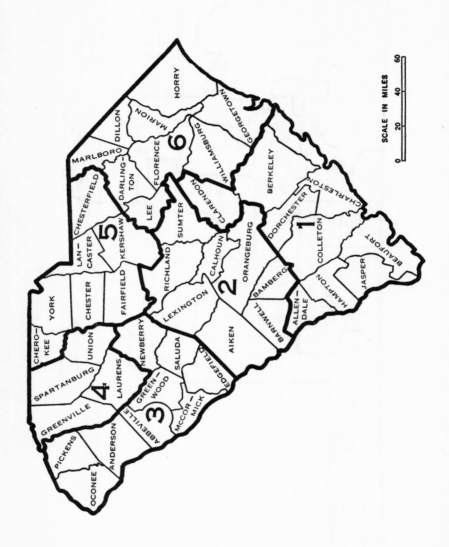

SOUTH CAROLINA (6 districts)

TENNESSEE (9 districts)

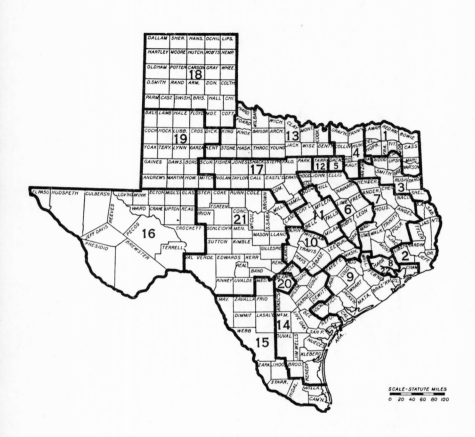

TEXAS (22 districts)

VIRGINIA (10 districts)

HANCOCK

BROOKE,

OHIO

1 MAR-SHALL

WETZEL

MONON-GALIA

MARION

PLEASANTS

TYLER

PRESTON

TAYLOR

MOR-GAN

BERKE-LEY

JEFFER-SON

WOOD

RITCHIE

DOD-DRIDGE

HARRI-SON

BARBOUR

TUCKER

GRANT

MINERAL

HAMPSHIRE

HARDY

WIRT

CALHOUN

GILMER

LEWIS

UPSHUR

2

RANDOLPH

PENDLETON

MASON

JACKSON

ROANE

3

BRAX-TON

4

PUTNAM

KANAWHA

CLAY

WEBSTER

POCAHONTAS

CABELL

LINCOLN

6

NICHOLAS

WAYNE

BOONE

FAYETTE

GREENBRIER

LOGAN

MINGO

WYOMING

RALEIGH

SUMMERS

MONROE

McDOWELL

5

MERCER

SCALE IN MILES

0   20   40   60

WEST VIRGINIA (6 districts)

INDEX

pansion Acts, preliminary issues, record on, 122; renewals, record on, 119, 120

Louisiana Congressional districts: District 1, 127, 147, 148 (*see also* Multilateral districts); District 2, 127, 147, 148 (*see also* Multilateral districts); District 3, 131, 139 (*see also* Wavering districts); District 4, 131, 214, 215, 217 (*see also* Wavering districts); District 5, 132 (*see also* Ideological districts); District 6, 130, 146, 206-207 (*see also* Pragmatic districts); District 7, 131, 207-208 (*see also* Wavering districts); District 8, 131, 139 (*see also* Wavering districts)

Louisville, 148, 150, 183, 233 (*see also* Kentucky District 3)

Lubbock, 148, 234

Marshall Plan, 61, 70, 274; Southern support of, 39, 56, 58

Memphis, 148, 150, 233, 235

Miami, 148, 149, 150, 272

Middle East, 57

Midwest (U.S.), 15, 36, 54, 63, 65, 66, 127, 290; "isolationism" of, 35, 288-289; versus the South, on foreign aid, 67-71; and the South, on foreign policy, 104-106

Militarism, 53

Milwaukee, 236

Mississippi, 24, 81, 110, 113, 115, 116, 131, 133, 152, 165, 268; foreign aid, position on, 74, 76, 78, 79; foreign aid authorizations, record on, 72-73, 93, 112, 114; industrialization in, 225-231; international issues, record on, 108-109, 110, 112, 114; Negro population of, decline in, 232, 233; rural-urban trends in, 222-224; Trade Agreements and Expansion Acts, preliminary issues, record on, 122; renewals, record on, 119, 120

Mississippi Congressional districts: District 1, 133, 135 (*see also* Ideological districts); District 2, 131, 201 (*see also* Ideological districts); District 3, 127, 147, 152, 211, 217 (*see also* Multilateral districts); District 4, 117, 133 (*see also* Ideological districts); District 5, 117, 133, 135 (*see also* Ideological districts); District 6, 133, 135, 138, 209 (*see also* Ideological districts)

Mobile, 235

Montgomery, 142, 239 (*see also* Alabama District 2)

Multilateral districts, effects of change on, 278-281; listed, 127-128; model of, 205-206; Negro population of, 151-152; per capita income of, 202, 204; population growth in, 190; position of, defined, 127; "stalwarts," 147-151, 154; criteria for selection of, 147; susceptibility to change of, 209-213, 217; urbanization in, 193, 196; value added by manufacturing in, 197, 200; voting patterns of, presidential elections, 154-155, 156

Multilateralism, 21-22, 24, 25-26, 28, 40-41, 47, 57, 59, 96, 98, 101-102, 192, 196, 273-274, 287-288 (*see also* Internationalism)

Multilateralists, 161-163, 165-168, 170-172, 174, 176, 178, 184, 277, 278, 282-283

Mutual Education and Cultural Exchange Act, 100, 102, 105; Southern Congressional record on, 103

Mutual Security Program, 57

Myrdal, Gunnar, 245

Nashville, 239, 240

National Association for the Advancement of Colored People (NAACP), 245, 257

National defense, Southern dedication to, 37-39, 56

Negroes, Southern, 13, 14, 54; district distribution, significance of, 151-153, 216-217; impact of, 151, 284; increased mobility of, 231;

DATE DUE

			Printed in USA